Making Microsoft Office Work

About the Author:

Ralph Soucie is the author of two books on Microsoft Excel, and has contributed to other best-selling books on Excel, Windows, and Word for Windows. For several years he was a contributing editor and lead commentator on spreadsheet and accounting applications for *PC World*. Ralph has published over 50 articles in *PC World*, *PC Computing*, *The Quantum PC Report for CPAs*, and other publications.

Ralph owns Onset, Inc., a technical services firm and publisher of the OfficeNinja newsletter.

You can reach Ralph Soucie on CompuServe at 72411,2545 or on MCI Mail at 356-6514.

Making Microsoft Office Work

Ralph Soucie
(with Tim Tow, CPA)

Osborne **McGraw-Hill**

Berkeley New York St. Louis San Francisco Auckland Bogotá Hamburg London Madrid Mexico City
Milan Montreal New Delhi Panama City Paris São Paulo Singapore Sydney Tokyo Toronto

Publisher *Lawrence Levitsky*	Osborne **McGraw-Hill** 2600 Tenth Street Berkeley, California 94710 U.S.A.
Project Editor *Bob Myren*	
Computer Designer *Roberta Steele*	For information on software, translations, or book distributors outside of the U.S.A., please write to Osborne McGraw-Hill at the above address.
Illustrator *Marla Shelasky*	Making Microsoft Office Work
Quality Control Specialist *Joe Scuderi*	Copyright © 1995 by McGraw-Hill, Inc. All rights reserved. Printed in the United States of America. Except as permitted under the Copyright Act of 1976, no part of this publication may be reproduced or distributed in any form or by any means, or stored in a database or retrieval system, without the prior written permission of the publisher, with the exception that the program listings may be entered, stored, and executed in a computer system, but they may not be reproduced for publication.

1234567890 DOC 9987654

ISBN 0-07-881188-0

Information has been obtained by Osborne **McGraw-Hill** from sources believed to be reliable. However, because of the possibility of human or mechanical error by our sources, Osborne **McGraw-Hill**, or others, Osborne **McGraw-Hill** does not guarantee the accuracy, adequacy, or completeness of any information and is not responsible for any errors or omissions or the results obtained from use of such information.

Series Design: Seventeenth Street Studios

To Linda and Brooke

CONTENTS AT A GLANCE

I BASIC PRINCIPLES AND TECHNIQUES

1	WELCOME TO YOUR NEW OFFICE	3
2	HOW OLE HELPS IN SHARING DATA BETWEEN APPLICATIONS	19
3	SHARING DATA BETWEEN EXCEL AND WORD	39
4	MANAGING LINKED AND EMBEDDED OBJECTS	71
5	TAPPING DATABASES WITH QUERY	99
6	AN INTRODUCTION TO MICROSOFT ACCESS	129
7	WORKING WITH GRAPHICAL DATA	155

II PUTTING OFFICE TO WORK

8	CREATING PUBLICATION-QUALITY REPORTS	179
9	CREATING A FORM LETTER USING A MAILING LIST IN EXCEL	201
10	GENERATING SALES ACTIVITY REPORTS	219
11	MAILING, ROUTING, AND FAXING DOCUMENTS	241
12	AUTOMATING SALES PROPOSAL CREATION	269
13	PRESENTING A PROPOSAL WITH POWERPOINT	293

III ADVANCED EXAMPLES

14	BUILDING A RAPID RESPONSE INTERFACE WITH EXCEL	319
15	ADVANCED TOPICS AND TROUBLESHOOTING	351
16	CREATING SOLUTIONS WITH VISUAL BASIC FOR APPLICATIONS AND OLE AUTOMATION	367
17	THE ULTIMATE OFFICE	391
	INDEX	547

CONTENTS

ACKNOWLEDGMENTS, *XIX*
INTRODUCTION, *XXI*

BASIC PRINCIPLES AND TECHNIQUES

1 Welcome to Your New Office   3

Spending a Typical Day in the Office, 4
Just What Is Microsoft Office, Anyway? 5
Working with Microsoft Office, 6
   Boosting Your Production with Office, 6
   Understanding the Roles of the Applications, 11
   How Office Helps Your Applications Share Data, 12
   Orienting Toward the Job Rather Than the Computer Application, 13
   Automating Operations, 14
   Using the Microsoft Office Manager, 14
Setting Up Office, 16
   Minimum System Requirements, 16
   Installing the Office Program Suite, 17
Conclusion, 17

2 How OLE Helps in Sharing Data Between Applications   19

Understanding Objects, 21
   Making Data Smarter, 21
   How OLE Works, 22
What Is Shared Data? 23
   What Is Linked Data? 24
   What Is Embedding? 25
   What Is a DDE Link? 25
   What Are the Source and Destination Documents? 26
   What Is a Compound Document? 26

A Simple Example, 26
    Sharing an Excel Range, 27
    Transferring Data to Another Application, 28

Working with Shared Data, 30
    Using Linked Objects, 30
    Using Embedded Objects, 31
    Editing Linked or Embedded Objects, 31
    What Happens When You Save a Compound Document, 32

3 Sharing Data Between Excel and Word   39

Specifying What Kind of Data You Will Share, 40
    Types of Shared Objects, 40
    Selecting the Excel Object Type to Put into Word, 43

Embedding an Excel Range, 45
    Embedding a Worksheet Object, 46
    Embedding a Picture of the Data, 47

Linking an Excel Range, 48
    Linking a Worksheet Object, 48
    Protecting the Source Data, 49

Inserting an Excel Range While Word Is Active, 50
    Inserting a Worksheet Object with the Toolbar, 50
    Inserting a Worksheet Object with the Menu, 51
    Inserting Worksheets from Existing Files, 52
    Inserting a Range from an Excel File, 54

Linking and Embedding Excel Chart Objects, 56
    Embedding an Excel Chart, 56
    Inserting an Excel Chart, 58
    Embedding a Chart as a Picture, 60
    Linking a Chart, 61

Editing Objects, 62
    Editing Embedded Excel Objects, 62
    Moving Around the Source, 63
    Editing Linked Excel Objects, 63

Using Word as a Server for Excel, 64
    Pasting Text into a Cell, 64
    Inserting Word Files with Excel Commands, 67

Deleting Objects, 68

Conclusion, 68

4 Managing Linked and Embedded Objects   71

Managing Embedded Objects, 72
    Realizing the Power of Embedding, 72
    Understanding What Embedding Can't Do, 74

  Minimizing the Memory and Storage Costs of Embedding, 75
  Dealing with Large Excel Objects, 76
  Converting Objects, 77
Understanding Excel-to-Word Links, 79
  Understanding Word Fields, 79
  Keeping Control of Linked Objects, 81
Modifying Links, 82
  Changing an Automatic Link to a Manual Link, 82
  Redirecting Links, 85
  Editing LINK Fields Directly, 86
  Opening a File That Contains Links, 87
Using Excel Data in Word, 87
  Making Sure Recipients Have Access to the Source File, 88
  Copying Objects, 88
  Using Excel's Copy Picture Command, 89
  Pasting from a Chart in Its Own Sheet, 90
Using Word Data in Excel, 91
  Pasting Text into a Cell Formula, 91
  Sharing Long Text, 92
  Sharing Tabular Data, 94
  Managing Word Objects in Excel, 95
  Saving Time When Printing Compound Documents, 95
When Things Go Wrong, 96
Conclusion, 97

5 Tapping Databases with Query 99

Why You Would Need to Query a Database, 100
  Understanding Database Management Systems, 101
  Understanding Queries, 102
  Microsoft Query and the ODBC Standard, 102
Creating Queries, 103
  Installing the Query Add-In, 103
  Specifying a Data Source, 104
  Setting Up for a Simple Query, 105
  Creating and Executing the Query, 110
  Using "Or" Criteria, 120
Putting Query Results into Excel and Word, 121
  Sorting Results, 123
  Returning Data from Microsoft Query, 124
  Updating Query Results, 126
  Copying Data from Microsoft Query, 126
  Saving and Opening Queries, 126

Editing a Data Source, 127

Conclusion, 127

6 An Introduction to Microsoft Access — 129

Opening Access Files, 131

Viewing and Editing Data, 132
- *Viewing Tables, 132*
- *Editing Data in Tables, 133*
- *Working with Forms, 135*

Accessing Data in Other Database Programs, 138
- *What Is ODBC? 138*

Attaching Tables, 138
- *Installing ODBC Drivers, 139*

Creating Queries, 141
- *Adding Fields, 141*
- *Adding Fields and Criteria, 143*
- *Using Query Wizards, 144*
- *Using Functions, 144*
- *Managing the Query Window, 145*
- *Querying Multiple Data Sources, 146*
- *Creating Queries from Other Queries, 146*
- *Saving Queries, 146*

Moving Access Data to the Other Office Applications, 147
- *Understanding Recordsets, 148*
- *Using the Access Exporting Buttons, 148*
- *Using the Merge It Button, 149*
- *Customizing the Access Toolbar, 150*

Creating Reports, 151

Conclusion, 152

7 Working with Graphical Data — 155

Drawing Graphic Objects in the Client Application, 157
- *Using the Drawing Toolbar, 157*
- *Understanding Drawn Objects, 158*
- *Layering Drawn Objects, 159*

Putting Objects into Client Applications, 161
- *Creating Objects with the Embedding Applications, 161*
- *Inserting Objects, 162*
- *Using Third-Party Drawing Programs, 163*
- *Using Graphics in Access Tables, 165*
- *Inserting Pictures, 165*

Using Clip Art, 167
- *Using the Microsoft ClipArt Gallery, 167*

Using Clip Art in Access, 168
Creating Picture Charts in Excel, 170

Some Techniques for Using Graphics in Word, 171
Putting Embedded Graphics into Frames, 171
Putting Graphics in Text Boxes, 172
Using Graphics in Tables, 172
Using Dingbats Instead of Graphics, 173

Conclusion, 175

PUTTING OFFICE TO WORK

8 Creating Publication-Quality Reports   179

The Scenario: The Monthly Mutual Fund Report, 180
Creating the Body of the Report, 181
Using WordArt to Create a Company Logo, 181
Using Drop Caps, 187

Creating the Worksheet That Calculates the Return to Investors, 188
Creating the Worksheet, 188
Recording a Visual Basic Macro to Update the Figures, 190
Assigning the Macro to a Button, 191
Bringing the Excel Worksheet into Word, 192

Integrating the OLE Objects with the Text, 192
Using Frames, 193
Adding Captions to Objects, 194
Using Reverse Type, 196
Using Microsoft Graph, 197

Conclusion, 199

9 Creating a Form Letter Using a Mailing List in Excel   201

The Scenario: Sending Out a Press Release, 202

Creating the Main Document, 203

Specifying the Data Source, 205

Merging the Name and Address Data, 207
Using the MailMerge Toolbar, 207
Adding Merge Fields to the Main Document, 208
Checking for Errors, 209
Printing the Letters, 212
Merging to a Document, 212

Creating Mailing Labels, 213

Conclusion, 216

10 Generating Sales Activity Reports   219

The Scenario: Informing Customers About Their Buying Activity, 220

Creating the Main Document, 221

Finding the Data You Need, 222
   Understanding Crosstab Queries, 222
   Modifying the Quarterly Orders by Product Query, 224

Using an Access Query as a Data Source, 225
   Connecting to Access with the Mail Merge Wizard, 227
   Adding the Merge Fields, 227
   Merging from Access, 227

Performing Computations in Word, 229
   Computing the Base Period Order Level, 229
   Computing the Base Period Average, 230
   Hiding the Computations, 231
   Computing the Current Sales Level, 231
   Viewing the Computations, 232
   Allowing for International Addresses, 232

Selecting Specific Customers, 234
   Selecting Records with SKIPIF Fields, 235
   Merging the Records, 236

Printing Envelopes, 237

Conclusion, 239

11 Mailing, Routing, and Faxing Documents   241

Sending Messages, 243
   Composing a Message, 244
   Creating a Personal Address Book, 245
   Sending a Note to a Group of Recipients, 246
   Attaching Files and Objects to a Message, 247
   Sending a Document, 250

Routing Documents, 252
   Adding a Routing Slip to a Document, 252
   Responding to a Routed Document, 254

Reading Messages, 255
   Replying to a Message, 255
   Deleting Messages, 255
   Storing Messages in Folders, 256
   Searching for Messages, 259

Faxing Messages, 260
   Setting Up for Fax Messaging, 260
   Faxing a Message, 262
   Faxing Documents, 263

    Entering Fax Addresses in Your Personal Address Book, 264
    Reading Fax Messages, 265
    Opening Documents Sent via Microsoft PC Fax, 266
Conclusion, 266

12 Automating Sales Proposal Creation   269

The Scenario: The Computer Consulting Proposal, 270

Automating Entry of Client Information, 272
    Prompting for Input with ASK Fields, 272
    Using REF Fields to "Reference" Text, 275
    Adding Intelligence with IF Fields, 276
    Personalizing the Document, 277
    Enhancing Accuracy, 278

Linking Computations from Excel, 279

Linking Rate Information from an Access Database, 281
    Inserting a Database, 281
    Selecting Fields to Be Inserted, 285
    Working with DATABASE Fields, 286

Adding the Final Touches, 287
    Adding More Automation, 287
    Putting Your Logo in the Document Header, 288

Conclusion, 290

13 Presenting a Proposal with PowerPoint   293

The Scenario: Presenting a Proposal, 294

Creating a Presentation, 295
    Assigning a Template, 295
    Choosing a Slide Layout, 297
    Augmenting Slides with the Pick a Look Wizard, 298
    Using an Outline to Organize the Content, 299

Refining the Presentation, 304
    Reorganizing the Presentation, 304
    Linking Slides to Spreadsheets and Tables, 307
    Adding Effects, 308
    Rehearsing the Presentation, 310

Making the Presentation, 311
    Printing Handout Material, 311
    Using a Service Bureau to Print Slides, 311
    Running a Presentation from a PC, 312

Creating Future Presentations, 313
    Opening an Existing Presentation, 313
    Getting a Head Start with the AutoContent Wizard, 313

Conclusion, 315

ADVANCED EXAMPLES

14 Building a Rapid Response Interface with Excel — 319

Creating Your Own Operations and Command Center, 321
  Monitoring Operations by Computer, 321
  Understanding the Components of a Rapid-Response System, 322
  Creating a Rapid Response Workstation with Office and Visual Basic for Applications, 324

The Scenario: Monitoring a Manufacturing Process, 325
  Making Sweet Stuff: The Megachunk Chocolate Factory, 325
  Recording Data During Processing, 325
  The Workstation in Action, 326

Looking at the Entire Macro, 329

Taking a Closer Look at the Macro, 335
  Disguising Excel, 335
  Designing the Main Screen, 340
  Creating a Production Line Detail Screen, 344
  Creating the Supplementary Screen, 349

Conclusion, 349

15 Advanced Topics and Troubleshooting — 351

Nesting Objects, 352

Packaging Objects, 353
  Why Would You Package Objects? 353
  Understanding the Object Packager, 354
  Packaging Documents, 354
  Packaging a DOS Program File in a Mail Message, 357
  Selecting Your Own Icons, 358
  Editing an Existing Package, 358

Restoring a Corrupted REG.DAT File, 358
  Rebuilding REG.DAT for the Applications, 360
  Restoring REG.DAT to the Default Setup, 361

Troubleshooting Common OLE Problems, 362
  Losing the Formatting of Linked Excel Objects, 362
  Linking the Same Item More Than Once, 362
  Making Corrections When Excel Feeds "Incorrect" Data to Word, 363
  Speeding Up File Saves, 364

16 Creating Solutions with Visual Basic for Applications and OLE Automation — 367

Getting Started with OLE Automation, 369
    Understanding Controllers and Objects, 369
    Understanding Object Models, 370
    A Simple Example, 370

Manipulating Objects in OLE Automation, 376
    Creating and "Getting" Objects, 376
    Using Object Libraries in VBA, 378
    Controlling Embedded Applications, 380

Solving Business Problems Using OLE Automation, 381
    Automating the Creation of a Word Document from Excel, 381
    Controlling Excel with Access, 382
    Embedding an Excel Object in an Access Form, 385

Conclusion, 389

17 The Ultimate Office — 391

What You Need to Know, 392
Analyzing Investment Data at the Touch of a Button, 393
The Scenario: The Money Manager, 393
Setting Global Options for the Application, 395
Entering Transactions, 396
Analyzing Investment Data at the Touch of a Button, 398
Printing Reports for Clients, 405
Creating Your Own Solutions, 409

Index — 411

Acknowledgments

I would like to thank Cindy Brown, Managing Editor, for handling technical and administrative issues and numerous scheduling changes with considerable aplomb. Cindy also scored a coup by recruiting veteran *PC World* columnist Scott Spanbauer as part of the editing team. Scott's take-no-prisoners comments made this a much better book.

Project Editor Bob Myren brought much-needed production experience to the latter editing stages. Thanks also to Jeff Pepper, John Ribar, Scott Rogers, Lisa Kissinger, and Kathryn Hashimoto. And thanks to everyone for their patience.

I would also like to thank the following contributors: Tim Tow, CPA, created the Visual Basic and Access Basic examples in Chapters 14, 16, and 17, and assisted with Chapter 6. Tim is a systems consultant for Intergraph Corporation in Huntsville, AL, where one of his specialties is integrating Windows applications with relational databases. Tim is a frequent contributor to (and MVP Award winner in) CompuServe's Excel Forum. A founding member of the Internet Excel Developer's Mailing List, Tim remains an active participant on the Internet. Tim has also contributed to an advanced book on Excel.

Shane Devenshire, who wrote the bulk of Chapter 8, is a partner in MAR&SHA Corporation, a computer consulting and training company, where he specializes in project management and spreadsheet consulting. Shane has written more than 80 articles on computers and software for more than a dozen different publications, including *PC World* and *PC Computing*.

Steven Nameroff contributed the PowerPoint tutorial material in Chapter 13. Steve is the author of *QuickBASIC: The Complete Reference*, and co-author of *WordPerfect 6: The Complete Reference* and *Turbo Pascal 7: The Complete Reference*. Steve works as a consultant for Rational Software Corporation, specializing in complex software development using object-oriented methodologies.

Introduction

Of the thousands of pages of documentation included with the Microsoft Office suite of programs, only a small percentage show how to use multiple applications to solve business problems. *Making Microsoft Office Work* fills that gap by demonstrating how to harness the full power of the Office applications to solve business problems.

A Manual on Application Integration

Early on, we determined that readers don't need another fat book full of warmed-over tutorials on the popular Excel and Word programs. Accordingly, this book focuses on showing you how to *integrate* Word, Excel, and the other Office applications (Access and PowerPoint) to solve business problems. As you can see from a brief review of the outline, most of the chapter titles describe business needs—such as keeping in touch with customers—rather than program operations. Instead of calling this book a "how-to" guide, call it a "get-it-done" guide.

Though the material assumes you know how to use Word and Excel, it includes instructions on Microsoft Query, Access, PowerPoint, and Mail. (Mail is covered because purchasing the Office suite entitles the user to connect to a Mail server. Any PC running Windows for Workgroups can be a Mail server; and since more users are currently buying Windows for Workgroups than single-user Windows, using Mail leverages the productivity gain you get from the other Office application programs.)

What's In This Book

Though this is a solutions-oriented book, you do need to understand some basic principles concerning how data is shared among applications. You can then implement the business solutions with some understanding of the inner workings of OLE. That understanding will better enable you to adapt the solutions presented in this book to your own particular needs.

Part I: Basic Principles and Techniques

The first four chapters constitute a reasonably complete course on linking and embedding. As noted at the outset, OLE 2.0 doesn't have an interface. Instead, it borrows the interfaces of application programs such as Excel and Word that support the OLE 2.0 standard. Chapters 1 through 4 explain what OLE 2.0 can do, then show you how to make OLE 2.0 work via application programs. Most of the examples in these introductory chapters feature Excel and Word, the most widely used applications in the Office suite.

Chapters 5 and 6 cover the database beat. Chapter 5 shows you how to use Microsoft Query, a data access tool that brings external data from databases into Excel and Word. Chapter 6 provides a brief tutorial on using the Access database program (included with the Professional edition of Office only). The chapter focuses on entering data and creating queries and reports.

One of OLE's leading benefits is the ability to embed graphics in documents. Chapter 7 provides a short course in creating and using graphics in the Office suite.

Part II: Putting Office to Work

Part II shows you how to attack some common business problems with the Office suite. Chapter 8 shows you how to combine Excel objects and various types of graphic objects to create a professional-looking report in Word. Chapter 9 demonstrates how to generate form letters using a mailing list in Excel. Chapter 10 covers the same topic from a different perspective, showing how to generate form letters for selected customers based on accounting information from an Access database.

Chapter 11 provides a basic tutorial on using Microsoft Mail to communicate with others in your workgroup, including how to use the Microsoft PC Fax utility.

Chapters 12 and 13 present a scenario in which your goal is to persuade someone (in this case a prospective client) to take action. Chapter 12 shows how to automate the creation of a sales proposal. Chapter 13 uses the same scenario to show you how to create an effective sale presentation with PowerPoint.

Part III: Advanced Examples

The four chapters in the last part are technically demanding. Chapter 14 shows you how to use Excel and embedded graphics to create a point-and-click interface for a sophisticated data collection and analysis system. Chapter 15 covers various advanced topics such as packaged objects and the object registration database. Chapter 16 is an introduction to OLE Automation—the facility (in Visual Basic and Access Basic) for taking programmatic control of other application programs.

The book's final chapter requires strong knowledge of Access and familiarity with Access Basic. The example in Chapter 17, which combines the Access database with Excel's recalculation engine, shows just how much productivity you can wring out of the Office suite if you learn the macro languages and OLE Automation.

Conventions Used in This Book

To help you identify special types of information, this book uses certain type styles, as described below:

Type of Information	How Displayed
Text that the reader is instructed to enter	**Bold type**
File names	ALL CAPS
New terms	*Italic type*
Macro code listings	`Special (monospace) type`

The following conventions are used in instructional sequences:

- Individual keys in keystroke combinations are separated by plus signs, as in CTRL+SHIFT+F9

- Individual commands in command sequences are separated by commas, as in "Choose File, Edit." (Occasionally, however, sequences are described more fully, as in "from the File menu, choose Edit.")

Scattered throughout the text you will find helpful Notes, Tips and Cautions:

note *Notes provide supplementary information on related matters or help you understand subtle distinctions.*

tip *Tips suggest convenient techniques or shortcuts.*

caution *Cautions help you avoid common problems such as inadvertently deleting data that has not been saved.*

Disk Offer

This book contains several examples and macros that require significant keyboard input. If you wish to use those examples and macros, to minimize your time spent keying in data, you can order, for $15, a 3 1/2-inch diskette with example files for Chapters 10, 12, 14, 16 and 17. Just fill in the order blank on the next page and mail it, along with your payment, to the address shown. If your PC does not have a 3 1/2-inch drive, please contact the author via CompuServe at 72411,2545.

I have enclosed payment of $15 ($20 for a foreign order). Please send me a 3 1/2-inch source code disk for the examples in chapters 10, 12, 14, 16 and 17 of *Making Microsoft Office Work*. (Foreign orders: Checks must be drawn on a U.S. bank.)

_____
Name

_____
Address

_____
City   State   Zip

_____
Telephone

Send payment to:

Onset, Inc.
H.C. 32, Box 52
Sullivan, ME 04664

This offer is subject to change or cancellation at any time. This is solely the offering of the author. Osborne/McGraw-Hill takes no responsibility for the fulfillment of this offer. Please allow two weeks for delivery.

Part I

Basic Principles and Techniques

CHAPTER 1

Welcome to Your New Office

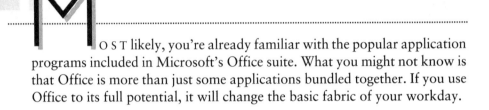

MOST likely, you're already familiar with the popular application programs included in Microsoft's Office suite. What you might not know is that Office is more than just some applications bundled together. If you use Office to its full potential, it will change the basic fabric of your workday.

Spending a Typical Day in the Office

No matter what your position, you're increasingly expected to perform a wide variety of tasks, and to perform them at a high level. Whether you're a manager, professional, salesperson, or an administrative assistant, your job very likely requires you to communicate with a variety of people in and outside your department. You also probably have to deal with numeric and text-based information.

A typical workday likely calls for you to carry out many of the following activities in some form:

CHECKING THE IN-BASKET When you arrive at the office, you generally find several letters, interoffice memos, and/or telephone messages of varying degrees of importance. You usually check them for pressing items and follow up quickly on these. Nonurgent items must wait until later—but you have to make sure you don't lose track of them.

ANALYZING FIGURES To help your department head make decisions, you pore through reports, tables, and financial schedules, and project results of various courses of action in a spreadsheet such as 1-2-3 or Excel.

DOING RESEARCH Some of your analysis requires you to dig up economic statistics and sales information going back several years. You obtain this data from a variety of sources within and outside your organization. Sometimes you have to sweet-talk the accounting or MIS departments into providing financial data in ASCII format, which you import into a spreadsheet. You then have to incorporate that data into your analyses.

SENDING REPORTS AND MEMOS   Once you have completed your analysis, you send memos to colleagues. The memos consist of one-page summaries of the key points or conclusions, followed by supporting schedules, prose, and/or graphics.

FILLING OUT FORMS   From time to time you have to fill out forms relating to travel expenses, time spent on various activities, and acquisition of equipment.

PRESENTING RESULTS   Sometimes you have to make standup presentations at management meetings, which means you spend a fair amount of time drafting text in word processing and working with your graphics department to design visual displays.

CONVERSING WITH COLLEAGUES   You spend a lot of your time exchanging information with co-workers verbally, both in person and on the phone.

Just What Is Microsoft Office, Anyway?

Interestingly, you won't find a direct answer to this question in the Microsoft Office documentation, though the exterior packaging is pretty clear about what programs are included. The Standard Edition of Office contains the following programs:

- Microsoft Word
- Microsoft Excel
- Microsoft PowerPoint
- Microsoft Mail (license only)

The Office product does not include the Microsoft Mail software per se; only a license to use it. That is, if you already own the server version of Mail (included with Windows for Workgroups, versions 3.1 and higher), purchasing Office legally allows you to copy the Mail workstation software to your PC and to connect to a Mail server.

The Professional Edition of Office adds the Microsoft Access program to the Standard Edition.

In addition to the applications, you get a couple of other bonuses. First, you get the Microsoft Office Manager, a toolbar that offers a handy way to start Office applications and some Windows utilities. (You'll learn more about the Microsoft Office Manager later in this chapter.) Moreover, when you buy Office, rather than the individual applications separately, you will be able to install all the applications in one fell swoop.

Working with Microsoft Office

Using Microsoft Office as it is meant to be used changes your thinking about the applications. They look and act the same, but once you've completed this book they will take on a different aura. Instead of merely using Word or Excel individually you'll start thinking in terms of using Office to attack business problems, rather than using Word or Excel individually.

Boosting Your Production with Office

Let's look at some practical examples of how Office can help you get through your busy workday.

Checking Your In-Basket

Once you and the others in your workgroup are connected by a network and have installed Office, you can check messages very quickly. With Microsoft Mail, you can receive electronic messages that cut down on telephone tag and are easier to answer (Figure 1-1).

Mail is tightly integrated with the other Office applications. You can, for instance, create a message from within Excel and attach the current workbook to a Mail message.

Analyzing Figures

When it's time to put some cost figures together for management decisions, Office can eliminate awkward exporting routines for converting data from spreadsheet format to text. All you need to do is copy the desired Excel range, then activate Word and paste the range where you want it in the document. Figure 1-2 shows an Excel range embedded in a memo in Word.

If you have both an Excel window and a Word window open on the screen, you don't even have to copy and paste. You can simply highlight the range, drag it into position in the Word document, and drop it into place, as illustrated by Figure 1-3.

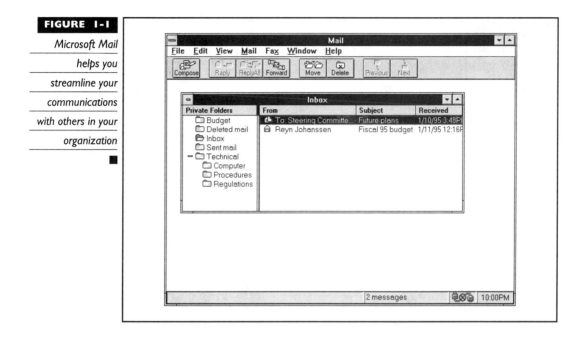

FIGURE 1-1

Microsoft Mail helps you streamline your communications with others in your organization

Researching and Assembling Historical Data

If your position requires that you obtain information from a database or from the company's accounting system, Office can help you dip into these

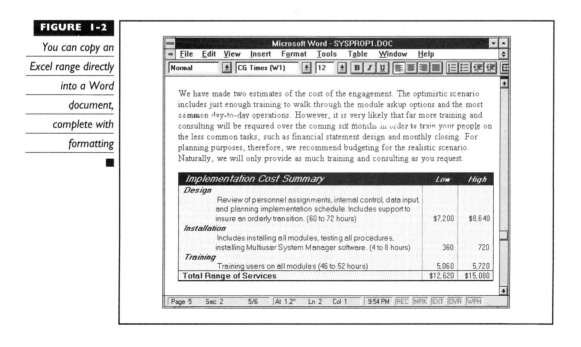

FIGURE 1-2

You can copy an Excel range directly into a Word document, complete with formatting

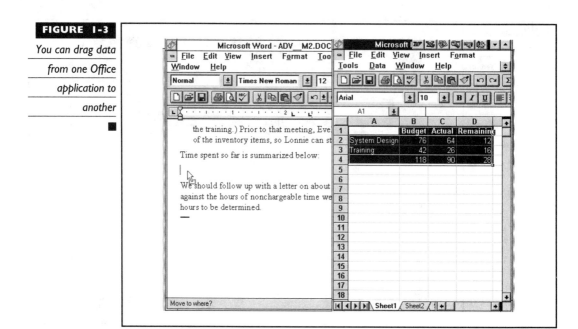

FIGURE 1-3

You can drag data from one Office application to another

larger pools of data. The Microsoft Query program allows you to examine and query databases created in Paradox, dBase, and databases on larger computer systems. Query's capabilities actually are borrowed from Microsoft's full-function Access database program, which is included with the Professional Edition of the Office suite.

An important advantage of using Query is that you can start it from within Excel. Once Query has returned the information you want, as in Figure 1-4, you need only choose the Return Data to Excel command from Query's File menu. That copies the query results into the active range in the workbook.

Even without using the Query tool, you can view data from other applications with the Insert Object command, which pulls the specified data directly into the active document.

Sending Reports and Memos

If you use Windows for Workgroups version 3.1 or higher, you can use its electronic mail capability to speed the delivery of forms and other documents. Just choose the Send command from the File menu of Excel, Word, or PowerPoint to send files to someone else in your organization. Alternatively, you can create an electronic routing slip (shown next) to route such documents in sequence to a series of recipients.

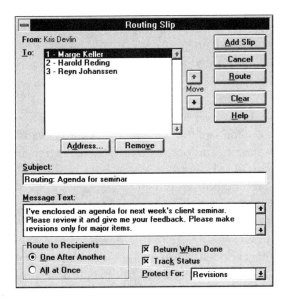

Filling Out Forms

Office provides some tools to automate the completion of paper forms like requisitions and timesheets. You could, for instance, fill out a timesheet in Excel and route it to the time clerk with Mail. Microsoft also sells a

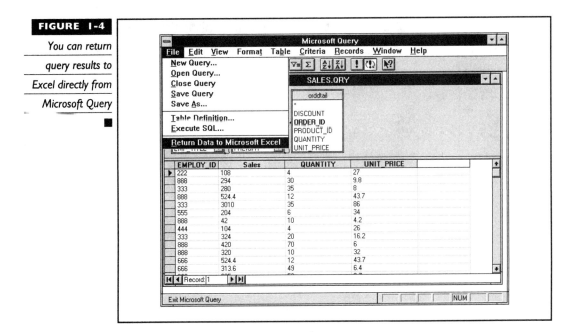

FIGURE 1-4

You can return query results to Excel directly from Microsoft Query

separate program, Electronic Forms Designer. Within a short time, a variety of similar forms programs will be available from other vendors as well.

Presenting Results

Instead of having to rely on specialists to create presentation materials, you can use PowerPoint's striking presentation graphics to polish up your speeches and proposals. If you've created an outline in Word, you can open the Word file from within PowerPoint to transform a text document to a presentation, as in Figure 1-5.

Not only that, but you can make your presentation very dynamic by attaching Excel workbooks to the PowerPoint presentation. If one of your audience asks a what-if question, you can double-click on the embedded Excel document to bring it up on the screen.

Another key benefit of the tight integration between PowerPoint and the other Office applications is that it enhances accuracy. When you are presenting budget figures, you want to be sure that they agree with the numbers you worked up in Excel. If your Excel workbook itself is embedded in your PowerPoint presentation file, you won't have to worry about discrepancies.

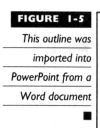

FIGURE 1-5

This outline was imported into PowerPoint from a Word document

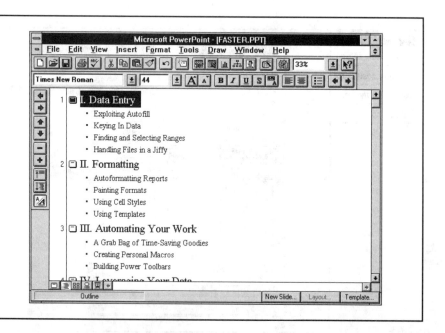

Conversing with Colleagues

At this time, technology cannot substitute for the comprehensive visual and auditory feedback you get when you talk to someone in person. However, Office can increase the efficiency of interpersonal communication by making it easier for the conversing parties to stay well informed. When people are equipped with the same background data, they can get to the bottom line more quickly. Moreover, by providing easier access to the organization's informational assets, Office can marginally reduce the need for face-to-face meetings, which can sometimes be difficult to arrange.

Understanding the Roles of the Applications

To better appreciate the benefits of Office's "working together" style, reflect for a minute on the roles played by common productivity applications.

Microsoft Access

Database management systems such as Microsoft Access store and classify relatively large amounts of data. Most of this data is stored internally in the form of tables and lists. Access does more than simply manage lists, however. It keeps track of the relationships among tables, making it possible to create sophisticated reports and compute statistics. Like most relational databases, Access provides programming tools to automate data entry, analysis, and reporting.

Microsoft PowerPoint

At the opposite end of the spectrum from Access is PowerPoint, which is designed to present data. If Access is the back end, PowerPoint is the quintessential front end. It possesses no capability to process data other than outlining major points to be presented visually. Essentially, PowerPoint takes data created by other programs and makes it look good.

Microsoft Word

Like PowerPoint, Word can be seen as a presentation tool, but one that presents data in "written" form. Being a word processing program, it's designed to handle a greater amount of detail, mostly in the form of text, than PowerPoint. Its role also differs from PowerPoint in that Word is heavily used to generate original data. In general, though, Word's job is to create a package in which other data, such as database, spreadsheet, or graphical data, is often contained.

Microsoft Excel

Excel occupies an intermediate position along the continuum from data crunchers to presentation tools. As the leading spreadsheet program, Excel boasts an extremely powerful recalculation engine. Often, though, it is used as an ad hoc tool for making relatively undemanding mathematical computations such as addition and multiplication. Its formatting and "pretty-making" features are also extensive, so it's also a capable presentation tool. For creating business-oriented reports, though, Excel usually serves up numerical data in the form of tables and graphs, and Word provides the text "wrapper" that goes around the data "package."

How Office Helps Your Applications Share Data

In a minute you'll see some examples of how Office can change how you work. First, though, let's take a closer look at your current work activities.

Since desktop computers became commonplace in business, millions have enhanced their productivity. But even in the most heavily computer-mediated environments, most workers spend a great deal of their time translating data among verbal, hard-copy, and various electronic formats. When you key data into a spreadsheet, you are transcribing data from a printed page or from your own intellectual knowledge base (your brain, that is). When you fill out a paper form, you are often transcribing data from electronic form to hard copy. When, having queried a database, you advise your manager of the results, you are transliterating electronic data into the spoken word. Importing an ASCII file into a worksheet is a translation of data from one electronic format to another.

When you reflect on all of this translating activity, you will realize that it takes up quite a lot of time from a great many educated and experienced people. Yet workers are expected to produce ever-better results in an ever-shrinking amount of time. Moreover, we as consumers expect better and faster service from the companies we do business with. Consider, for instance, the person you talk to when you call the customer service number for one of your credit cards. You have never spoken to this person before, and probably never will again. Yet this person knows where you buy your gasoline, where you stayed in Florida, and where you rent videos—and is momentarily one of only a handful of people who know your mother's maiden name. If the representative *doesn't* have all of this information at his or her disposal, in fact, you're likely to be somewhat annoyed.

We receive this level of service courtesy of a highly integrated computer system that makes key information easily available. Similarly, Microsoft intends with the Office suite to make key information more readily available to the various application programs you use to process that information. Office's ability to move data around among Word, Access, Excel, and PowerPoint reduces the need for your personal intervention in translating the data from one electronic format to another. Office automates the process so you don't have to handle the data as much.

As for the process of translating data between electronic and physical form, the Office suite provides the ability to greatly reduce the reliance on paper and oral conversations to convey information. In the case of formal presentations, Office minimizes the time you must spend in preparing an effective presentation, and can even help you create automated desktop presentations that do not require a human presenter.

Orienting Toward the Job Rather Than the Computer Application

In general, personal productivity software has steadily gotten better and easier to use since the introduction of the IBM Personal Computer in 1981. Microsoft in particular has publicized its efforts to improve usability, even creating a trademark name, IntelliSense, to describe features that make it seem that the computer knows what you want to do before you've done it.

Whatever label you attach to the concept of computer software "intelligence," there are limits to how much of it can be provided within the confines of a single application program. Human beings don't segregate intellectual work into "text processing" and "numerical analysis" sessions, so it's a bit unnatural for us to apply stand-alone computer applications to multifaceted business problems.

To address this problem, Microsoft developed the OLE (Object Linking and Embedding) standard to enhance the ability of application programmers to get their programs to cooperate better. You'll learn more about OLE in the next two chapters, but the key point is that much of Office's seamless integration is made possible by the "plumbing" Microsoft has put in place to facilitate interprocess communication.

OLE provides a number of powerful benefits. It makes it possible for applications to share not only data, but common program operations. The Find File dialog boxes of all the Office applications use the same program code. That makes for more efficient use of programming resources by software developers, and helps conserve memory and disk space on your computer. (Granted, conservation of disk space is not the first concept that comes to mind after one has installed the complete Office package. Nevertheless, the suite would occupy even *more* space if the applications did not share some common code.)

When you only have to learn one spell-checking routine and one file-search procedure, you can get productive faster—especially when the common elements are well designed. But regardless of how cleverly Office implements OLE, an application wouldn't do a user much good if its own native features weren't well designed. The core productivity applications, Excel and Word, lead the competition in both sales and in the independent reviews. Access and PowerPoint are also usually rated at or near the top of their class.

It takes a solid standard (OLE), clever use of the standard in integrating the components, and good application program design to make a top-notch suite of programs. Office has all three. Combine that with the inherent advantage of each of your applications "knowing" with certainty which other applications are installed on your system, and you have arguably the most powerful single software product available.

Automating Operations

Office offers another important bonus: version 2.0 of OLE. OLE 2 facilitates the ability of one application program to control another application, using the latter as a sort of assistant. OLE Automation, as it is called, requires good knowledge of either Microsoft's Visual Basic, Applications Edition macro language, or one of the native macro languages of the individual applications. At this point, Excel and Access are the only Office applications that can control other applications. However, the Office applications are farther along than any other competing products in the extent to which they take advantage of OLE Automation. You will see some examples of OLE Automation in Chapters 16 and 17.

Using the Microsoft Office Manager

One of Office's niftier design elements is the Microsoft Office Manager toolbar:

By default, the setup program places the Microsoft Office Manager toolbar onto the Windows title bar.

The toolbar stays in position no matter what Windows program you switch to. Clicking the last button on the toolbar brings up the following menu:

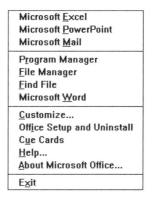

From this menu you can start application programs as well as help and setup utilities.

The Microsoft Office Manager also has a special help facility, which includes special Cue Cards:

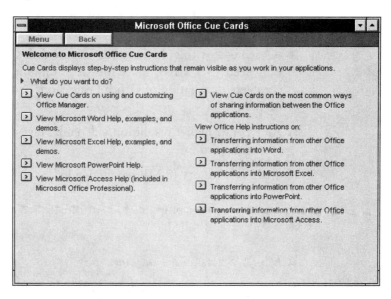

The options on the right portion of the Cue Cards window contain instructions on applying multiple Office applications on specific tasks.

The problem with the Microsoft Office Manager toolbar is that it uses some of your system resources, the most precious part of your computer's memory when running Windows. Most people who have more than one

Windows application running simultaneously will be better off removing the Microsoft Office Manager in order to recover the system resources. This will avoid the slow performance and error messages that are the hallmarks of low memory resources.

Setting Up Office

Before you can get started, naturally, you must first install the Office suite on your computer. You need to have a capable computer system to run Office.

Minimum System Requirements

To run Office, your computer system must have the following:

- Generally, an 80386-based processor capable of running Windows. (Officially, Office will run on 80286-based computers if you don't plan to run Microsoft Access. For practical purposes, however, you should consider a 25-Mhz 80386-based computer as the minimum requirement.)
- A hard disk with at least 50 MB of free disk space. (Officially, you only need 15.5 MB of space for the minimum installation, but a complete installation of Office Professional Edition will take up over 60 MB.)
- An EGA or higher resolution video adapter (VGA or higher recommended).
- 4 MB of memory (8 MB recommended).

In addition, your computer system must have the following operating system software installed:

- MS-DOS version 3.1 or later.
- Microsoft Windows version 3.1, Windows for Workgroups version 3.1 or higher, Windows NT 3.1, or Windows Advanced Server 3.1.

To use Microsoft Mail with the Office suite, you must have Windows for Workgroups or Windows NT installed.

Installing the Office Program Suite

The installation program for Microsoft Office will install the Office Manager software and all the application components in one single setup session. Of course, unless you install from a CD-ROM, installation involves handling a great many floppy disks.

You start floppy disk–based installation by inserting the Setup disk in a disk drive as you would for any other Windows application programs from Microsoft. Then follow these steps:

1. In the Program Manager, choose the File Run command.

2. In the Command Line box, enter the drive identifier (such as **a:** or **b:**), followed by the word **setup**.

3. The Setup program will prompt you to enter or select options and to insert additional disks.

4. When you have completed the installation, the Setup program will display a message. Choose OK.

For each application you install, Setup will ask you to choose from three installation routines: Typical, Complete/Custom, and Laptop (Minimum). The Typical option is often the best for a computer with plenty of hard disk space. Keep in mind, though, that certain potentially useful features, such as the Query tool and certain add-in programs for Excel, are not installed by the Typical option. If you choose the Complete/Custom option, you can specify exactly which components you want to install. The Laptop option installs only the minimum files needed to run the application.

Conclusion

Each of the Office applications works splendidly on its own. Starting with version 4.2, though, Office boasts a greatly enhanced ability for working in harmony as a single product. You will see numerous cross-application examples in this book. The first step, though, is to understand the basis of Office's data-sharing mechanism, OLE 2.0. That is the subject of Chapter 2.

CHAPTER 2

How OLE Helps in Sharing Data Between Applications

THE old way of computing on PCs was similar in some ways to operating in a manufacturing plant. For years, users have been processing data by moving it into and out of various application programs. Think of a machine shop, where a part might move from an injection molding machine to a boring mill, then to the welding station, then to packaging. Every time the part moves to a different station, the operator reads the paperwork associated with the job, sets up the machine, and performs the operation. Finally, the part is moved to the next operation shown on the routing document.

Microsoft Office automates your desktop "factory" by putting a full complement of compact, high-tech tools within easy reach. With these tools, you can personally perform the entire "manufacturing" job from molding to packaging. To draft a budget, you can use the Query application to bring raw numbers from the corporate financial database into Excel. You can use Excel's statistical functions to develop projections. To get input from colleagues, you can route the worksheets and have them automatically returned to you. When you complete your analysis, you can drag an Excel range containing summary figures directly into a report you prepared in Word. If you have a network or Windows for Workgroups installed, you can send the finished product out the door electronically with the help of Microsoft Mail

In the future, the documents you create will increasingly be mixed-format documents blending numbers, graphics, and text. You will build these documents by assembling pieces constructed in different application programs. However, the technology that enables the more efficient integrated environment is complex. To take full advantage of Office's tools, you need to understand the Object Linking and Embedding (OLE) standard, which undergirds Office's data-sharing mechanism.

Understanding Objects

Before the introduction of OLE and its predecessor, Dynamic Data Exchange (DDE), the "machine shop" method of processing data caused inefficiencies. Suppose you wanted, for instance, to bring tabular data in your spreadsheet program into a word processing document. You had to export the spreadsheet file, or part of it, to a universal file format such as DIF or ASCII. Then you would start the word processing program and open the exported file. You might even need to run a separate import procedure before opening the file. Then you might have to reformat the imported data in some way.

Making Data Smarter

As software developers searched for remedies to this problem, they concluded that the way programs interact with data had to change. No longer could programs be allowed to make cavalier assumptions about data. To achieve the goal of one-stop data processing, programmers—as well as the users themselves—now have to think of data items as smart little creatures that have a lot to say. Using the format prescribed by the OLE standard, programmers must ensure that data items (called *objects*) carry little business cards and brochures, just in case they encounter a program that wants to make use of them.

You might think of OLE as a computer dating service for objects and application programs. The OLE specifications prescribe a format for data to talk about its qualities, and for programs to describe what kind of data interests them. As application developers become more adept with OLE, data will grow ever more independent of any single application program. As a result, users will no longer think of being "in" Excel or Word; instead, they will feel more as if they are in particular business processes.

Microsoft Office is one step along this road. In Office, the data, just as much as the application, controls what you see on the screen. More precisely, the combination of data and what you would like to do with it is the center of attention. Depending on the context of the business problem you are trying to solve, the application program (as represented by the menu and toolbar system that surrounds the data on the screen) will change.

While this helps users do their jobs more easily, designing applications becomes very complex. Consequently, it will be a while before application programs deliver OLE services to their full potential. Application designers have to determine which aspects of the data they want to make available to other applications, and what they would like their applications to do to OLE objects from other applications. Following the OLE guidelines, they will cause the applications to *expose* objects to other applications. Remember the dating service analogy? Exposing an object is a little bit like an individual videotaping his or her pitch for potential suitors. Until the programming community masters the art of OLE implementation, however, commercial software releases will occasionally fall short of expectations.

How OLE Works

Windows uses the OLE 2 standard to register objects, thus making them known to whatever applications might want to make use of them. When you start Windows, all the object types available from your currently installed OLE-capable applications are registered, so that Windows knows what kinds of objects might later float around among applications. When you link or embed an object, the application that created the object (called the *server* application) negotiates with the application that would like to use the object (called the *client* or *container* application) to determine the boundaries of what can be done.

Examples of Objects

Common examples of data objects include

- A spreadsheet range or a single cell
- A chart
- A database record or field value
- A graphic object (vector or bitmap)
- A page, paragraph, line, or word of text in a word processing document
- An entire database, spreadsheet, text, or graphical file

note *The term "object" might be a bit confusing for readers who generally use the term to describe graphical objects such as clip art and geometric shapes on a computer screen. Do not confuse the onscreen object, which is a representation of the data, with the data object behind it. The onscreen object is analogous to the menacing projected image of the Wizard of Oz. The real object—the data—is "the man behind the curtain."*

The Hierarchy of Objects

Obviously, when you deal with objects that might be spreadsheet cells, presentation slides, tables in a database, text, or graphic or sound recordings, some kind of classification scheme is necessary for the application programs to identify particular objects. Under the OLE standard, objects are identified by the application, topic, and item.

The application in which the object was created is the most basic identifier. The topic is generally the particular file in which the object resides. The item identifies the particular data item in the file or document (such as a particular row or cell in an Excel workbook, or a bookmark in a Word document).

As you will learn in the following chapters, data links are sometimes inadvertently severed. Repairing the broken connection requires some ability to identify the "lost" source item by filename and by item (cell reference or range name in Excel, or bookmark in Word).

Apart from the broken-link situation, you generally won't have to worry too much about OLE's application/topic/item nomenclature. Just be aware that Windows keeps track of every object in use by a non-native application, and the object's type often limits what you can do to that object. For instance, you won't be able to use Word's spell-checking function to check the spelling of text in an embedded clip art object. Even if the onscreen object contains text, the characters are not represented as text internally.

If you use OLE's facility for controlling an application from another application (known as OLE Automation), you will need to know precisely how to identify objects by application, topic, and item. You'll see examples of OLE Automation in Section III of this book.

What Is Shared Data?

There are a few different ways that the data created in a given application can be used by another application under OLE. This book refers generically to all forms of interapplication data exchange as *sharing* data. Data passed from one application to another is called *shared* data. In the context of a particular task, though, shared data under OLE is described as either *linked* or *embedded* data.

What Is Linked Data?

OLE allows you to *link* data between applications. For instance, you can link a range in Excel to a Word document, as illustrated in Figure 2-1. You might think of the link as a porthole into the Excel document, through which anyone who views or reads the Word document can see what's going on with that Excel object. If the source data—the range inside the Excel worksheet—changes, the change can be instantaneously reflected in the Word document.

Linking data provides real-time update capability in many, though not all, cases. It can also conserve memory and disk space, because the destination document stores only the information necessary to re-create the link to the source file. It also helps ensure that documents contain the up-to-date, officially sanctioned data.

Linking, however, involves risks. If users don't follow certain rules concerning moving and deleting source files, they can break the links between source and destination documents. When that happens, the destination document displays an error message, or—perhaps worse—erroneous data. You'll learn more about broken links and how to reestablish them in this chapter and in Chapter 4.

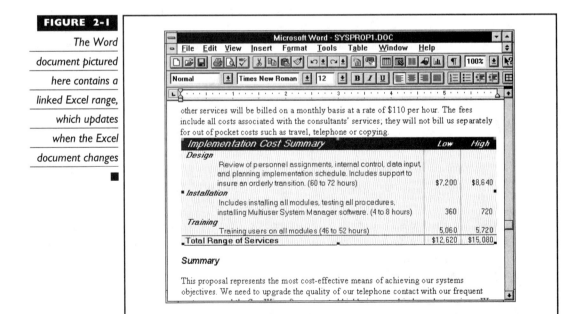

FIGURE 2-1

The Word document pictured here contains a linked Excel range, which updates when the Excel document changes

What Is Embedding?

When you embed an object, you are essentially pasting a snapshot of it in the client application. Though an object's appearance is the same whether it is linked or embedded, there is a major difference. Embedded objects are not linked to the server application, so changes in the source document will not be reflected in the destination document. That does not, however, mean that the object can't be changed. You'll see how to edit an embedded object in the next chapter.

Client applications have to store all the information necessary to edit or format embedded objects. That's more information than is needed to store linked objects. As a result, embedded objects generally take up much more space in files than do linked objects. (An embedded object can increase the size of the destination document by more than the size of the source file.)

Embedding offers two major advantages:

- You don't have to worry about inadvertently deleting or moving source files.
- You can send a document with an embedded object to anyone who has access to a computer running the source application, regardless of whether he or she can access the source document.

If, for instance, you need to send a text document that contains some clip art to a print shop, you should embed the clip art object into the document.

What Is a DDE Link?

Dynamic Data Exchange (DDE) is a somewhat primitive precursor to OLE that lives on in Windows applications, including those in the Office suite. Essentially, DDE offered users the ability to install a sort of pipeline between two applications, so that the server application could pass values to the client application. In general, DDE's functionality is available through OLE. Moreover, DDE has always been somewhat complicated, so most users rarely bother with it. DDE can, however, be very useful in setting up Office applications to automatically receive incoming data from applications that do not support OLE. For instance, you could use DDE to have Excel receive financial quotations as they come in from a communication program. DDE macro commands are also available in application programs that offer both a macro language and DDE support.

FIGURE 2-2

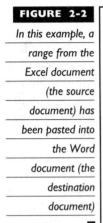

In this example, a range from the Excel document (the source document) has been pasted into the Word document (the destination document)

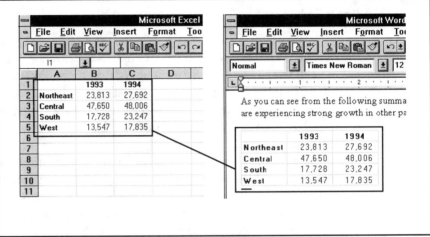

What Are the Source and Destination Documents?

A *source* document is a document whose data has been pasted, embedded, or linked to a client application's document (the *destination* document). In the diagram in Figure 2-2, an Excel worksheet (at left) is the source document. A Word document (at right) is the destination document. The specific data that is being shared is called the *source data*.

What Is a Compound Document?

A *compound* document is a document containing linked or embedded data, or a DDE link to a file, created in another application. A memo with an embedded Excel range and a PowerPoint presentation linked to an Excel workbook are two examples of compound documents. Compound documents will become more commonplace in the coming years.

A Simple Example

It's time to look at the actual process of creating a compound document. Suppose your department is planning to install a new computerized customer service system, and you're involved in the planning. You've used Excel to summarize cost figures for hiring consultants, and you've drafted a report that's ready to send to your superiors for review.

FIGURE 2-3

Cost estimates to be included in a report

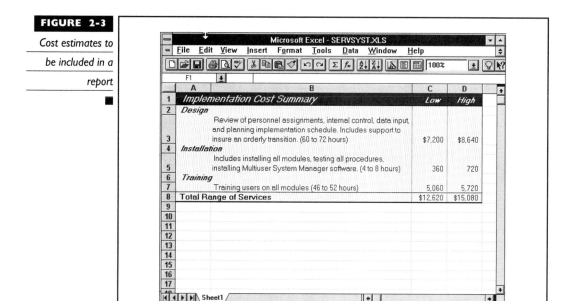

Sharing an Excel Range

Figure 2-3 shows the cost figures in cells A1:D8. You want to include this summary in your report, which you've drafted in Word.

Follow these steps to embed the summary into your Word document:

1. Select the range you want to copy.

2. From the the Edit menu, choose the Copy command, or use the CTRL+INSERT or CTRL+C shortcuts.

3. Activate the Word window and position the insertion point where you want to insert the summary.

4. From the Edit menu, choose the Paste Special command.

5. This brings up the Paste Special dialog box shown on the following page, which displays the Formatted Text (RTF) option selected by default. Notice also that the upper-left corner of the dialog box contains useful information about the object you are about to paste. Select the first type listed in the box (Microsoft Excel 5.0 Worksheet Object).

```
┌─ Summary Info ─────────────────────────┐
│ File Name:  COMPSALS.XLS         [ OK ]│
│ Directory:  C:\EXCEL\ANALYSIS          │
│ Title:      [Sales trends      ] [Cancel]│
│ Subject:    [               ]    [ Help ]│
│ Author:     [Dave Gray      ]          │
│ Keywords:   [               ]          │
│ Comments:   [Delete after 3/31/95  ↑]  │
│             [                      ↓]  │
└────────────────────────────────────────┘
```

6. Choose OK to embed the range as an Excel object.

The resulting compound document is shown in Figure 2-4.

Transferring Data to Another Application

Once you have copied data, you have three different ways to place it in another application:

- You can simply plain-paste it by choosing Paste from the Edit menu. Plain-pasting converts the data to the client application's native format. Text, for example, is native to Word.

- You can embed it. Embedding leaves the data in its original "foreign" format. That is, it's in a form that can't be directly edited in the client application.

- You can link it as either native or foreign data, depending on the type you select in the Paste Special dialog box.

Relating these operations to the options in the Paste Special dialog box can be confusing at first, because the dialog box seems to offer only two options: Paste and Paste Link. Actually, what happens to the data depends on your choice of action (Paste or Paste Link) and your choice of data type. If you select Paste Link, the object will always be linked. If you select Paste, you will plain-paste the data if you've selected a data type (such as Text or Formatted Text when you are pasting into Word) that is native to the client

FIGURE 2-4

A report with an embedded Excel object

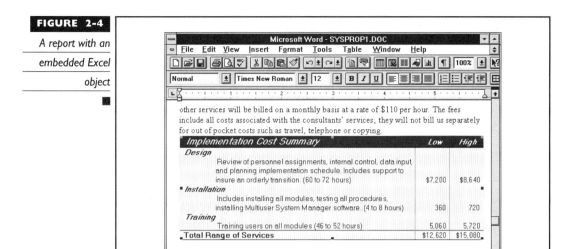

application. You will embed the data if you've selected a data type that is foreign to the client application.

The following table summarizes how Paste Special options affect data copied from Excel and put into Word.

	Type of Data Selected	
Action Selected in Paste Special dialog box	**Native to Word (Text, Picture, or Bitmap)**	**Foreign to Word (Worksheet or Chart)**
Paste	Plain-pasted	Embedded
Paste Link	Linked	Linked

You determine the type of object you are sharing by selecting a type from the As list. Select Paste to embed the object; select Paste Link to link it. If you paste-link the object, you have various update-frequency options (Automatic, Manual, and Locked).

The object types shown in the As list will vary depending on the type of data you copied from the server application. To complicate matters even further, the As list usually contains a default object type that, if selected, results in a conversion and a plain paste, rather than an embed or a link. Selecting the default options shown in Figure 2.4 would have pasted the Excel data into Word as a Word table.

Working with Shared Data

Most of this book is devoted to telling you how to share data among applications to make your job easier. As with any other power tool, following certain guidelines will help you achieve the desired results.

Using Linked Objects

As you saw earlier in the example, linking data in Office involves three basic steps:

1. Copying the data in the server application to the Clipboard using normal command methods (such as choosing Edit, and then Copy, using a keyboard shortcut, or clicking the Copy button on a toolbar).

2. Activating the client application.

3. Pasting the selection using a special paste command or option. The exact procedure depends on the particular client application. In all the Microsoft Office applications, you choose the Paste Special command from the Edit menu, then select the desired options from a dialog box. (Occasionally, however, you might encounter applications that, instead of Paste Special, have a Link or Paste Link command on the Edit menu.)

When you paste-link data, you have several options depending on what you intend to do with the shared data afterward. A common option is to paste-link an Excel range into a Word document as an Excel object. The object will be updated dynamically whenever the source data changes in Excel.

Suppose, for instance, you are working with others in your department to create a report that contains extensive financial data. While both the financial data and the accompanying text are being assembled, you want the continuous-update feature of OLE's linking capability. In that event, you would paste-link an Excel worksheet object, as demonstrated in "A Simple Example," earlier in this chapter.

From this procedure, you can get a hint of OLE's complexity. The ways in which you can manipulate shared data depend not only on the particular client and server applications, but on the type of object you create when pasting the data into the client application. For instance, when you paste-link an Excel object into Word, Word creates a LINK field. What you can do with the linked data depends on the attributes of Word for Windows fields—not on the capabilities of Excel.

Naturally, the things you want to do to shared data depend on the particular business task. We could describe several variations on the earlier example, each of which would dictate a different type of linked object—but that is, after all, what the rest of this book is about.

Using Embedded Objects

The demands of the particular business situation might point to embedding an object in, rather than linking it to, the client application. This would be the case when you are pasting graphical data, such as clip art or a corporate logo, into a document that you will send out to be printed. Once you send the compound document out of your workgroup, a linked object will not contain the information required for the recipient to print or display it.

To embed the graphical object into Word, you would use the default Paste option in the Paste Special dialog box rather than Paste Link. In the As box, you would select the type of object that suits your immediate purpose. If you are about to finalize a document before sending it out for printing or processing, you would probably select Picture, which minimizes the size of the destination document while retaining the best-quality formatting information.

tip *You don't always need to link or embed data. Often, the recipient will not need to edit an embedded object using the server application; in that case the best solution is to plain-paste the object into the destination document. To create a Word table from Excel data, copy the desired range in the Excel worksheet and paste it into Word with the Paste command from the Edit menu or the* CTRL+V *or* SHIFT+INSERT *shortcut.*

Editing Linked or Embedded Objects

You learned earlier in this chapter that the behavior of a linked or embedded object depends on several factors: the client application, the server application, the type of data represented by the object, and the type of link, if any. "Behavior" means, essentially, how the object looks or reacts when you do something to it. In most cases, there's quite a bit you can do to linked or embedded objects. Often when you have linked or embedded data into a text or a presentation document, you're most interested in modifying the object's appearance. You can usually expand or reduce objects in size and put borders around them. You can also stretch them vertically and horizontally, and apply colors and patterns.

To do more than that, however, you often need to use the tools and commands that belong to the source application. Suppose, for instance, you want to format the axes of an embedded Excel chart in a Word document.

Word has no commands for formatting chart axes, but that's not a particular problem; OLE 2.0 allows you to format the chart with Excel commands without leaving the Word document.

If you double-click an Excel object embedded in a Word document, the title bar shows the client application (in this instance, Word) and the menu and toolbar change to those of Excel, as shown in Figure 2-5.

You can then revise and edit the range in much the same way you would any Excel range. When you finish editing the object, click outside the object to continue editing the destination document.

This is an example of *in-place activation* (sometimes called "editing in place").

What Happens When You Save a Compound Document

When you save a document that contains an embedded object, all the information necessary to display, print, or edit the object is saved along with the file. In effect, the client application saves the entire source file—no matter how large—along with the destination document.

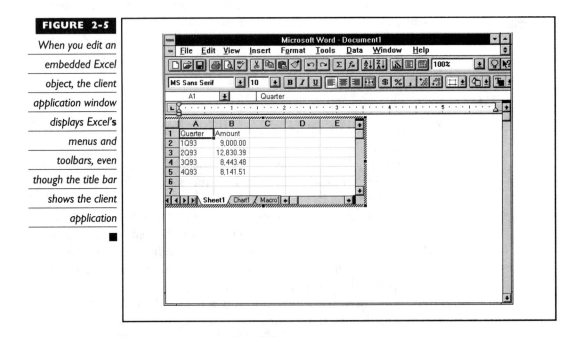

FIGURE 2-5

When you edit an embedded Excel object, the client application window displays Excel's menus and toolbars, even though the title bar shows the client application

caution *To avoid wasting disk space, follow this rule of thumb: if it takes more than 10 seconds to open a source file, think carefully before embedding any data from this file.*

You can save disk space by linking data; when you save a document that contains a link, you are saving only a reference that points to the source file. As a result, however, linking carries with it a heavier responsibility: to make sure source documents will always be available to supply data during the expected "life" of the destination document.

Opening a Compound Document

You open a compound document as you would any ordinary document. What happens next, however, could vary depending on several factors:

- The update frequency you specified when you created the link. For instance, if you selected manual updating, changes to the source data are not reflected until you recalculate or update the object in the client application.

- Whether you have set the client application to update links upon opening the file. For instance, you can tell Excel not to update links in newly opened files by deselecting the Ask to Update Automatic Links option in the Edit tab of Excel's Options dialog box (available by choosing Tools, then Options).

- Whether the linked data has changed in the source document since you last saved the destination file.

- Whether the server application is set to communicate changes. (It's possible to set the server application to ignore requests for updates from other applications.)

More often than not, the client application will update all links whenever it opens a file. For example, if you open an Excel document containing automatic links (that is, links whose updating is set to Automatic rather than Manual), Excel will display a dialog box asking you if you want to reestablish the link to the source document.

Breaking Links

When you create links, be careful when moving or renaming source files. Unfortunately, OLE 2 does not enable application programs to monitor the movement of source files from one subdirectory to another. If you have a Word document that's linked to an Excel document on the C:\EXCEL subdirectory, moving the document to the D:\FINANCE\95TAX subdirectory will break the link. (Renaming a source file will also break OLE links.) If you subsequently open the Word document after moving or renaming the source Excel file, the Word document will no longer be linked to the Excel file.

caution *Because the current version of OLE lacks safeguards, link breakage will inevitably become a problem in large organizations. The mere act of moving or renaming a source file will not generate a warning message. (This is true whether you use DOS, the Windows File Manager, or a third-party utility to move, delete, or rename the file.) Worse yet, a severed link arising from moving or renaming a source file will not generate an error message in the client application.*

The only clue to a lost link will be the failure of the linked object to update when it should. If you suspect that a link to an Excel file has been severed, for instance, follow these steps to check out the link:

1. Select the linked object.
2. Choose Edit, then Linked Spreadsheet Object.
3. From the submenu that appears, choose either Edit or Open.

If the link is intact, you will be able to edit the object. If it has been severed, the client application will display a message stating that the client application cannot edit the Excel worksheet.

Practicing Safe Linking

Given the fragility of OLE links and the absence of error messages to alert you to their existence, it's vital to protect against inadvertently breaking a link. Set up one or more subdirectories with names like \SOURCDAT, \DSERVER, or \REFERNCE, to house your important source documents. Then avoid (like the plague!) moving or renaming the files on this subdirectory. Also consider other application-specific security measures, such as cell protection and write-reservation passwords. These help protect the data inside the files from inadvertent errors that can ripple through to destination documents.

Another good practice is to set up "expiration dates" for source files. When you save your source files, you can indicate an expiration or purge date in the Comments box in the Summary Info dialog box, as shown here:

Chapter 2: How OLE Helps in Sharing Data Between Applications **35**

[Summary Info dialog box]

Make sure you advise colleagues who use documents with links of any time limits on the source data.

note   *If two linked files reside in the same directory and are moved simultaneously to a new directory, the integrity of the link(s) will be preserved. However, you should always consider that a source file might contain a link to another file that could be broken when you move the former file.*

Redirecting and Modifying Links

If, despite your best efforts, an OLE link is broken, all is not necessarily lost. You might be able to restore the link.

You can view information about any of the linked objects in any destination document by choosing the Links command (located on the File or Edit menu, depending on the application). This will display a dialog box similar to the one shown here.

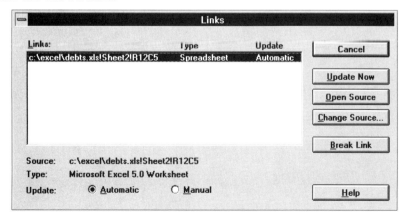

In the Links dialog box, you can reconnect a link to a source file that has been moved or renamed. You can also modify various aspects of links—change updating from Automatic to Manual, for instance. You can also purposely break a link in order to finalize the value or other data supplied by the source document. You'll learn these procedures in the next chapter.

What you've seen in this chapter is an example of embedding Excel data into Word. You've also learned about some of the more important options you have when you need to share data. Just as importantly, you now have a grasp of the technical underpinnings of Office's data sharing capability. This basic understanding will be helpful in resolving problems that might pop up as you employ some of the advanced capabilities of OLE.

The variety of different options in sharing data is much broader than you've seen in this chapter. Chapter 3 will cover a wide range of possibilities and show you how to maintain the integrity of data links between applications.

CHAPTER 3

Sharing Data Between Excel and Word

In the previous chapters, you learned you have many options in deciding what data you want to share in the client application. Most server applications are capable of sharing their own data in multiple forms. For instance, having copied an Excel range, you can choose to link (or embed) that data as either a worksheet object or a picture object. The particular object types available (sometimes called *data types*) vary depending on the nature of the copied data.

This chapter will explain the various Excel data types and demonstrate how to share them in Word.

Specifying What Kind of Data You Will Share

As you put Office to work, keep in mind the fundamental rationale for *sharing* data, as opposed to simply *pasting* it. Sharing the data keeps it closely associated with the server application. Whether an object is linked or embedded, you can reconnect it with the server application at any time by double-clicking the object. If, on the other hand, you simply paste the data, you will not subsequently be able to modify it using the editing tools of the server application.

Types of Shared Objects

Office applications can handle a wide variety of data types. The particular data types presented as options in the Paste Special dialog box (shown on the following page) can vary, depending on the server application and the nature of the copied item.

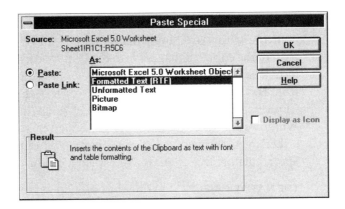

To get a general idea of the variety of data types you might encounter, display the Registration Info Editor window. (Choose File, then Run while in the Program Manager, then enter REGEDIT in the dialog box that appears.) Registration is a procedure performed on Windows startup that identifies the types of objects that might be generated by the particular OLE-capable programs installed.

Your Registration Info Editor window should look something like that shown in Figure 3-1. (While the displayed list might look daunting, it's usually not necessary for you to deal with OLE objects at this level of abstraction. However, a glance at this list gives you a hint of the behind-the-scenes object management done that Windows performs using the OLE 2.0 standard.)

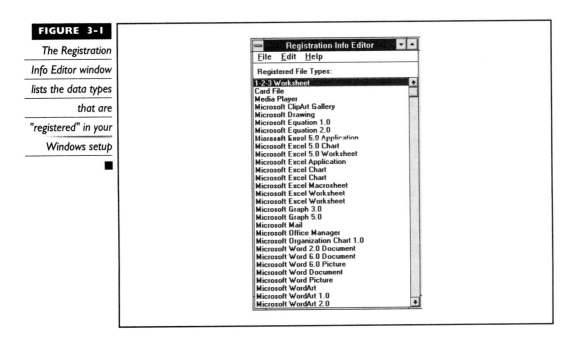

FIGURE 3-1

The Registration Info Editor window lists the data types that are "registered" in your Windows setup

If you're curious about the nature of data you have copied, simply view it in the Clipboard. Immediately after you've copied, but before you've pasted, the copied data goes into the Clipboard, the universal waystation for recently cut or copied data. Until you choose the Paste Special command from the Edit menu in the client application, the copied data resides in the Clipboard. Figure 3-2 shows an Excel range in the Clipboard window of Windows for Workgroups Clipboard Viewer.

Let's get an overview of the object type options available in the Paste Special dialog box after you've copied a cell or range in Excel.

THE NATIVE OBJECT Sharing the object in its native format puts the greatest possible amount of information into the client application. Examples of native objects are Excel 5.0 worksheets, Excel 5.0 charts, WordArt text, and PowerPoint slides. (Of course, it's the particular object type you copy that determines the types offered in the As list of the Paste Special dialog box.)

Sharing the native object puts into the destination document all information that the server application needs to edit the object. If you link the object, the document stores a link to a source document. If you embed the object, it contains all the attributes to make it behave normally if you activate it for in-place editing. Whether you have linked or embedded the object, double-clicking an Excel worksheet object allows you to revise the data and format its appearance just as if you were running Excel.

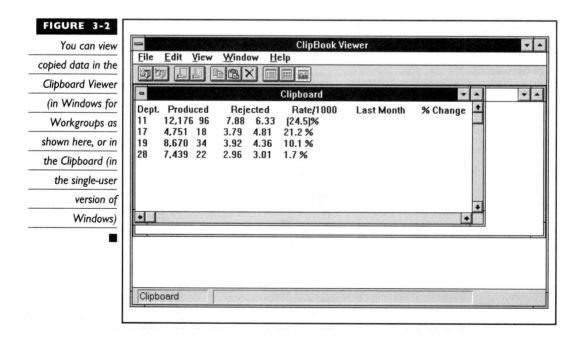

FIGURE 3-2
You can view copied data in the Clipboard Viewer (in Windows for Workgroups as shown here, or in the Clipboard (in the single-user version of Windows)

FORMATTED AND UNFORMATTED TEXT Embedding formatted text puts the copied text, together with all the formatting attributes applied, in the server application. Office applications, along with most other application programs that use OLE, use Rich Text Format (RTF) codes to store formatting attributes. RTF is a quasi-universal standard for converting formatting information into coded instructions that can be read by client applications.

Generally, selecting a text option in the Paste Special dialog box plain-pastes, rather than embeds, the data. If you paste an Excel worksheet object, cell formulas are converted into their returned values, and you lose the ability to edit the object in Excel. If you select Formatted Text, the cell values are placed in a Word table. For unformatted text, Word will paste characters only, without any formatting. The rows in the copied range will be separated by paragraph characters; the columns will be separated by tabs.

You can also link Excel data to Word as text. You'll find a detailed discussion of this topic, including some background information on how Word handles linked Excel data, in Chapter 4.

PICTURES OF THE DATA Select the Picture option to convert the copied object (cell, range, or chart) into a graphical object that you can resize or edit. Pictures are vector graphic images; that means they use mathematical algorithms to determine how to redraw the image after you have modified it. You can resize a picture object as many times as you want without distorting its appearance or losing resolution. You can also edit pictures with the Microsoft Draw tools. Pictures, moreover, use less memory than bitmaps.

You can link or embed Excel cells, ranges, or charts as picture objects.

BITMAPS Select the Bitmap option when the Picture option is not available in the Paste Special dialog box. This puts a bitmapped graphic into a document. The problem with bitmaps is that sizing and scaling can introduce fuzziness and distortion into the graphic.

Selecting the Excel Object Type to Put into Word

Because programming with OLE 2 is still somewhat new, many applications are fussy about what kind of shared data they accept from a server application. Your choice of data type in the Paste Special dialog box might be limited to text and bitmap only, for instance—or native object and picture. The Excel-to-Word connection is much richer than for most client-server application pairs. Consequently, when you paste an Excel range into a Word document, you have a wide range of choices.

Table 3-1 summarizes the important characteristics of the five data type options that appear in Word's Edit Paste Special dialog box when you've just copied an Excel range.

Option	Use	File Storage Requirements	Editable with Word Commands?
Excel 5.0 Worksheet	When you think you might have to revise the formulas in the source document	Potentially large	No
Formatted text (RTF)	When you want to manipulate an Excel range as a Word table	Small	Yes
Unformatted text	When you only want to pull in values (with cell values separated by tab characters, and rows separated by linefeeds)	Small	Yes
Picture	When you need a graphic image and need to save memory	Small	No
Bitmap	When you need a graphic image and all other object types are unsuitable or unavailable	Large	No

TABLE 3-1 *Effects of Different Data Type Options When Pasting an Excel Range into Word* ∎

tip *One factor that might influence your decision whether to paste a worksheet object or formatted text is the respective Autoformat feature of Excel and Word. If you prefer Word's table Autoformat, which offer a greater variety of options, paste the object as Formatted Text. If you like Excel's more accessible and colorful Autoformat, paste the object as an Excel worksheet.*

Embedding an Object as an Icon

When the data you want to share is large—an entire document, for instance—you might prefer to embed an object as an icon. That way, the large embedded object won't obscure the rest of the document. Figure 3-3 shows an Excel workbook embedded as an icon in a Word document.

Anyone who has the current version of Excel can display the embedded workbook by double-clicking on the icon.

Plain-Pasting the Data

Remember the basic principle mentioned earlier: you share data when you want to maintain a connection between the object and the editing tools in the server application. If, on the other hand, the data you want to paste is in final form, the command to choose from the Edit menu is Paste, rather than Paste Special. In fact, in some cases Paste creates an embedded object

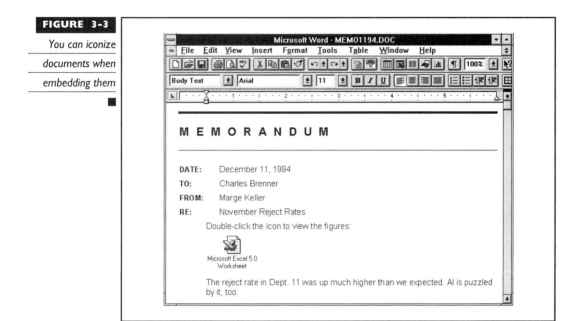

FIGURE 3-3

You can iconize documents when embedding them

by default. (This is the case, for instance, when you paste an Excel chart into Word.) No matter what you paste, though, choosing Edit, then Paste has the same effect as selecting the default data type shown in the As box of the Paste Special dialog box and the default Paste option.

Embedding an Excel Range

Much of what you have learned so far has been a bit abstract. It's time to walk through a realistic example illustrating your many data-sharing options.

Here's the scenario: One of your duties is to monitor yield rates from a certain manufacturing operation in your company. Every week, you enter production and defect numbers into a summary worksheet in Excel. You usually print the sheet out and send it to your boss with a transmittal letter. The following example illustrates how embedding can improve your work product.

Assume that you have already summarized the results for the current period, as shown in Figure 3-4.

At this moment, you believe the figures in the worksheet to be final. Occasionally, however, you have been asked to reformat financial schedules for appearance, so you decide to embed the Excel range in the cover letter.

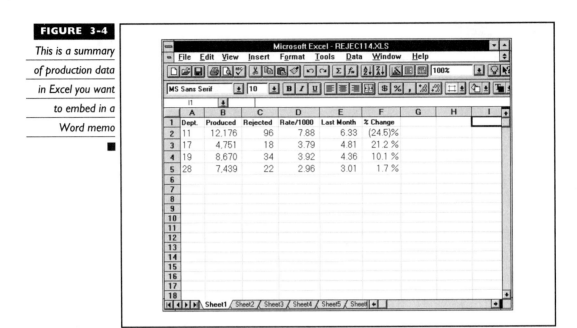

FIGURE 3-4

This is a summary of production data in Excel you want to embed in a Word memo

That way, if you're asked to do more work you'll be able to use Excel's formatting tools, and even add additional computations.

Embedding a Worksheet Object

To embed the Excel range in a Word document, follow these steps:

1. Select the range A1:F5.
2. Choose Copy from the Edit menu.
3. Start Word and open the desired Word document.
4. Position the insertion point in the desired location.
5. Choose Paste Special from the Edit menu.
6. In the As list of the Paste Special dialog box, select Excel 5.0 Worksheet.
7. Choose OK.

Figure 3-5 shows the resulting compound document.

Now you can send a printed copy of this document to your associates while retaining a copy on disk just in case changes are needed. Even better, you could send the Word file, which essentially contains the whole of the

FIGURE 3-5

The Word memo with embedded Excel data

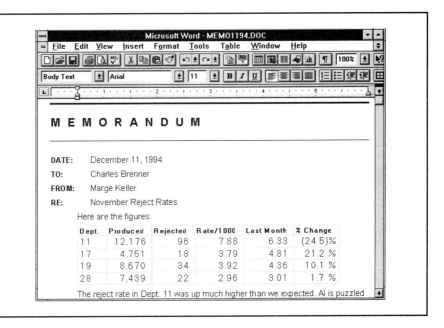

source Excel file within it. The recipients can then make changes without having to wait for your response. Changes made to the embedded Excel object will not affect the source document—which, incidentally, you might not have saved anyway.

Embedding a Picture of the Data

On the other hand, you might not be particularly concerned about having to change the embedded Excel range. Often, the primary purpose for a report is to be archived in a filing cabinet. In that case, consider plain-pasting the object into the memo as a picture to save disk space.

To paste an Excel range as a picture, follow these steps:

1. Copy the range and activate the Word document.
2. Display the Paste Special dialog box. (From the Edit menu, choose Paste Special.)
3. In the As list, select Picture.
4. Choose OK.

Your Word document looks like Figure 3-5 with one exception: when you paste a range as a picture, the gridlines are not included in the object.

The picture and bitmap formats look identical when you paste an Excel range into Word. In general, though, you should favor the "smarter" Picture option over Bitmap. (Remember, a picture is stored as mathematical data, whereas a bitmap file contains data on each screen pixel in the object.) When the Picture option is not available, you will have to resort to a bitmap.

note *Before you insert an object, you must have started the server application at least once since the current version of the server application was installed. Starting the server application registers its objects. Think of how you register for a seminar. When you check in and sign your name, the seminar sponsors know you are present; they check you off the list, hand you your printed materials and name badge, and usher you into the seminar. Registering objects is likewise necessary for Windows to keep track of what type of objects can be created by the programs installed on your computer.*

You'll come back to the example of the monthly yield report later in the chapter.

Linking an Excel Range

As you learned a moment ago, embedding an object is useful when you have to send the entire destination document to a recipient who might not have access to the source document. One problem, however, is that the embedded data gets "severed" from the source document. If you revise the source Excel range in the example, you would have to send an updated copy of the memo to all recipients—or your organization would run the risk of relying on incorrect information.

Another disadvantage of embedding is that your hard disk could become cluttered with duplicate embedded data. Over time, you could end up storing several hundred megabytes worth of redundant embedded objects.

For these reasons, consider *linking* extensive or very complex data rather than *embedding* it into the client application. Also consider, however, that you must be careful after creating a link that you don't break it by moving the source file. You'll learn how to minimize this type of problem in Chapter 4.

Linking a Worksheet Object

To link the Excel range in the example to the Word memo:

1. Select the range A1:F5 in the worksheet.

2. Choose Copy from the Edit menu.

3. Start Word and activate the Word document.
4. Position the insertion point in the desired location.
5. Choose Paste Special from the Edit menu.
6. In the As list, select Excel 5.0 Worksheet.
7. Select the Paste Link option.
8. Choose OK.

The results are identical to those in Figure 3-5.

note *If you're pasting to a non-Microsoft application program, the Edit menu might not have a Paste Special command. In that case, look for a Paste Link command.*

Objects created in non-OLE 2 server applications cannot reliably be linked into Office client applications. For instance, linking objects created in some server applications to Word results in linked objects that do not update until you save the source document that contains them. In other applications, you might not be able to link objects at all. To complicate matters further, there is no indicator that tells you whether the server application is OLE 2-enabled, so you will inevitably have to learn by a certain amount of trial and error.

Though you can't see any difference between an embedded Excel range and a linked Excel range, there's a major difference below the surface. Generally, once you've linked the Excel and Word documents, any change in the source Excel range will automatically be reflected in the memo, as long as the object is set to automatically update. (You'll learn how to control updating of a linked object in Chapter 4.)

Protecting the Source Data

Establishing a link to the source document minimizes the chance of multiple electronic versions of the report floating around, but it raises other concerns. For instance, you should password-protect the source Excel document in a situation like this. Otherwise, someone else could enter or change erroneous figures without your knowledge. Then a memo with incorrect figures could circulate while your name is still associated with it.

If you and your colleagues are not in the habit of password-protecting files, the transition to tighter security procedures might be initially uncomfortable. However, independent surveys and anecdotal evidence indicate that spreadsheet files across corporate America are rife with errors. Used carelessly, linking and embedding could cause those errors to proliferate more rapidly.

note *All this talk about serious errors may have you wondering why Microsoft hasn't done something to reduce the chances of something going wrong. In fact, they are working on an operating system that will provide a better way of keeping track of objects. Code-named Cairo, the new operating system is scheduled for release in 1996.*

Microsoft Office offers a variety of options for controlling the way data in client applications is updated. See Chapter 4 for more information.

Inserting an Excel Range While Word Is Active

When you want to share data, you don't necessarily have to start by activating the server application and copying the object. With the Object command on the Insert menu, you can create a non-native object, such as an Excel chart in a Word document, from within the client application. This is helpful for creating quick embedded objects when you don't need great precision or extensive formatting.

Inserting a Worksheet Object with the Toolbar

To embed an Excel worksheet object in Word, follow these steps:

1. Position the insertion point where you want the object.
2. Point to the Insert Microsoft Excel Worksheet button (shown here) on Word's Standard toolbar, then press and hold the mouse button.

Insert Microsoft Excel Worksheet

This displays a pull-down grid for specifying the size of the inserted Excel object (shown here in the top-right corner of the screen).

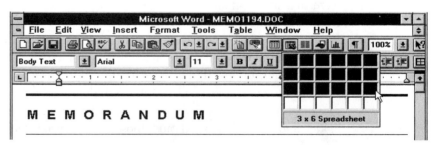

3. Drag the mouse pointer down and to the right to define the size (in rows and columns) of the Excel object. Each cell in the grid represents a cell in the inserted worksheet object. The grid shown in the screen above defines a range consisting of three rows and six columns.

4. Click outside the worksheet object on the client application window. If you realize that you want a larger worksheet range, adjust the object in the usual manner.

5. When you have finished entering the values and formulas you want in the embedded worksheet object, reduce the size of the worksheet object by dragging the borders until no blank rows or columns are visible. Otherwise the inserted worksheet will include the surrounding blank cells.

6. Click outside the worksheet object on the client application window.

Word embeds a blank worksheet object having the specified number of rows and columns.

Inserting a Worksheet Object with the Menu

You can also use menu commands to insert an embedded Excel worksheet object in Word. Follow these steps:

1. Position the insertion point where you want the object.

2. Choose the Object command from Word's Insert menu. Word displays this Object dialog box:

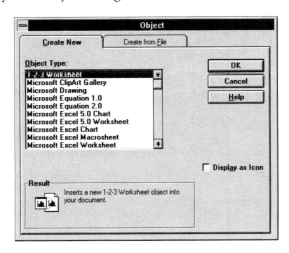

3. Click on the Create New tab, if it is not already in the foreground.

4. In the Object Type box, select Microsoft Excel 5.0 Worksheet. Word embeds an Excel worksheet object in the document and opens a blank worksheet for editing, as shown in Figure 3-6.

note *Excel worksheet objects created with the Insert Object command contain one sheet only. You can add more sheets to the object—to create and organize supporting computations, for instance—but only the active sheet will be visible in the destination document.*

caution *If you choose File Close and confirm the action while editing an embedded object, Word will close the destination document. That's because the document itself, and thus the Close command, are still "owned" by Word.*

Inserting Worksheets from Existing Files

You've just learned how to create *new* Excel objects while you are in Word. With the Object command from the Insert menu you can also insert data from *existing* Excel files.

Suppose, for instance, you need to insert a budget computation for 1995 from a worksheet named SALESBDG.XLS.

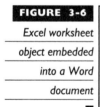

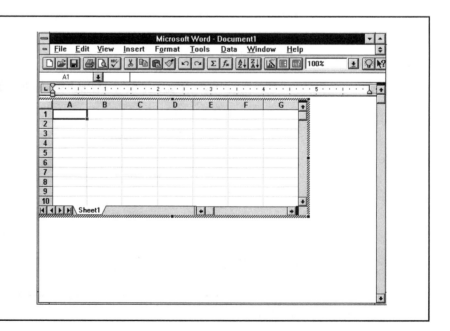

FIGURE 3-6

Excel worksheet object embedded into a Word document

To insert the computation into your Word document, follow these steps:

1. Position the insertion point where you want the object.
2. Choose the Object command from Word's Insert menu. Word displays the Object dialog box.
3. Display the Create from File tab shown below. This tab is very similar to the dialog box displayed by the File Open command in all of the Office applications.

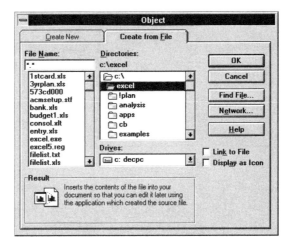

4. Enter or select the file you want to embed.
5. Choose OK.

A worksheet displaying the data in the active sheet of the Excel document is inserted in the Word document. The entire document is embedded, but only the range you specified is visible on the screen.

As it appears in the client application, the embedded object (Figure 3-6) will contain a range large enough to include all cells containing data (which includes formatting attributes) in the active sheet in the source document. If only one or two cells contain data, the embedded object might contain a few blank cells. Obviously, it's not a good idea to embed a worksheet (like the one in Figure 3-7) that is too large to fit comfortably into a text document. In Chapter 4 and in some of the examples in Part II you will learn strategies for dealing with large embedded objects.

If, after inserting an Excel document, you decide you need only part of the data, you can copy a range from the object. The simplest method is to activate the linked or embedded object, select the range you want to copy,

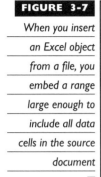

FIGURE 3-7

When you insert an Excel object from a file, you embed a range large enough to include all data cells in the source document

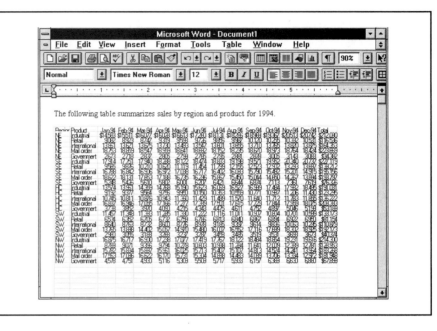

and drag it to the desired location in the destination document. (Alternatively, you can use the Copy/Paste Special procedure from the Edit menu to paste the selected range from the object into the client application.) You can then delete the original Excel object if it is no longer needed.

note *If you decide you want to save an inserted object as a separate file, you must start the server application and copy the object into a new document.*

Inserting a Range from an Excel File

Word offers another command on the Insert menu, File, for inserting Excel objects from existing files. With this command you can specify a range. However, inserting with the File command automatically converts the Excel data into formatted text. You can plain-paste or link data, but not embed, with the File command.

Follow these steps to insert an Excel range as formatted text:

1. Place the insertion point in the desired location in the Word document.

2. From the Insert menu, choose File. This brings up the following dialog box.

Chapter 3: Sharing Data Between Excel and Word 55

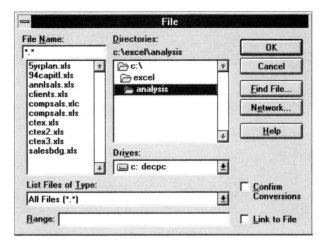

3. Select the All Files option in the List Files of Type box, so that files other than Word documents will be listed.

4. In the File dialog box, select the directory path and filenames. If you want to link the data, select the Link to File option.

5. Choose OK. Word displays the Open Workbook dialog box.

6. Select the sheet containing the range you want to insert.

7. Choose Open. Word displays the Open Worksheet dialog box:

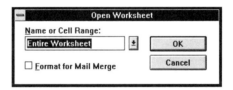

8. Display the Name or Cell Range list by clicking the adjacent arrow.

9. Select the range you want to insert.

10. Choose OK.

The data in the specified range is inserted in the Word document as a Word table. That is the same result you would obtain if the range had been copied in Excel and pasted into Word using the Paste command from the Edit menu. However, if you are using Word and Excel is not running, the File command on the Insert menu will save you the time it would have taken to start Excel and copy the range over to Word.

note *If you're inserting data from a non-Office application, you might want Word to display a confirmation message before it converts the foreign file. See Chapter 6 for more information on the subject of file conversion.*

If you find you've inserted the wrong range, you can change the range by following these steps:

1. With the inserted object selected, press F9. This displays the Open Workbook dialog box again.
2. Select the desired sheet and choose Open.
3. In the Open Worksheet dialog box select another range to insert.

Follow these principles when deciding whether to use the Object command or the File command:

- If you want to create a new object, choose Object.
- If you want to insert an object from an existing file as an Excel worksheet object, a picture, or a bitmap, choose Object.
- If you want to insert an object from an existing file as formatted text, choose Object if you know the name of the range you want to insert. Otherwise, choose File, which allows you to select a range name from a list.

Linking and Embedding Excel Chart Objects

In general, the procedures for sharing Excel charts and sharing worksheet ranges are similar. Many of the options require you to balance the same kinds of decision factors as with worksheet objects. To illustrate chart linking and embedding you'll come back to the yield report memo you looked at earlier in this chapter (Figure 3-5).

Embedding an Excel Chart

Suppose you want to put a chart of results for the prior three months in the memo. The following sheet contains production and scrap figures (computed as reject percentage rates) for the current month and the prior three months:

Chapter 3: Sharing Data Between Excel and Word

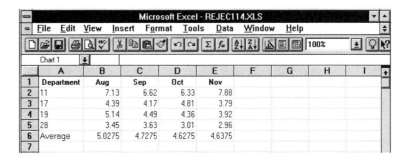

To embed the Excel chart in a memo, follow these steps:

1. Select the chart.
2. Choose Copy from the Edit menu.
3. Activate the Word document.
4. Position the insertion point in the desired location.
5. Choose Paste Special from the Edit menu.
6. In the As list, select Microsoft Excel 5.0 Chart Object.
7. Choose OK.

Excel inserts the chart in the memo, as shown in Figure 3-8.

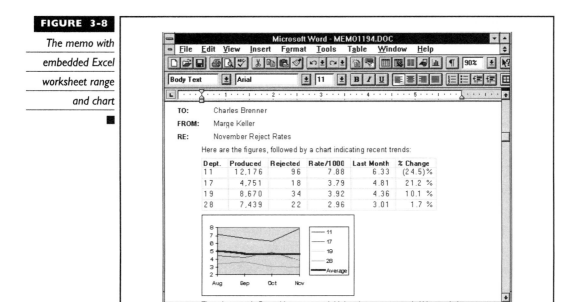

FIGURE 3-8

The memo with embedded Excel worksheet range and chart

To activate the chart for formatting with Excel commands, double-click the chart object. Once you've activated the object, you can also change the worksheet data supporting the chart.

Inserting an Excel Chart

You can create an Excel chart and insert it in a memo by following these steps:

1. With the memo document open in Word, position the insertion point where you want the chart.
2. Choose the Object command from the Insert menu. This displays the Object dialog box.
3. Select the Microsoft Excel 5.0 Chart option from the As list.
4. Choose OK.

This inserts an Excel object with two sheets: a chart and a worksheet with some sample data, which is shown in Figure 3-9. (You might find it initially disconcerting to see that you've inserted an Excel object with travel expense figures. However, Microsoft felt that that was preferable to embedding a completely blank chart sheet and worksheet, which would leave many users wondering what to do next.)

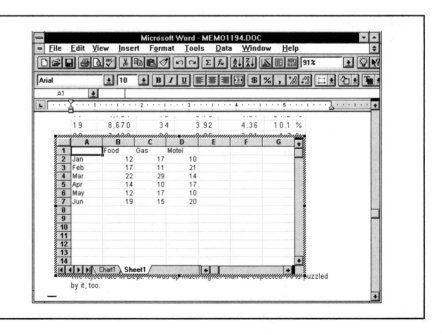

FIGURE 3-9

When you insert a chart object, it comes complete with this sample data, which you must modify

Replace the sample data with your own data, adding or deleting rows and columns as necessary. If you delete any rows, you must follow these steps to modify the chart:

1. With the embedded chart activated for editing, select the sheet containing the chart. (This sheet is labeled Chart1 when you first insert the chart.) Excel will display a message.

2. Click OK to clear the message. The data series corresponding to the deleted rows are effectively deleted from the chart. However, "orphans" of the deleted rows remain in the chart. The first group of data markers (labeled "Food" in the figure shown here) contains stubby remnants of the markers for the deleted rows; the legend displays **#REF!** values in place of the deleted row headers.

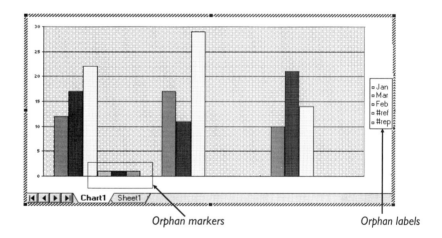

Orphan markers   Orphan labels

3. Click on one of the orphan markers in the first group chart and press DELETE. The marker disappears and the chart spacing adjusts accordingly. The corresponding label in the legend also disappears.

4. Delete the rest of the orphan markers in the same manner.

tip *To save time, consider creating a quick chart in Microsoft Graph. Graph-created charts look the same as Excel charts, and Graph uses fewer system resources than Excel. The main drawback is that the supporting data does not reside in Excel. You'll learn how to use Graph (one of the OLE-embedding applications that comes with Word) in Chapter 8.*

Embedding a Chart as a Picture

In the previous example, it was assumed that you wanted to embed the chart data as a chart object. That would allow you to use Excel to edit the chart. However, editing or changing the size of an embedded chart object in Word changes the "focus" of the displayed object relative to the entire worksheet contained in the object. Normally, changing the size of the object causes it to display only part of the chart, as shown in figure 3-10.

Moreover, embedding a chart from a large Excel file can add significant bulk to the destination file. It will also use scarce system resources.

To avoid these drawbacks, consider embedding the chart as a picture. You can scale embedded chart pictures and stretch them vertically or horizontally without worrying about inadvertently cropping them. The savings in file size can also be significant, depending on the relative sizes of the embedded object and the source file. If, for instance, you embed a small chart from a 100K source file, you'll increase the size of the destination file by about 100K. If, on the other hand, you embed a picture of that cell, the size of the destination file might only increase by 5K or so.

The only problem with using a picture is that you will only be able to edit the object with Word's own small picture-editing application. As you can see from Figure 3-11, you can format individual objects (such as labels) within the picture; this can be useful when you are forwarding the Word document to someone who does not have Excel. If you anticipate having to edit the chart with the aid of Excel, though, paste the chart as a chart object.

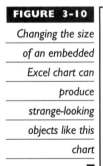

FIGURE 3-10

Changing the size of an embedded Excel chart can produce strange-looking objects like this chart

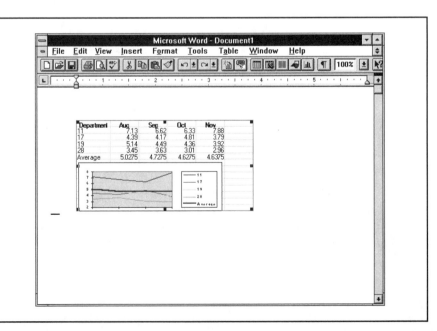

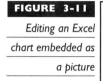

FIGURE 3-11

Editing an Excel chart embedded as a picture

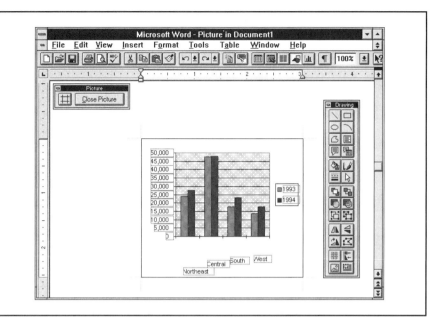

A chart pasted as a picture will be treated like any picture created in Word. For instance, if you select Picture Placeholders in the View tab (which allows the screen to refresh faster by suppressing the display of graphics), a placeholder will appear in place of the chart. You can suppress printing of the chart if you select the Draft Output option in the Print tab of the Options dialog box (which prevents pictures in the document from printing).

Linking a Chart

Linking requires less file space for destination documents than does embedding. When you link a chart object, it doesn't matter whether you link it as a picture or as a native object. Either way, you get a linked picture that you can activate and edit in Excel.

To link a chart to Word, follow these steps:

1. Copy the chart in Excel.
2. Display the Paste Special dialog box from the Edit menu in Word.
3. Select the Picture option in the As box.
4. Select Paste Link. (It doesn't matter what data type is selected in the As box.)
5. Choose OK.

This will link a picture of the chart in the Word document; you can scale the object without inadvertently cropping it. When you activate the object for editing, you will be able to edit the source document in Excel.

Editing Objects

One of the most profound advances in Office's implementation of OLE 2 is also one of the simplest to use: editing objects in place. All you have to do is double-click the object to be able to modify and format the data (whether linked or embedded) using the commands and tools of the server application.

Editing Embedded Excel Objects

To edit an embedded Excel object, double-click the object. This activates the object for editing in its native environment. The Word main menu and toolbars are replaced by their Excel equivalents (Figure 3-12). Scroll bars also appear in the object.

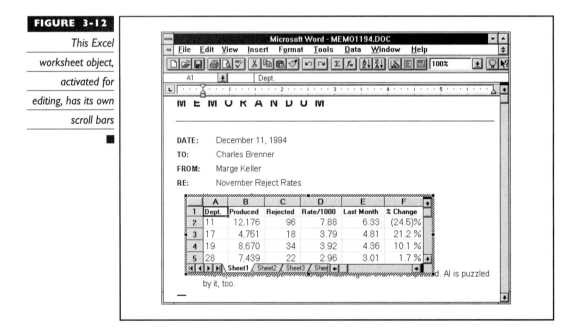

FIGURE 3-12

This Excel worksheet object, activated for editing, has its own scroll bars

tip *The Office applications provide two alternatives to the double-click procedure for editing a linked or embedded object. One method is to click the object with the right mouse button to bring up a shortcut menu of editing options. You can also choose the Object command from the Edit menu for editing the object. (The exact name of this command depends on what type of object is selected. If an Excel object embedded in Word is selected, for instance, choose Edit, then Spreadsheet Object.)*

The menus and toolbars of the client application change only when the object is truly *foreign*—that is, not native to the client application. If you paste an Excel range into Word as formatted text, it becomes a (native) Word table. Since you can edit the table within Word, double-clicking the table will result in no change to Word's menu or toolbars.

Moving Around the Source

Once you have activated an embedded Excel object, you are not limited to editing the original source range. You can scroll anywhere in the current sheet, or select other sheets in the workbook. You can add or delete sheets. To sum it up, it's as if you have opened the document in Excel—because that's exactly what OLE 2 allows you to do.

When you have finished editing an embedded object, click outside the object to return to the client application. All changes you made will be reflected in the embedded object.

Editing Linked Excel Objects

When you double-click a linked object, the client application's menus remain in place. The server application starts up in its own window and opens the source document (Figure 3-13). As with embedded objects, you have full access to the entire source document. You can even open another document, since the server application is actually running.

When you have finished editing a linked or embedded object, click outside the object to return to the client application. Generally, changes you make to the source document are controlled by the Automatic, Manual, and/or Locked options in the Links dialog box. However, this setting can be overridden by setting certain options in the Options dialog box of the client or server application. You will see how updating can be suppressed for linked Excel and Word objects in Chapter 4.

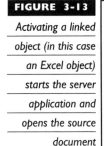

FIGURE 3-13

Activating a linked object (in this case an Excel object) starts the server application and opens the source document

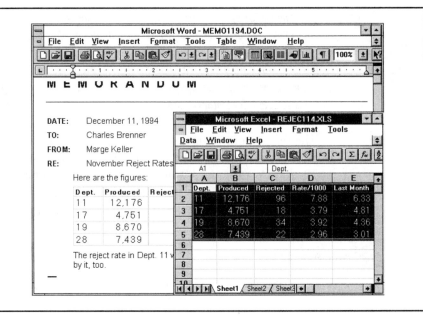

note   *You can add formatting that "surrounds" the object without resorting to in-place activation. For instance, you can use Word's Format Borders command to add a border around embedded pictures, Excel worksheets, and Excel chart objects.*

Using Word as a Server for Excel

There are two primary reasons to use Word as a server application: to pass text contained in a Word document to another application and to add explanatory or decorative text. The former is done by paste-linking a word or phrase into a cell formula; the latter involves pasting picture objects onto worksheets.

Pasting Text into a Cell

If you often use a certain Excel worksheet together with a particular Word document, you might want the worksheet to capture some key pieces of data from the Word document. Suppose, for instance, that when you send out a notice of an upcoming meeting, you usually attach a small Excel worksheet that summarizes the allotted time for each topic on the agenda. You can paste-link text that you use as a template for creating the meeting notices from the Word document to the Excel worksheet.

Figure 3-14 illustrates how text data from Word can be linked to a cell in a worksheet. (Notice the formula in Excel's formula bar.)

To paste-link text into Excel, follow these steps:

1. Select the text in the Word document you want to link.
2. Choose Copy from the Edit menu.
3. Open (or activate) the Excel worksheet that will contain the schedule for the meeting.
4. Select the cell in the workbook you want to contain the linked text.
5. Choose Paste Special from the Edit menu.
6. In the Paste Special dialog box, select Text from the As list.
7. Select the Paste Link option.
8. Choose OK.

The description of the meeting ("Partner's Meeting") in the Word document illustrated in Figure 3-14 is linked to the active cell (B2) in the Excel worksheet. Though you can't tell from the diagram, the date (1/9/95) shown in the Word document is also linked to the worksheet (cell B3). The links

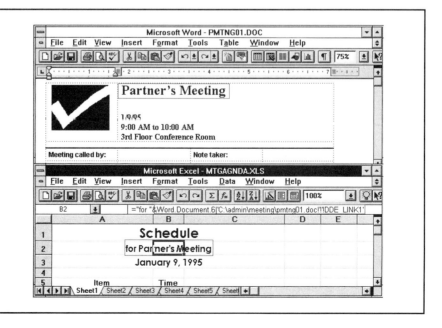

FIGURE 3-14

You can paste-link specific Word text to a cell value so that Word essentially passes a variable to Excel

preclude the possibility of mismatched date and title information in the Word and Excel documents.

As you can see from the formula bar in Figure 3-14, paste-linking the Word text in this manner creates a DDE link to the Word document while it enters a formula in the selected cell. That's because Excel can act as an OLE client application for graphic objects only; you cannot create an OLE link to a cell entry. (You can use OLE to link or embed Word text to an Excel document, but the text is encapsulated in a picture object.).

To implement the DDE link, Word creates a bookmark with a name like DDE_LINK1 in the source document. Bookmarks are the only mechanism available in Word to ensure that an Excel formula can refer to certain selected text. Bookmarks are essentially Word's equivalent to Excel's named ranges.

caution *You must save the Word document after you create the link to save the bookmark and preserve the link.*

If you want to use logical or mnemonic names when you link to Word text, you can create your own bookmarks in the Word template, such as Client for the client's name. See Chapter 13 for more details.

You can search for bookmarks in a Word document by following these steps:

1. Press F5 twice to display the Go To dialog box.

2. Select Bookmark in the Go to What list. The Go To dialog box looks like this:

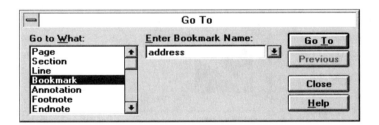

3. In the Enter Bookmark Name box, enter the bookmark name or click the arrow and select the name from the drop-down list.

4. Choose Go To.

Word selects the text defined by the bookmark. (If the bookmark contains a field, it selects the field.)

Inserting Word Files with Excel Commands

Earlier in this chapter, you learned how to link and embed Excel objects from existing files using Word's Insert Object command. You can also do the converse: insert an existing Word document, or part of one, into Microsoft Excel.

Follow these steps to insert an existing Word document into an Excel document:

1. Select the cell where you want the upper-left corner of the document to appear.

2. From the Insert menu, choose Object. This brings up the Object dialog box.

3. Display the Create from File tab as shown here.

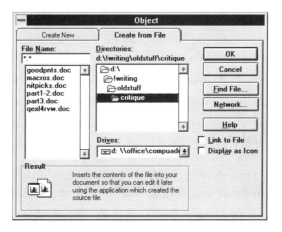

4. Enter or select the drive and directory in the usual manner.

5. If you want to insert a linked object, select the Link to File option.

6. When you have finished, choose OK.

Microsoft Excel inserts a picture containing the selected text file into your Microsoft Excel worksheet.

You can only insert entire documents—not selected text—with Excel's Insert Object command.

Deleting Objects

To delete an object from a destination document, simply select it and press DELETE. Be aware, however, that if no other copy of the object exists, you will receive no warning.

You might want to delete an object from a document but first save a copy in a separate file, just in case you need to use it again. Follow these steps:

1. With the object selected, choose the Object command from the Edit menu. Most likely, the word "Object" will be preceded by the object's type. For instance, if you have selected an Excel object, the command will be Spreadsheet Object.

2. Choose the Open command from the submenu. This starts the server application and opens the source document.

3. In the server application, choose File Save Copy As.

4. In the Save As dialog box, enter the filename and directory in the usual manner.

5. Choose OK.

Conclusion

In this chapter, you learned the procedures for linking and embedding objects in Excel and Word, both by copying data from the server application and by pulling in source data while running the client application. You also learned how to activate linked and embedded objects for editing, which is one of the most advanced features of OLE 2.

The next chapter will also show you some of the finer points of the Excel-to-Word OLE connection. You will also learn how to minimize the risks inherent in data sharing.

CHAPTER 4

Managing Linked and Embedded Objects

As you continue working with linked and embedded objects, you will encounter increasingly complex and challenging situations. As advanced as it is, OLE 2 can still confound users in seemingly ordinary data-sharing operations. You can minimize problems, though, if you make judicious decisions as you share data between applications. This chapter will add to your knowledge base by covering linked and embedded objects in greater depth.

In this chapter, you will learn

- Factors to consider when you're deciding how to share data (for instance, whether to link or embed)
- How to modify and manage links between applications
- A variety of techniques for solving problems and for getting the best results out of the Excel-to-Word data connection

Managing Embedded Objects

As you learned in the previous chapter, embedded objects require you to make tradeoffs. The most costly tradeoff is the potentially large amounts of memory and disk storage requirements of embedded objects. This section will help you find the most efficient way to share data in a variety of situations.

Realizing the Power of Embedding

It's well worth repeating that embedded objects are much more than the small snippets of data that appear in the client application. As you learned in the previous chapter, when you embed an object, you embed the entire source document—no matter how large or complex—in the client application. Consequently, you can do virtually anything to an embedded Excel object in the client application once you activate the embedded object for editing.

To see a simple example of the versatility of embedding, follow these steps:

1. Open (or create) an Excel document that contains data in more than one region within a sheet—with the ranges fairly close together—as shown here:

	A	B	C	D	E	F	G	H
1			1993	1994				
2	Wages		23,052.00	13,847.00				
3	Schedule C Income		21,541.36	37,679.00				
4	All Other		(2,724.00)	938.00				
5	Adjusted Gross Income		43,862.36	54,458.00				
6								
7								
8	Other Income:							
9	Interest		65.00	614.00				
10	Dividends		211.00	324.00				
11	Capital loss		(3,000.00)	0.00				
12			(2,724.00)	938.00				
13								

2. Copy one of the ranges containing data (such as A1:D5 as shown in the above screen) and paste it into Word as an embedded Excel 5.0 Worksheet object. The Excel object displays the range you copied—in this case, A1:D5.

3. Activate Word and double-click the Excel object.

4. Expand the size of the object by dragging the bottom-right selection square down and to the right. Expand the boundaries far enough to make room for the second data area. The Excel sheet tabs will appear at the bottom of the object.

5. Click outside the object. The embedded Excel object will now display the second data area. Figure 4-1 shows the result of the procedure on the given example.

The range displayed by the object now includes the second data area. As you can see, embedded objects are not "what you see is what you get" entities; what you actually get is *more* than what you can see.

The implications are profound. The recipient of your document has much more direct control over the appearance of the compound document than you might appreciate from the simple example you just looked at. If she thinks the embedded object includes too much detail, she can "narrow" it down to a smaller range. She can add summary computations to the

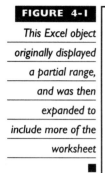

FIGURE 4-1

This Excel object originally displayed a partial range, and was then expanded to include more of the worksheet

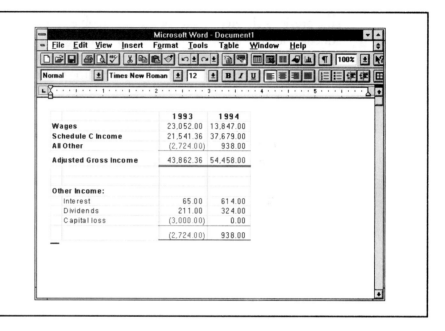

embedded object and display those in place of the range you embedded. She can activate a different sheet in the embedded workbook. She can create new scenarios with the Scenario Manager. She can even run a macro that's contained in the embedded document.

The list of operations you can perform on an embedded object can actually become almost dizzying. In effect, you can do virtually anything, even something that doesn't make sense, because that's the nature of embedding in OLE 2.

Keep this capability in mind when you send or submit Word documents with embedded Excel data. In the Word text, you can include instructions for the recipients to examine assumptions and even test results of different assumptions (as long as they don't save over your data).

Understanding What Embedding *Can't* Do

The freedom to roam all over an embedded Excel object when editing it carries responsibility. When you have finished editing, you must be sure to return to the range you want displayed in the destination document. Remember that the displayed object reflects the portion of the source document displayed when you finish editing it.

One thing you can't do in an embedded object is open another file within the object. The Open command from the File menu is still "owned" by the client application, so any new documents you open will be in the client application rather than the embedded object. If, while editing an embedded Excel object, you take any action that would result in opening another Excel document—such as double-clicking a cell containing a reference to another Excel workbook—Excel will display an error message.

Though you can display an Excel object that includes both cell data and an embedded chart, you wouldn't want to. You can produce a superior-looking document by sharing the chart and the supporting data as two separate objects. You should also consider linking, rather than embedding, the two objects to preclude any possible discrepancies between the two.

You cannot link or embed Excel modules. (Modules are sheets containing Visual Basic, or VBA, code). You can, however, copy text from modules into Word. Since modules contain only VBA code in the form of text, there would be no need to paste a "module object." While editing an Excel object, you can, however, run a macro (Visual Basic or Excel 4.0 style) that is contained in an embedded Excel object.

Minimizing the Memory and Storage Costs of Embedding

Along with all their power and richness, embedded objects carry some heavy baggage. Even if what appears in the destination document looks minor, the embedded object can inflate the size of destination documents. Copying a single cell from an 800K Excel file increases the size of the destination document by about 800K because (remember?) the embedded document contains all the information necessary to edit it with the server application's tools. Once people in a large workgroup catch on to the power of embedded objects, server disk storage requirements could soar. It's not unthinkable that organizations might have to institute procedures to limit the use of embedded objects.

Considering the disk space required by embedded objects, you should try to link rather than embed, unless the source document is relatively small. You should also delete unused sheets from Excel workbooks before embedding any data from them.

At the same time, you should note that embedded objects do not always use more disk space than linked objects. When you are linking or embedding a "native" object in the client application (such as formatted text in Word), embedding has the same effect on file size as does linking, because native objects contain less data than foreign objects. Also, in the case of large Excel worksheet objects, linking will save slightly less space than when the object is small. Finally, if the source document is very small, a link will be slightly more costly in terms of disk space than an embedded object.

Naturally, there will still be instances where linking is not practical—when you need to send a compound document off site, for example. If you must embed a small amount of data from a huge Excel document, consider one of the following space-saving techniques:

- Paste the Excel object as a picture. This saves space, but also means no one will be able to use Excel's capabilities to format the object.

- If retaining full formatting capability is important, paste the desired range into a new Excel workbook. (You might have to paste values rather than formulas.) Then paste the data from that "minimalist" workbook into the Word document. That way the recipient can double-click the object to format it. (Curiously, deleting sheets from a document that has already been embedded does not reduce the size of the destination document.)

Sending separate copies of the destination document to multiple recipients could be a major source of "object pollution" on the network. You can combat the proliferation of large objects by *routing* compound documents rather than sending out multiple copies. You'll see an example of document routing in Chapter 11.

note   *You can share drawing objects you create in Excel (such as lines and circles) by copying them into Word, but it's more efficient to create them with Word's own drawing tool. You'll learn how to do this in Chapter 7.*

Dealing with Large Excel Objects

If you're preparing a document for upper management, any Excel data you need to add to a report or memo will likely be summary data that fits nicely within a single page. Occasionally, however, you want to provide detailed Excel data within a printed document. If the data is larger than the confines of a single page, one of the following strategies might enhance the appearance of the printed compound document:

- If the sheet is only barely larger than a single page, you can set off the object with section breaks, then adjust the margins so it will fit on one page. If this still does not provide enough room, Word will shrink the document proportionately, as shown in Figure 4-2. The effect is similar to what you get when you fit a document to a single page in the Page tab of Excel's Page Setup dialog box.

- You can link or embed a series of smaller portions of the Excel document so that each shared object will fit on a single page of the Word document.

If you are submitting the document electronically, you can

- Embed the Excel object as an icon.
- Embed a small part of the Excel document and advise the recipient to edit the object in place so he can view the entire document.

tip *Saving files that contain OLE objects to a floppy disk can be surprisingly slow, because of the way Windows stores these files. One way to speed up the process is create a floppy disk cache with SmartDrive. See Chapter 15 for more information.*

Converting Objects

Earlier in this chapter, you learned that one way to save disk space is to link or embed an object type that carries less information "luggage" with it. Usually, selecting a native object type (like text or picture objects when Word is the client application) will require less disk space, subject to some exceptions that were discussed earlier in this chapter.

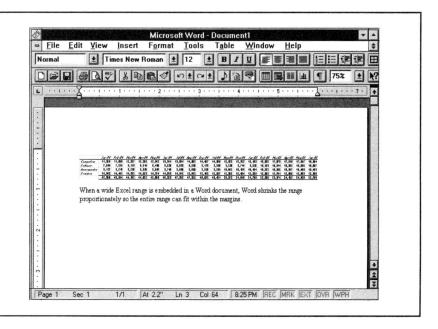

FIGURE 4-2
Word reduces the font size of large Excel objects to fit them on a single page

To a limited degree, you can convert one type of embedded object to another. You might want to do this to save memory or disk space. Embedded objects use at least as much file space as the entire source document, so every instance of embedding essentially doubles the storage space occupied by the source document. However, converting an embedded Excel object to a picture can save space.

To convert a linked or embedded object in Word to an embedded picture, select the object and press CTRL+SHIFT+F9. Breaking a link in Word also converts the object to an embedded picture. You'll learn how to break a link later in this chapter.

None of the Office applications, however, offers a Convert command that converts an OLE object into an object that is native to the client application. If you are working in a client application other than Word, you might have to use the following workaround procedure:

1. In the client application, select the linked or embedded object.
2. From the Edit menu, choose Copy.
3. Click on the destination document at the point where you want to place the copied object.
4. From the Edit menu, choose Paste Special.
5. In the Paste Special dialog box, select the desired datatype. (For instance, if the original object is an Excel chart, select Picture.)
6. Choose OK.
7. Delete the original object if it is no longer needed.

note *If you select an object, then display the Edit menu and choose Worksheet Object or Chart Object (depending on what object type is selected), the client application will display a submenu with a Convert command. The Word manual, on page 608, says you can use this procedure to convert a worksheet object to text, or to convert a chart object to a picture. The manual, however, is in error on that point. Microsoft has acknowledged that the section, "Converting an Embedded Object to a Graphic," on pages 608-609 is incorrect. Due (apparently) to bugs or omissions, the Convert command essentially does not work.*

Understanding Excel-to-Word Links

Though the OLE standard sets guidelines for interapplication data sharing, each client application employs different methods in implementing links. Word, for instance, uses *fields,* which will be explained momentarily. The client application's particular method of implementing links controls how the object reacts to editing and other operations. To fully exploit the Excel-to-Word data connection, you have to learn how Word fields work.

Understanding Word Fields

Most OLE client applications provide some kind of referencing device to "point" to the source data. In Excel, that device is the cell formula. In Word, this task is carried out by fields.

Like Excel formulas, fields accept arguments, reference other items, and can perform calculations. Fields are often used in creating form letters and in inserting dates and page numbers. When you paste-link data into Word as you did in Chapter 3, you create a LINK field.

Creating EMBED Fields

When you embed an object in Word, Word creates an EMBED field. You can think of the EMBED field as a "slot" into which Word fits embedded objects of all types. (Incidentally, you can only create an EMBED field by using the Insert menu's File or Object commands, or by creating an object in a server application. You cannot create an EMBED field with the Insert Field menu's command.)

Generally, Word displays the results of fields. You can, however, view the *field codes* in a document by pressing ALT+F9, which toggles back and forth between field code view and normal view. ALT+F9 is the Word keyboard shortcut for selecting the Field Codes option in the View tab of the Options dialog box.

As the term "field code" suggests, fields contain text codes that determine what the field displays in the Word document. Figure 4-3 shows the Word memo with field codes displayed. Viewing the field codes is helpful in discovering what is wrong when you don't get the results you intended. You will learn more about field codes in later chapters.

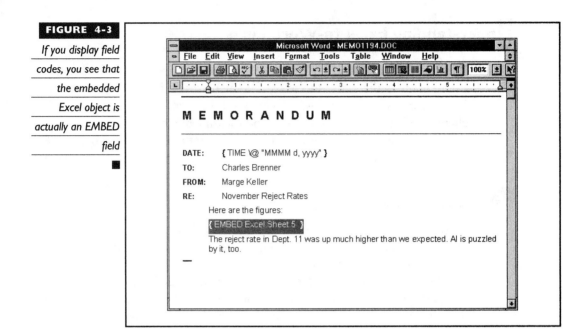

FIGURE 4-3

If you display field codes, you see that the embedded Excel object is actually an EMBED field

Creating LINK Fields

Like embedded objects, linked objects in Word are contained in fields. The following LINK field code is an example:

```
LINK Excel.Sheet.5 "C:\\EXCEL\\ADMIN\\CFO\\CAPCONTR.XLS"
"CAPCONTR!R26C3" \a \p
```

Being more complex than EMBED fields, LINK fields have more parameters. In many cases, you can go about your linking activities blissfully unaware of the complexities of LINK field syntax. However, complications can arise, so it's best to learn how to work with LINK fields in Word.

Understanding LINK Field Syntax

The syntax of a LINK field is as follows:

```
{link class_name file_name [item] [switches]}
```

The *class* name represents the data type, such as Excel.Sheet.5 for an Excel 5.0 worksheet object or Word.Picture.6 for a picture. This is determined by your selection in the As list of the Paste Special dialog box. The *file* name is the name of the source file; the *item* is the sheet and cell reference.

note *Remember from Chapter 2 that OLE organizes objects by the application, topic, and item? You can see from the syntax in the LINK field how Word implements this referencing method. The* class name *parameter is roughly equivalent to the application. The* file name *is the topic, and the* cell or range *is the item.*

Switches are used by Word in fields to indicate preferences. Table 4.1 explains the switches available for the LINK field.

You'll learn more about the LINK field and its parameters in several examples in Part II of this book. Sometimes the fastest way to get the desired result from an embedded object is to edit the field codes. You'll learn how to do this later in this chapter in the section "Editing LINK Fields Directly."

Keeping Control of Linked Objects

Be sure to keep in mind while you are editing linked Excel objects that what you are changing is not an independent, freestanding object; it is the source document itself. Your changes will cause changes to any and all destination documents that are linked to any of the cells you change. Even though it looks like you are acting locally, your changes can have a global effect, rippling through a series of destination documents. Moreover, this

Switch	Effect
\a	Updates LINK field automatically when source data changes
\b	Displays a bitmap
\d	Does not save the graphic data with the file, which saves disk space
\p	Displays a Word picture
\r	Displays formatted text
\t	Displays unformatted text

TABLE 4-1 *Effects of Switches in LINK Fields* ∎

will occur without any warning message. This is good reason to consider sequestering important source documents in a single directory and protecting them from unauthorized changes by limiting access to those files.

If you're concerned about unauthorized changes affecting your destination documents, you can always break all links to the source document. Of course, you will then lose automatic updating, which might be critically important in some situations. A less drastic alternative is to lock linked objects, but that only postpones the day of reckoning. In most cases, you eventually have to jump one way or the other. Either you break the link and give up your update capability, or leave the link in place and give up a certain amount of assurance that no one will mess with the source data for the linked objects.

tip *Consider applying one of Excel's AutoFormats before pasting an Excel object in Word. Unless you paste it as Formatted Text (or paste-link a picture), you won't be able to format the gridlines or patterns in Word.*

Modifying Links

The rationale behind OLE is that shared data is plastic; it will change over time. A linked object in one of your destination documents might change without your intervention because someone has changed the source data; at other times you will change the shared data by editing it directly.

It's often useful to be able to transform a shared object into a different type of shared object as your work projects move from prototype to draft stage, and then to final form. In the early stages of creating a report in Word, you might embed an Excel worksheet object. Later, when you're sure you won't need to edit the object in Excel anymore, you might convert it to a picture to save disk space. There might be times when you need links to be updated rapidly, and other times that you'll want to minimize the link "traffic" between documents.

Changing an Automatic Link to a Manual Link

By default, Office applications create *automatic* links. That means that the client application constantly polls the server application to see if the source data has changed. When there's a change, the client application reads the revised data and updates the linked object.

While automatic links are gratifyingly sophisticated, they tend to slow down processing. As a result, changes in source data might take several seconds before they are reflected in the client application. Such delays are especially noticeable when a document contains several links. Sometimes you might want to streamline things by changing the update method.

To change an automatic link in a Word document to a manual link, follow these steps:

1. Select the linked object you want to modify.

2. From the Edit menu, choose Links. This brings up the Links dialog box, as shown here:

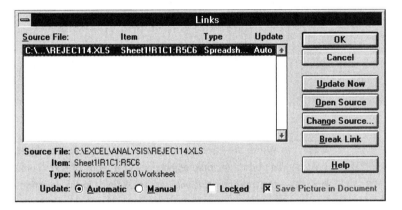

3. If you did not select the linked object you want to modify earlier, select it now from the list. If the document contains multiple links, you can add to the selection by clicking additional link(s) while pressing CTRL.

4. Select the Manual option.

5. Choose OK.

To change a manual link to an automatic link, follow the same procedure, but select the Automatic option in step 4.

note *If you open a destination document while the source document is open, and the open document differs from the saved version, the client application updates the linked object from the open document. If you close the source document without saving the changes, interestingly, the linked object will not revert to the saved version until you update it manually, or until you close and reopen the destination file.*

caution *When your document contains worksheet and chart objects reflecting the same data, make sure you use the same updating method for both objects. If one updates automatically and the other manually, you might have to explain some embarrassing discrepancies in your reports or presentations.*

Updating a Manual Link

If your document contains manual links, you obviously need to update them before submitting the document to someone else. To update a manual link, follow these steps:

1. Choose Edit, then Links.
2. Select the link(s) you want to update, if they are not already selected.
3. Choose the Update Now button.
4. Choose OK.

tip *In Word, the fastest way to update a single linked object is select the object, then press F9. To update multiple objects, select a block of text containing the objects and press F9—but note that this will update all fields in the selection along with the links.*

Locking a Link

In a Word document, you can *lock* linked objects individually to prevent updating, regardless of whether the links are set to Manual or Automatic. If your application is performing sluggishly, you might want to lock all links temporarily to improve performance. Locking prevents updating even when you try to update an object manually.

Locking is very useful when you want to globally suppress updating for all links in large portions of documents or entire documents. To lock all links in the current selection, press CTRL+F11. To unlock all links in the current selection, press CTRL+SHIFT+F11. Locking does not disturb the automatic or manual status of a link.

To lock a link individually, follow these steps:

1. In Word, choose Edit, then Links.
2. In the list box, select the link(s) you want to lock.

3. Select the Locked option.
4. Choose OK.

Breaking a Link

When a link has served its purpose and you want to finalize the object in its present form, you can break the link. Follow these steps:

1. Select the linked object you want to modify.
2. Choose Edit, then Links.
3. In the Links dialog box, choose the Break Link button.
4. Select Yes in response to the confirmation message. The link disappears from the list.
5. Choose OK.

tip *In Word, you can use the shortcut key for unlinking a field, CTRL+SHIFT+F9 instead of performing steps 2 through 5.*

The object does not appear to have changed. Display the field codes (by pressing ALT+F9), though, and you'll see that the object is now an embedded picture. In Word, breaking the link changes the datatype at the same time that it permanently severs the connection with the source file. For that reason, you should consider whether a less drastic measure such as locking or changing to manual updating better suits your purpose.

Redirecting Links

It's inevitable that someday you will inadvertently delete, rename, or move a source file. When this happens, you can restore the link (to the renamed or moved file), or redirect the link to another file.

Follow these steps to restore or redirect a link to an Excel range:

1. With the linked object selected, choose Edit, then Links.
2. In the Links dialog box, make sure the correct object is selected.
3. Choose the Change Source button. This brings up the Change Source dialog box shown on the following page.

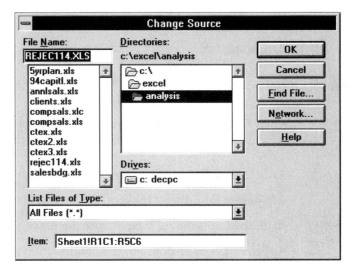

4. If you want to link to another file, or if you are trying to restore a severed link, select the file from the File Name box, changing drives or directories as needed.

5. Revise the Item entry if necessary, using the syntax *sheetname!reference*. (The sheet name is not required by the dialog box, but you should enter it for accuracy's sake. If you enter a cell reference only, the link will be to the active sheet when the object was last edited.)

6. Choose OK.

7. In the Links dialog box, change the update options as desired, then choose OK.

The worksheet object is now linked to the range you defined in the dialog box.

Editing LINK Fields Directly

You've learned to redirect links and change link parameters in the Links dialog box. You can also change the parameters by displaying field codes and editing the parameters in Word. Let's suppose you are looking at the following field code:

```
{LINK Excel.Sheet.5 D:\\EXCEL\\FY94\\BENEFITS\\HELIG02.XLS
Sheet1!Regpay \p}
```

The **\p** switch indicates that this is a picture object. You would like to change it to text. Follow these steps to change the object type:

1. Display field codes in the Word document, if they are not already displayed.
2. Delete the switch \p and replace it with \t.
3. Display field results.
4. Select the field and press F9.

Word now displays the object as unformatted text, using tabs and paragraph characters to separate the values.

If you link, the recipient can move around the workbook, and view and change different sheets. The one thing she won't be able to do, though, is select a different range to be displayed by the object.

Please note that when you link an object from an Excel file with the Insert menu's Object command, Word creates an INCLUDETEXT field in the following form.

{INCLUDETEXT C:\\EXCEL\\FY94\\BENEFITS\\HELIG2.XLS \c MSBiff }

The INCLUDETEXT field displays Excel worksheet data in the form of a table. INCLUDETEXT fields are always set to Manual update status, so you must press F9 to see changes immediately.

Opening a File That Contains Links

Be default, all links contained in a Word file are updated when you open the file. When you first install Word, the Update Automatic Links at Open option in the General tab of the Options dialog box (Figure 4-4) is selected. Clear this option to turn off automatic updating at opening. Before you do so, however, be aware that Word will not advise you when you open a file containing links.

Using Excel Data in Word

Word 6 is very adept at handling foreign data; however, it can get quirky in certain exotic situations. In this section, you'll learn how to deal with practical and technical issues that can arise when you share Excel data with Word.

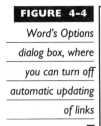

FIGURE 4-4

Word's Options dialog box, where you can turn off automatic updating of links

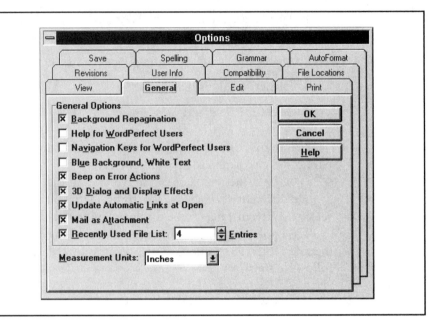

Making Sure Recipients Have Access to the Source File

Remember, every time you send a document that contains a link, you have to send the source file, or make sure the recipient has access to it. Otherwise, the recipient might receive an error message if he tries to access the source file, or he might simply open the destination file and not realize that he doesn't have current access to the source data.

If you receive a document containing links that cannot access a source document, you need to redirect the link. See the section "Redirecting Links" earlier in this chapter for instructions on how to do this.

caution It is possible to break a link without any sign of the broken link appearing in the destination document. If a link is broken by moving or renaming the source file while the destination document is not open, the latter document can be opened and the link updated without generating an error result or any other indication that the linked object is not actually linked to the source.

Copying Objects

If you want to create a copy of an embedded object to another document, simply choose Copy from the Edit menu while the object is selected, then paste it into the other document. You can also create multiple copies of the same object in a single document. You can also paste-link an object. This creates a DDE link to the original object. Changes you make to the original object will be reflected in any copies according to the same rules that apply to OLE links. If you double-click a linked object created in this manner, Word will select the original embedded object. If the source document is located in a closed file, Word will open it.

You can copy a linked object, too. If you plain-paste it, you create another linked object, identical in all respects to the original. From the Edit menu, if you choose Paste Special and then choose the Paste option, you embed a Word document object, formatted text, or a picture (depending on your selection in the As list of the Paste Special dialog box). If you choose Paste Link, you create a DDE link to the original object.

If you have received a compound document containing an embedded Excel worksheet you would like to save as a native Excel document, here's the easiest way to do it:

1. Activate the embedded object.
2. Copy the range you want to save.
3. Switch to the Program Manager and start another instance of Excel.
4. Paste the range into a blank worksheet and save the document under a different name.

Using Excel's Copy Picture Command

If you're working in Excel and you want to embed a picture of a range or a chart in Word, follow these steps:

1. Select the item (range or chart) you want to copy.
2. While pressing the SHIFT key, display the Edit menu.
3. Choose the Copy Picture command, which is displayed in place of the Copy command. This displays the Copy Picture dialog box.
4. Excel can copy the item in a form suitable for displaying on the screen (As Shown on Screen) or for printing (As Shown when Printed). Select the desired option and choose OK. (The effects of these options will be explained in a moment.)
5. Activate the Word document and position the insertion point where you want the copied picture to go.
6. From the Edit menu, choose Paste.

The effects of the As Shown on Screen and As Shown when Printed options are illustrated in Figure 4-5, which contains three picture objects created from the same Excel range. The first object on the left was copied using the As Shown on Screen option. The other two objects copied using the As Shown when Printed option. The difference between the second and third objects is due to different selected options in Excel's Page Setup dialog box at the time the range was copied. The second object was copied while gridline printing was turned on. When the third object was copied, gridline printing was turned off.

Pasting from a Chart in Its Own Sheet

Copying a chart in a chart sheet creates a strange result, at least initially. This action usually creates a chart that overflows the page in the client application. Fortunately, you can remedy this quirk easily. Simply double-click the embedded chart, then click the client application.

Copying from a chart sheet is ideal for linking or embedding charts that occupy the entire width of a page. However, it adds an \s switch to the EMBED field. The \s switch prevents picture or graphic objects from being resized. To resize the chart, you have to display field codes and manually remove the \s parameter from the field code.

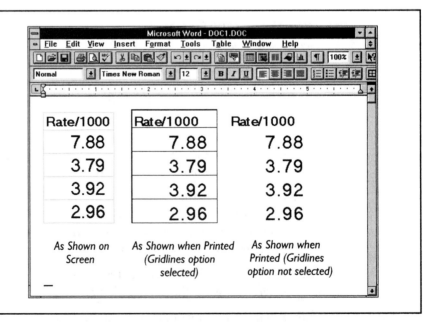

FIGURE 4-5

Three Excel objects copied as pictures, illustrating effects of the As Shown on Screen and As Shown When Printed options

Another solution to this problem is to paste the chart as a picture. The chart will be reduced in size as needed to fit in the margins.

Using Word Data in Excel

In Chapter 3, you learned how to use Word as a server application to pass key pieces of data to Excel formulas by pasting into a cell. While that is an important technique, there are more ways to share data coming into Word.

Pasting Text into a Cell Formula

Often, you want to use a text value from Word as an argument in an Excel formula. For instance, you might want to paste a date from Word, but convert the date into a number in Excel. If so, you can plain-paste text into the Excel formula bar. However, text pasted into the formula bar that exceeds 255 characters will be truncated.

If you paste text containing line feeds and tabs into a worksheet, Excel will paste each line of text into a separate row. Within each row, it will separate text into columns wherever it finds tab characters. Figure 4-6 shows how Excel breaks text into rows and columns.

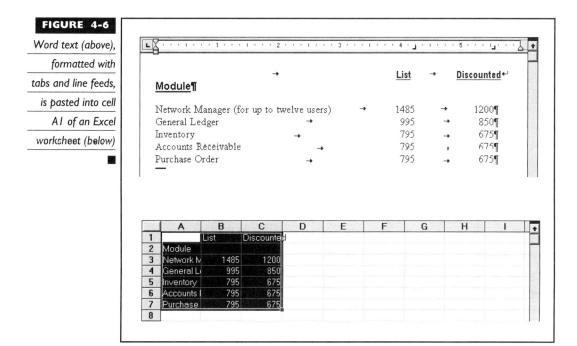

FIGURE 4-6
Word text (above), formatted with tabs and line feeds, is pasted into cell A1 of an Excel worksheet (below)

You cannot link text to the formula bar. However, you can paste text into a cell, then enter a formula referring to that cell in another cell.

Sharing Long Text

Sometimes you want to provide supplementary information to the viewer of an Excel document. Because Excel cells can contain at most 255 characters, you have to use Word objects or Excel text boxes to display long text.

Follow these steps to link or embed an entire Word document, or a large amount of text from a Word document, in Excel as a Word object:

1. In Word, select the text you want to link or embed. To select the entire document, hold down the CTRL key, then press 5 on the numeric keypad.

2. From the Edit menu, choose Copy.

3. Activate Excel and select the cell located at the upper-right corner of where you want the Word picture to appear.

4. From the Edit menu, choose Paste Special.

5. In the Paste Special dialog box, select Microsoft Word 6.0 Document Object from the As list. If you are linking the object, select Paste Link. Otherwise, leave the default Paste option selected.

6. Choose OK.

The text is linked or embedded as a full-page Word picture object, as shown in Figure 4-7. The object will retain all the formatting attributes, such as fonts, paragraph settings, and borders, that they have in the source document.

One disadvantage of Word objects containing a lot of text is that they occupy a lot of screen space. Unfortunately, you cannot scroll through Word objects. To surmount this problem, you can plain-paste the Word text into a text box (Figure 4-8) rather than linking or embedding a Word object. This allows you to keep the size of the text object to a minimum, while allowing the recipient to move through the text with the arrow keys.

Chapter 4: Managing Linked and Embedded Objects

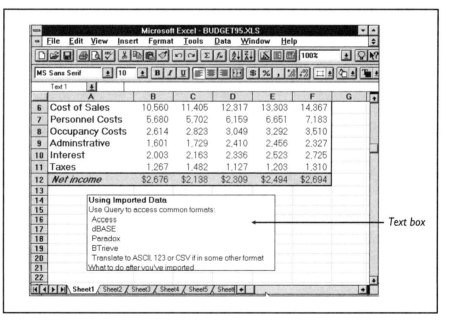

FIGURE 4-7
A Word picture object embedded in Excel

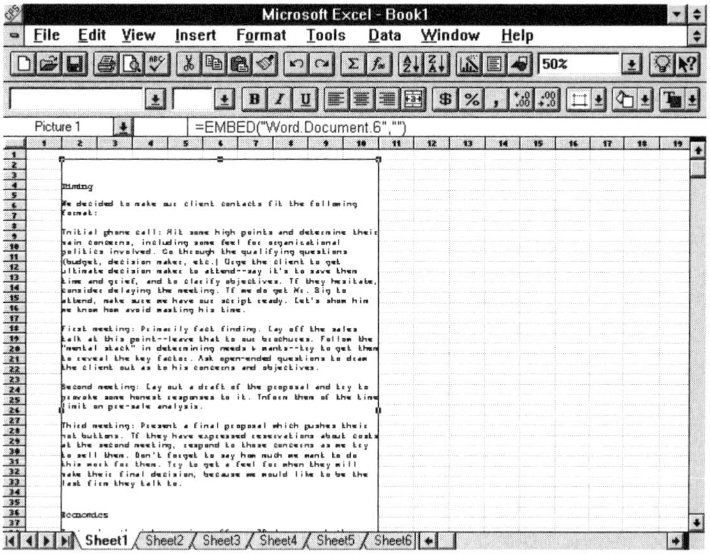

FIGURE 4-8
You can paste text from Word into a text box in Excel

The main drawbacks to this method are

- Formatting applied in the server application does not carry through to the Excel text box. Moreover, though line feeds and tabs work much as they do in Word, columns might not line up precisely within the text box.

- You can only plain-paste, not link or embed, Word text to an Excel text box.

note *You can move text from Word into formula bars and dialog box fields with OLE Automation. You'll learn how to do this in Chapters 14, 16, and 17.*

tip *If you want to identify all the bookmarks in a document—including DDE links—display the View tab of Word's Options dialog box and select the Bookmarks option in the Show area. All bookmarks in the document will be marked with heavy, square brackets.*

Sharing Tabular Data

Surprisingly, Word tables do not readily convert to Excel tables when embedded into Excel. In many cases, you will want to create a *list* in Excel from a Word table, with each of the cell values in the Word table contained in a separate cell in the Excel list. (As applied to Excel worksheet data, a "list" is roughly equivalent to a table in Word: a rectangular block of data with category names as column headers.)

The only way to create an Excel list from a Word table, however, is to plain-paste the table into a worksheet. This approach has one major drawback: it pastes only text, not table formulas. (Actually, the data is pasted as an array formula, but the effect is the same as if it were pasted as text.) If the Word table includes calculated amounts, such as row or column totals, the table formulas are effectively converted to numeric constants in Excel.

Unfortunately, there is no way to keep the table computations "live," as they would be in an Excel range. You can link a Word table containing formulas into Excel as a text or picture object. However, due to a minor bug in OLE 2.0, Excel will not update the table formulas within the object to reflect changes in the source document.

As you can see, copying tables from Word into Excel is only useful when you do not copy any table formulas. For the sake of accuracy, try to avoid copying tabular data from Word to Excel unless you're absolutely sure the copy range contains text or numeric constants only.

note *Whenever you paste an Excel range into a Word document as a table, Word inserts extra paragraph characters before and after the table. You cannot remove either of these paragraphs. The paragraphs are inserted automatically to prevent the possibility of pasting a table into a cell in another table.*

Managing Word Objects in Excel

Now that you've learned about linking and embedding Word objects in Excel, let's look briefly at what can happen in the document when you rearrange data in the worksheet. By default, Word objects in Excel worksheets move in tandem with the underlying cells when you insert rows or columns. This is helpful when you want an object to remain in close proximity to certain cells, but there will be other times when you want an object to remain in a fixed position.

To change the move and size properties of an object, follow these steps:

1. With the object selected, choose Object from the Format menu.

2. In the Format Object dialog box, display the Properties tab as shown here:

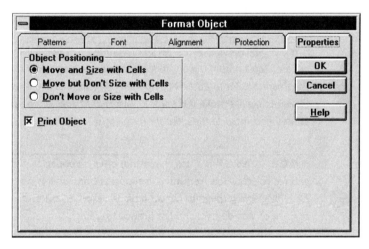

3. Select the desired option in the Object Positioning box.

In the Properties tab of the Format Object dialog box, you can also suppress printing of the object.

Saving Time When Printing Compound Documents

Because handling graphical data requires complex computations, Word documents that contain a large number of embedded objects can take a long time to print. One way to save printing time is to turn off printing of graphics in Word. Follow these steps:

1. Display the Options dialog box.
2. Display the Print tab.
3. Under Printing Options, select the Draft Output option.
4. Choose OK.

When you print, Word will omit the graphics, leaving blank the space(s) that would be occupied by the graphics. This can speed up printing considerably for graphics-intensive documents.

If you want rectangular placeholders to appear in the document to indicate the dimensions of graphic objects, follow these steps:

1. Display the Options dialog box.
2. Display the View tab.
3. Under Show, select the Picture Placeholders option.
4. Choose OK.

note *By default, Word does not update fields and links when documents are printed. You'll probably want to leave it this way (especially if linked objects in the document are set to Automatic updating, in which case they are always updated). However, always make it a point to ensure that links are updated before sending a printed document to the ultimate recipient(s).*

note *Unlike Word, Excel does not offer an option to globally suppress printing of graphic objects. However, you can suppress printing of a selected individual object in Excel by clearing the Print Object option in the Properties tab of the Format Object dialog box, which was described in the previous section.*

When Things Go Wrong

The OLE program that comes with the current version of Office is not a completely mature product, so you will run into undocumented problems from time to time. For help with some common problems, please refer to Chapter 15.

Conclusion

With this chapter, you've completed a short but intensive course on using OLE 2. Though you've worked mostly with Excel and Word, those two applications are the desktop productivity heart of the Office suite. As you begin working with the examples in Parts II and III of this book, don't forget to refer back to this chapter when you run into problems or confusing situations.

It's time now to move beyond the Excel-Word axis to the other programs in the Office suite. In the next chapter, you'll learn to use the Microsoft Query tool to bring database information into Excel and Word.

CHAPTER 5

Tapping Databases with Query

How many times have you wanted to analyze sales statistics in Excel, or send a form letter to all your company's suppliers in Word? Did you get frustrated because you couldn't readily access the large amounts of data required? The data might exist in your corporate accounting system or in a database; you might even be able to request a printed report. However, manually entering wage and tax information for, say, 200 employees into a spreadsheet from a hard copy would be extremely laborious.

To alleviate this "data lockup" problem, Microsoft included an add-in program called Microsoft Query to version 5 of Excel. Its primary purpose is to extract information created in other programs. Although Query is not a powerful relational database management system like Paradox or Access, it is a very useful tool.

In this chapter, you will see how to bring external data into Excel by learning

- Some basic facts about databases
- How to search for specific information in databases with Microsoft Query
- How to return the results of your Query to another application (such as Excel)

Why You Would Need to Query a Database

Among experienced spreadsheet users, the inability to conveniently access corporate data has been a time-honored complaint. If your job is to analyze large amounts of accounting and market research data, it's not practical to enter such data into your spreadsheet manually. Sometimes you can obtain corporate data in ASCII or comma-delimited format, which can be imported into Excel. Excel has some helpful tools for importing and formatting data, but the process can still be clumsy at times. Moreover, if you have to depend on the data processing department to provide the ASCII file, you might have to wait hours or days before you can look at the data.

Understanding Database Management Systems

If you work for an organization of more than, say, 200 employees, chances are the computer system has a database management system, or DBMS, that stores data in tables. You can use Query to pull data into Word or Excel from a DBMS. The first step in learning how is to understand the general structure of DBMSs.

note *The Professional version of Office includes the Microsoft Access program, a fully functional DBMS. Although Access can create more sophisticated queries, Query is faster and easier to learn. You'll learn about Access in Chapter 6.*

A table in a DBMS is much like a table in Excel or Word. (Figure 5-1 shows a customer table. This kind of data can easily be contained in a text document, a spreadsheet range, or a table in a DBMS.) Tables displayed in a DBMS generally have column headings across the top; the column headings correspond to *fields* in the table. Each row in the table contains values for the displayed fields for each *record*. (A record is the collection of field values for an individual instance or item in the table. The customer table, for instance, contains a record for each customer.)

FIGURE 5-1

Table containing customer data, typical of tables in a DBMS

Customer ID	Company Name	Address	City	Region	Postal
ALFKI	Alfreds Futterkiste	Obere Str. 57	Berlin		12209
ANTON	Antonio Moreno Taquería	Mataderos 2312	México D.F.		05023
AROUT	Around the Horn	120 Hanover Sq.	London		WA1 1DP
BERGS	Berglunds snabbköp	Berguvsvägen 8	Luleå		S-958 22
BLAUS	Blauer See Delikatessen	Forsterstr. 57	Mannheim		68306
BLONP	Blondel père et fils	24 place Kléber	Strasbourg		67000
BONAP	Bon app'	12, rue des Bouchers	Marseille		13008
BOTTM	Bottom-Dollar Markets	23 Tsawassen Blvd.	Tsawassen	BC	T2F 8M4
BSBEV	B's Beverages	Fauntleroy Circus	London		EC2 5NT
CACTU	Cactus Comidas para llevar	Cerrito 333	Buenos Aires		1010
CHOPS	Chop-suey Chinese	Hauptstr. 29	Bern		3012
COMMI	Comércio Mineiro	Av. dos Lusíadas, 23	São Paulo	SP	05432-043
CONSH	Consolidated Holdings	12 Brewery	London		WX1 6LT
DRACD	Drachenblut Delikatessen	Walserweg 21	Aachen		52066
DUMON	Du monde entier	67, rue des Cinquante	Nantes		44000
EASTC	Eastern Connection	35 King George	London		WX3 6FW
ERNSH	Ernst Handel	Kirchgasse 6	Graz		8010
FAMIA	Familia Arquibaldo	Rua Orós, 92	São Paulo	SP	05442-030
FOLKO	Folk och fä HB	Åkergatan 24	Bräcke		S-844 67
FRANK	Frankenversand	Berliner Platz 43	München		80805
FRANR	France restauration	54, rue Royale	Nantes		44000
FRANS	Franchi S.p.A.	Via Monte Bianco 34	Torino		10100
GALED	Galería del gastrónomo	Rambla de Cataluña, 23	Barcelona		08022

Sophisticated DBMSs store data in groups of related tables. These groups are generally called *databases*, though some DBMSs might use different terminology. Examples of these DBMSs, called *relational DBMSs*, include DBase IV, FoxPro, Paradox, Access, and Oracle. Relational DBMSs are able to meld groups of related tables into unified database systems by linking common fields among the various tables. Figure 5-2 illustrates how a DBMS can use key fields to link related tables.

A program can be a database even if not described as a database program. Most corporate accounting systems, for instance, store their data using relational DBMS methods. That means it's possible in many cases to access data from the accounting system via Microsoft Query.

Understanding Queries

Most relational DBMSs offer some capability to create *queries*. A query is a request to the database to provide certain selected information. When users talk about "accessing," "extracting," or "pulling in" data, they're implicitly talking about creating a query.

Microsoft Query and the ODBC Standard

Microsoft Query adheres to Microsoft's Open Database Connectivity (ODBC) standard. Relational DBMS vendors and third parties can create

FIGURE 5-2

How a relational DBMS links tables through common fields

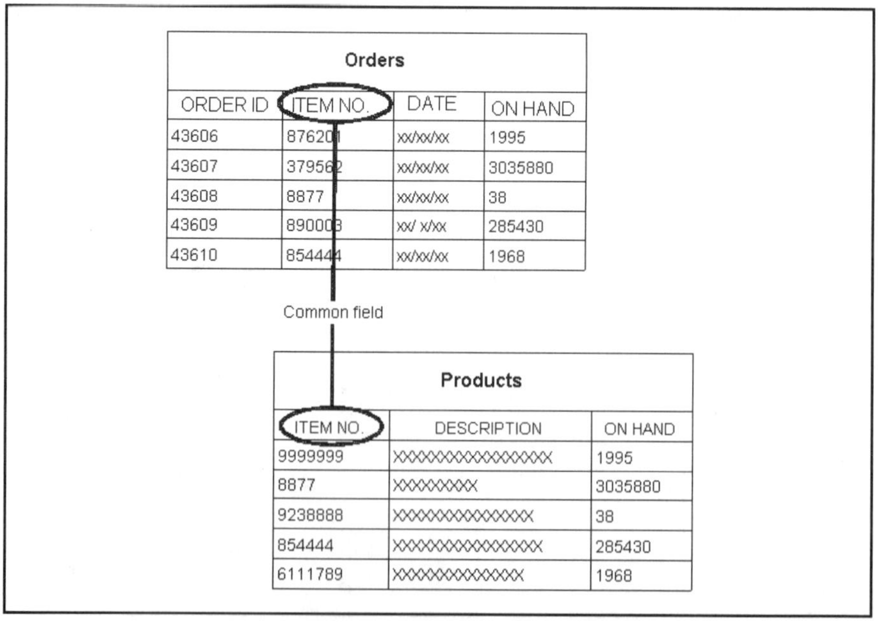

Orders

ORDER ID	ITEM NO.	DATE	ON HAND
43606	87620	xx/xx/xx	1995
43607	37956	xx/xx/xx	3035880
43608	8877	xx/xx/xx	38
43609	89000	xx/x/xx	285430
43610	85444	xx/xx/xx	1968

Common field

Products

ITEM NO.	DESCRIPTION	ON HAND
9999999	XXXXXXXXXXXXXXX	1995
8877	XXXXXXXX	3035880
9238888	XXXXXXXXXXXXX	38
854444	XXXXXXXXXXXXX	285430
6111789	XXXXXXXXXXXX	1968

"driver" programs that translate data into a form readable by Microsoft Query. It's not necessary to know anything about ODBC to perform the examples in this chapter, but you might eventually need to learn something about it to connect to some databases. Chapter 6 provides more information on the ODBC standard.

Creating Queries

One of the more common uses for Query is to pull database information into Excel. The examples in this chapter use the Query add-in for Excel. You can use Query as a stand-alone application by double-clicking the Query icon. (You'll find the Query icon in the same Program Manager group as the other Office applications.) However, it's easier to send query results to an application if you start Query from within that application. (You'll see why later in the chapter.)

note *As you learn how to use Query to bring data from Access and other databases into Excel, keep in mind that Query is essentially a tool for importing data. That is, Query converts and plain-pastes external data into the client application. You cannot use Query to link or embed data using OLE 2.*

Installing the Query Add-In

The Microsoft Query add-in ships with the Excel 5 program, but that does not necessarily mean that Query will be available. If the Get External Data command is present on Excel's Data menu, you can use the Query add-in immediately. The absence of the Get External Data command indicates one of two things:

- Query was not installed when the Office suite was originally installed. (That is, the person installing Office chose the custom setup option and chose not to install the Query add-in.)
- Query has not been added to the available list of add-ins in Excel.

The first step in remedying this situation is to choose the Add-ins command from the Tools menu. This brings up the Add-Ins dialog box shown on the next page:

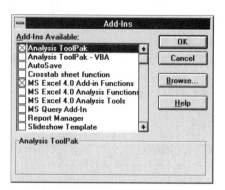

If the MS Query Add-In option is listed, click the name or the check box to select it, then choose OK. If this option does not appear in the list, you must install Microsoft Query. To install Query, follow these steps:

1. Run the Excel setup program. (Look for an icon called MS Excel Setup in the program group you specified when you installed Office.)

2. In the initial screen, select the Add/Remove button, then choose Continue.

3. In the second screen, select the Data Access option, then choose Continue.

4. Continue with setup, inserting disks as requested.

You don't have to restart Windows after closing the setup program.

Specifying a Data Source

The first step in creating a query is to specify a *data source*. (You can consider a data source to be equivalent to a database.) To query from Excel, choose the Get External Data command from the Data menu. This brings up the Select Data Source dialog box. If you have never used this command before, the Available Data Sources list will most likely have only the two items shown here:

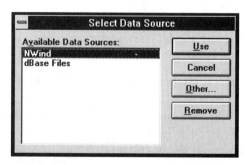

However, if anyone has previously accessed other data sources from Excel, more sources will be listed.

All the examples in this chapter use the Northwind Traders sample database that ships with Microsoft Access. (The sample data is identified as NWind in the Select Data Source dialog box.) This makes it easy for you to work through the examples exactly as they appear in the book. Although most of the transactions in the sample database are dated in 1989, the sample data is perfectly suitable for demonstrating all of the features of Query and Access.

Adding tables is the first step in creating the query for the data source you selected. Choose the Use button in the Select Data Source dialog box. This brings up the Add Tables dialog box shown here:

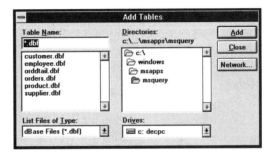

Setting Up for a Simple Query

Creating a query is simple enough in concept: it's simply a method of stating what specific data you want to look at. However, databases are intricate, highly structured entities, and you must be precise in "phrasing" your queries. Microsoft Query, while requiring you to operate within certain boundaries for precision's sake, offers point-and-click and drag-and-drop methods similar to those of Word and Excel.

Query creation involves two basic steps:

- Specifying which *field(s)* in which *table(s)* you are interested in
- Specifying which *record(s)* you are interested in

Each step might have a variety of substeps. This section demonstrates the first of these steps, and the next section demonstrates the second step.

Adding a Table

First, open the Northwind Traders sample database that comes with Microsoft Access. Next, you need to tell Query what table(s) within the database you want to query.

In the Add Tables dialog box, select the Orders.dbf table from the Table Name list, then choose Add. (For clarity, names of tables and windows are capitalized here, though not on the screen.) Behind the Add Tables dialog box, a query window opens up. The dialog box remains on the screen so you can add more tables to your query. Choose Close to close the dialog box.

Your query window should look like the one shown in Figure 5-3.

The top portion of the window is called the *table pane*. The bottom portion of the window (the *data pane*) is empty now, but will display the query results. The table pane contains a small window entitled Orders. This window, called a *field list*, contains a scrollable list of all field names in the Orders table.

Adding Fields

You start creating the query by specifying the fields you are interested in examining. The data pane always has one blank column, located at the extreme right, for adding fields to the query. The fastest way to add a field is to double-click the field name in the field list.

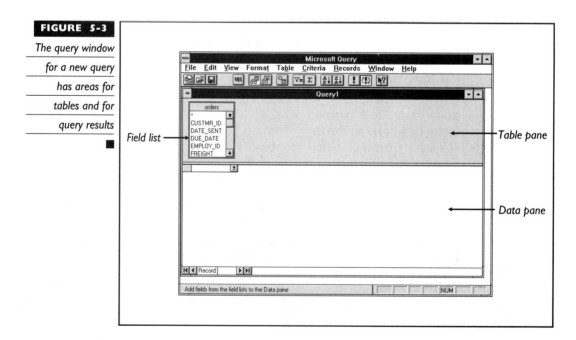

FIGURE 5-3
The query window for a new query has areas for tables and for query results

Add the following fields to the query by double-clicking them in the Orders field list in the sequence indicated:

- CUSTMR_ID
- ORDER_ID
- ORDER_DATE
- DATE_SENT
- ORDER_AMT

As you add each field, a corresponding column is added to the *result set* (the set of records displayed in the data pane). After you add each of the five specified fields, your query window looks like Figure 5-4.

You can also add a field to the data pane by dragging it from the field list to the blank column at the right, or by entering a field name in the blank column header.

Inserting Fields

Often you realize after you've added the initial group of fields that you want to insert a new field in the middle of two existing fields. You can do

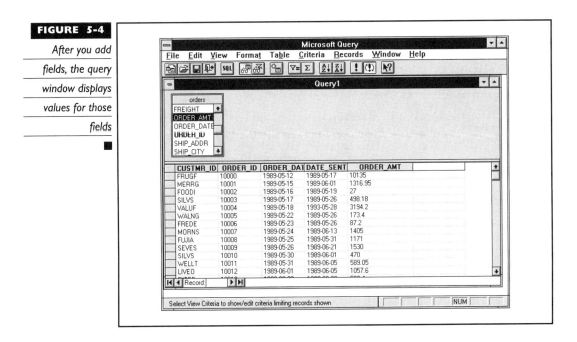

FIGURE 5-4

After you add fields, the query window displays values for those fields

this by simply dragging the new field from the field list to a column heading in the data pane. The field will be inserted to the left of the column.

To insert a blank field between two existing columns in the data pane with menu commands, follow these steps:

1. Click the column heading to select the column in the data pane.

2. Choose Insert Column from the Records menu. This brings up the Insert Column dialog box:

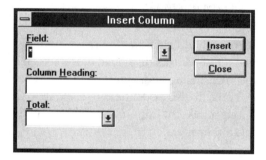

3. In the Field box, enter or select the name of the field you want to insert.

4. If you want a column heading that is different from the field name, enter the heading in the Column Heading box.

5. Choose Insert. Query inserts the new field to the left of the selected column.

6. Choose Close.

Adding All Fields in the Field List

Query offers a quick way to add all fields in the list to the result set: double-click the asterisk (*) in the field list, as shown here:

Alternatively, you can drag the asterisk to the empty field box in the data pane.

Managing Columns in the Result Set

Rearranging columns in the result set is very easy: simply select the column you want to move (by clicking on the column heading), then drag the column to the left or right, as you wish. As you drag, a thick black border will indicate the destination of the column.

To remove a column, select its column heading and press DEL.

To change the width of a column, move the mouse pointer over the right edge of the column heading until the mouse pointer changes as shown in the Sales column in Figure 5-5. Then drag the border to increase or reduce the column width. (Figure 5-5 shows a column being reduced in width.)

To change a column heading, double-click the column heading, which displays the Edit Column dialog box. Enter the new description in the column heading and choose OK.

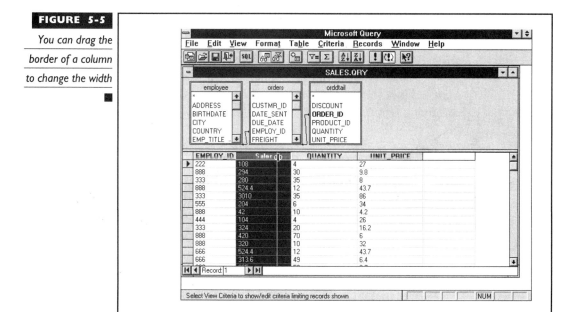

FIGURE 5-5

You can drag the border of a column to change the width

Creating and Executing the Query

You have now completed the first step in defining your query: specifying the table and fields. Now it's time to tell Query how to filter the result set, which currently includes all records in the table. First, though, you'll take a peek at the result set you have now.

Examining the Results

So far, this example has focused on the mechanics of creating a query. However, one critical question has been glossed over: What is it, exactly, that you hope to learn by creating this query? You have to know the question, naturally, before you can get a definitive answer.

To fill in the missing "motivation" for the example, suppose you are in charge of assuring customer satisfaction at Northwind Traders. You are querying the database because you want to know if customers are getting their shipments on time.

The fields in the current query contain key information on customer orders. Before filtering the list, browse through the result set (by clicking on the scroll bar at the right of the data pane) and look at the Date Sent column. You will see that there are very few orders that have not been shipped. Near the end, though, you find a few records with no data in the Date Sent column (such as 10031 and 10034 in Figure 5-6). This indicates that these orders have not yet been shipped.

Given the small amount of sample data you are using, you can find the answer to your question (which orders are behind schedule) by simply viewing the data. In all but the smallest businesses, however, the data is much more voluminous. In the real world, you need to filter the result set by specifying *criteria*.

Specifying Criteria

To specify which subset of the records you're interested in, you create criteria in the query window. Suppose it's July 31, and your immediate concern is whether Northwind Traders' current orders are on track for on-time delivery. You decide you'd like to focus on orders whose due date

FIGURE 5-6

You can scroll through the result set to look for orders that have not been shipped

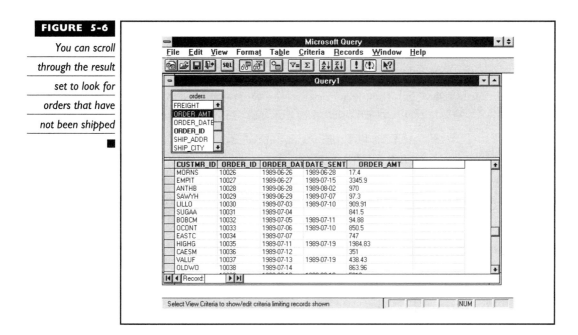

falls on or before August 9. This will require a *comparison criterion*, a common type of query criterion. Follow these steps:

1. Choose Add Criteria from the Criteria menu. This brings up the Add Criteria dialog box. The text boxes in the dialog box on your screen might contain different values from those shown here. The dialog automatically fills the boxes with default values based on the current selection in the data pane.

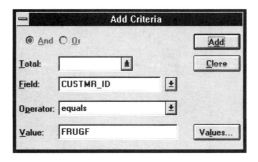

2. Click the arrow next to the Field box to display a list of fields in the result set.

3. Select DUE_DATE.

4. Click the arrow next to the Operator box to display a list of *comparison operators* you can apply to values in the result set.

5. Select "is less than or equal to", since you want orders due on or before August 9.

6. You can enter a value in the Value box, but if the result set happens to include a record with that particular value, you can select it from a drop-down list by choosing the Value button. Use this method to select the value 1989-08-09.

7. Choose Add. Behind the dialog box, Query filters the result set so that only records matching the criteria are displayed. The Add Criteria dialog box remains on the screen, in case you want to add more criteria.

8. Choose Close.

Your query window now looks like Figure 5-7. A third section, the *criteria pane*, has been added. The criteria pane provides the current criteria in a table format.

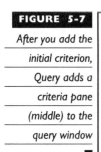

FIGURE 5-7

After you add the initial criterion, Query adds a criteria pane (middle) to the query window

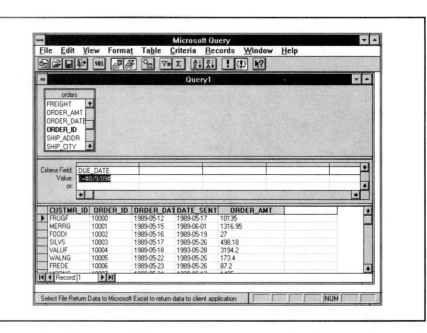

Remember, your purpose in adding this criterion was to narrow the focus to orders with looming due dates. You can see at a glance, though, that the result set includes numerous old orders that have already been filled. To really separate the wheat from the chaff, you'll have to add more criteria.

Using AutoQuery

Ordinarily, there isn't much to executing a query; it happens automatically as you make changes in the query window. This feature is called AutoQuery. With simple queries and relatively small data sources, AutoQuery is extremely convenient. However, if you are querying a large database, AutoQuery can slow down performance. You can turn it off by clicking the AutoQuery key on the toolbar, which looks like this:

If the AutoQuery button (right) is in the "on" position, as shown here, changes to criteria automatically update the results. If AutoQuery is off, you must click the Query Now button (left) to see the results of changes in your queries.

Adding Additional Criteria

If you could limit the result set to only those records that do *not* have an entry in the DATE_SENT field, you would have a list of unfilled orders due before August 9. Follow these steps:

1. Choose Add Criteria from the Criteria menu.
2. Select DATE_SENT from the pull-down list of fields in the Field box.
3. Display the pull-down list of comparison operators in the Operator box.
4. Scroll down to the bottom of the list and select "is Null". (Null means the field contains nothing.)
5. Choose Add, then choose Close.

Adding the second criteria has yielded the result you wanted: all unfilled orders due before August 9 (as shown in Figure 5-8).

FIGURE 5-8

A list of unfilled orders due to be shipped before August 9

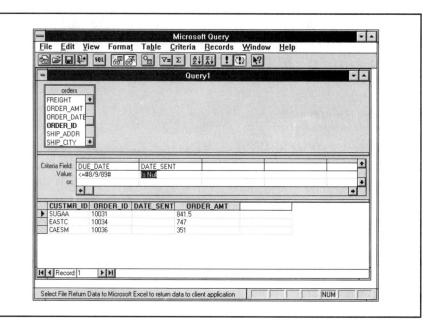

caution *A null value is not the same as a zero value. If you had selected equals in the Operator box and entered 0 in the Value box, you would have received an error message. That's because numeric data types such as zero are not compatible with dates. A thorough discussion of data types is beyond the scope of this book. However, you should be aware that comparison values you enter in the Add Criteria dialog box should be appropriate to the field. If the field contains text values, you should enter text values in the Value box.*

Sometimes the fastest way to add criteria is to enter them directly into the criteria pane. To enter the criteria in the preceding example, choose Undo Criterion from the Edit menu, then follow these steps:

1. In the criteria pane, click the box to the right of the DUE_DATE field (the top box in the second column). This displays a small arrow at the right of the box.

2. Click the arrow to display a list of available fields, as shown in Figure 5-9.

3. Select DATE_SENT.

4. Select the box in the Value row just below the DATE_SENT heading in the data pane. (You can do this by clicking the box or by pressing the DOWN ARROW key.)

5. Enter **is Null,** then press ENTER.

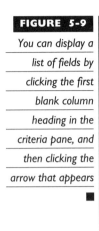

FIGURE 5-9

You can display a list of fields by clicking the first blank column heading in the criteria pane, and then clicking the arrow that appears

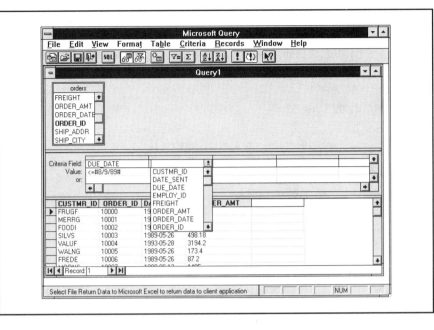

As soon as you press ENTER, the result set changes. Your query window should look like Figure 5-10.

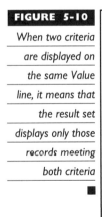

FIGURE 5-10

When two criteria are displayed on the same Value line, it means that the result set displays only those records meeting both criteria

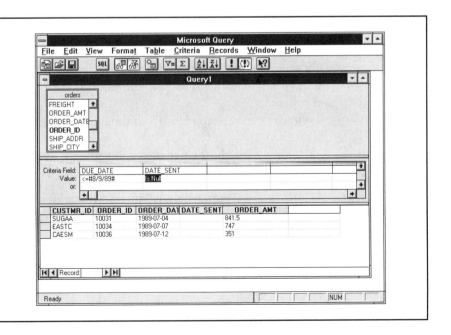

Note that the two criteria are displayed on the same Value line. That indicates that you want only records that satisfy both criteria. When you do not change the default And option in the Add Criteria dialog box, you will add an And criterion. Later in the chapter, you will learn how to add Or criteria.

Removing Criteria

Before you continue, return the result set to its initial all-inclusive state by removing the criteria. Follow these steps to remove criteria:

- To remove one specific criterion, click the column heading in the criteria pane (not the data pane) for the criterion you want to remove, then press the DEL key.

- To remove all criteria in the query, choose Remove All Criteria from the Criteria menu.

note *You can choose Edit, then Undo Remove Criteria to bring back a criterion immediately after removing it. Even better, you can save queries to disk, as explained near the end of this chapter.*

Creating a Super-Quick Query

You can quickly display all records matching a value in a specific record with the Criteria Equals button in the toolbar. Suppose you're looking at the result set in Figure 5-11 and something in one of the records looks wrong to you. You might want to look at all records for the customer who placed that order.

Follow these steps to view all shipments for Eastern Connection:

1. Select a box in the Customer_ID column in the data pane containing the value Eastern Connection, as shown in Figure 5-11.

2. Click the Criteria Equals button, which looks like this:

The query uses the selected value as an exact-match criterion and displays only records for Eastern Connection in the result set.

You can use the Criteria Equals button even if the value you want to specify is *not* shown in any of the records in the data pane. Simply click

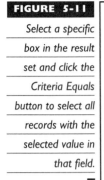

FIGURE 5-11

Select a specific box in the result set and click the Criteria Equals button to select all records with the selected value in that field.

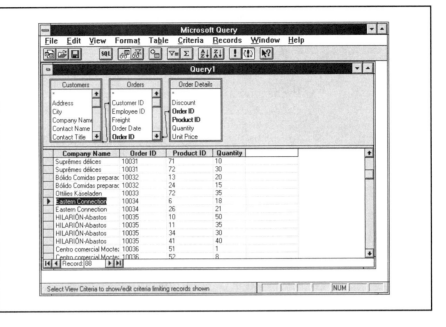

anywhere in the appropriate column and click the Criteria Equals button as in the preceding example. Then enter the desired criterion value in the Value row in the new column of the criteria pane.

note *This method of creating a query is an excellent example of "query by example," a concept that is implemented in various ways by many commercial DBMS programs.*

Adding Data from Another Table

So far you have only seen queries on a single table. Often, though, you need data from more than one table to get all the information you need. Relational databases use *key fields* to pull together information from separate but related tables.

It's often necessary to use multiple tables to get all the data you need into the result set. Using the previous example, for instance, suppose that you wanted to add company contact information to the order data you are requesting from Excel. If you scroll through the orders table, you won't find fields for company name or contact person.

To obtain company-specific data such as names, addresses, and phone numbers, you have to add the customer table to the query.

Follow these steps to add customers' company names and contact person information to your query:

1. Click the Add Table button in the toolbar.

2. In the Add Tables dialog box, select Customer.dbf, and then choose Add.

3. Choose Close. Query adds the table to the table pane. You also see a *join line* between the two field lists. The join line indicates that the two tables are joined by a common field.

4. Double-click COMPANY in the customer field list.

5. Double-click CONTACT in the customer field list. Query adds the company name and contact person to the data pane.

6. To make room for the new fields, delete the now-unnecessary DATE_SENT field from the data pane.

You can move field lists in the table pane. Move the customer field list to the right to make it easier to see the *join line* connecting the two field lists. Then scroll down the list to display the CUSTMR_ID field. Your screen should look like Figure 5-12.

The term *join* has a very specific meaning in relational database terminology. Tables in a database are not simply joined; they are joined in a specific

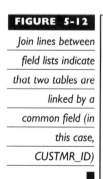

FIGURE 5-12

Join lines between field lists indicate that two tables are linked by a common field (in this case, CUSTMR_ID)

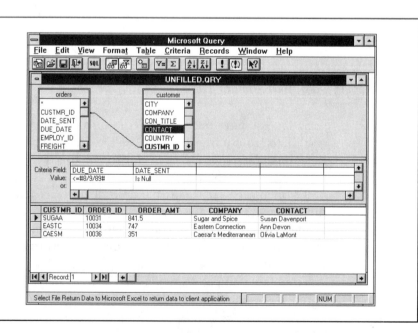

"place" by one or more common fields, as shown in Figure 5-2 at the beginning of this chapter. The join line in Figure 5-12 indicates clearly that the two tables are joined on the CUSTMR_ID field.

note *Successfully creating a query requires some prior knowledge of how the database is structured. There may be times you will need assistance from a database analyst or other technical expert to get the most out of your corporate database.*

Joining Tables Manually

As you saw in the preceding example, Query can automatically detect common fields and join them when you add tables to a query. Sometimes, however, Query is not able to join related fields automatically. (One simple example is when field names just aren't identical.) When this happens, you have to join the fields manually so that Query can pull related data from both tables.

Follow these steps to manually join fields in separate tables:

1. Use the scroll bars of the two field lists to display in each list the name of the fields you want to join.

2. Drag the field name from the first list over to the desired field name in the other list.

Query adds a join line between the two fields. To remove a join, click the join line. (The join line will become thicker.) Then press the DEL key.

More About Comparison Operators

Query provides an extensive selection of comparison operators you can use in creating criteria. Query offers the following mathematical operators for comparing numeric, date, and text values:

- Equals
- Does not equal
- Is greater than
- Is greater than or equal to
- Is less than
- Is less than or equal to

Query also offers nonmathematical comparison operators. These operators can search for embedded text within values or compare values to a list. Table 5-1 summarizes the nonmathematical comparison operators and describes how you can use them. As you refer to Table 5-1, please note the following:

- Each of the comparison operators has a corresponding negation operator (such as "Does not begin with") that will select records that do not satisfy the criterion.

- The comparison operators are case-sensitive, so you must use the correct capitalization when you enter the comparison value. Entering "fuller", for instance, will not select records with the value Fuller.

Using "Or" Criteria

Earlier in this chapter, you learned how to create And criteria so that Query would select records that meet *all* specified criteria. You can also

Comparison Operator	How Values Are Specified	What Records Are Selected
Begins with	Enter the text string in the Value box.	Records with values beginning with specified text
Ends with	Enter the text string in the Value box.	Records with values ending with specified text
Contains	Enter the text string in the Value box.	Records with values containing specified text
Is one of	Click the Values button, then double-click the desired values, or enter the values (separated by commas) in the Value box.	Records with values matching one of the specified values
Is between	Click the Values button, then double-click the desired values (two are required), or enter the values (separated by commas or the word *and*) in the Value box.	Records with values falling between the two specified values
Like	Enter the text string in the Value box, followed by the wildcard character %, or bracketed by wildcard characters.	Records beginning with the specified text string (if string is followed by the wildcard character), or record containing the specified text string (if string is bracketed).
Null	No value is required (the Value box is dimmed).	Records with blank entries.

TABLE 5-1 *Using Query's Nonmathematical Comparison Operators* ■

create Or criteria to select all records that meet *one*—but not necessarily *all*—of the specified criteria.

Suppose, for instance, that you want a list of all customers in California, Oregon, and Washington. Assume also that you are starting a brand new query, not adding to the one used in the preceding examples. Follow these steps:

1. Open a new query and add the Customers table.
2. Choose Add Criteria from the Criteria menu.
3. Select the Or option.
4. Click the arrow next to the Field box to display a list of fields in the result set.
5. Select "Region" (or whatever name is used for the field containing the state code).
6. Select "is equal to" from the Operator list.
7. Enter **CA** in the Value box.
8. Choose Add.
9. Add the state codes for Oregon and Washington as you did for California in steps 7 and 8.
10. Choose Close.

Your query screen will then look something like Figure 5-13. When you add Or criteria, Query places them on separate rows in the criteria pane.

As you might surmise, you can also combine And and Or criteria to create very complex queries.

Putting Query Results into Excel and Word

Let's return now to the Northwind Traders database and your effort to create a list of customers with pending shipments. Before you send the query results to an Excel worksheet, take a look at the data pane. The first column, CUSTMR_ID, is no longer needed. After all, you might be planning to pass the information on to an assistant who will actually call the customers; all he needs is the company and contact person. You should delete the

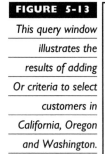

FIGURE 5-13

This query window illustrates the results of adding Or criteria to select customers in California, Oregon and Washington.

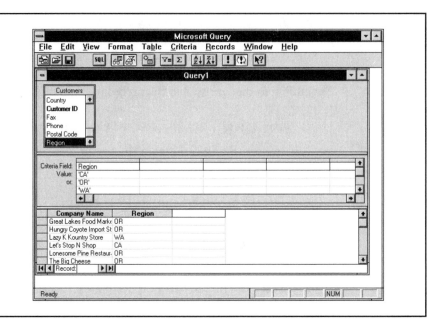

unnecessary columns and rearrange the remaining ones. Figure 5-14 shows the query results after putting the columns in a more logical sequence.

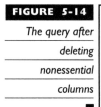

FIGURE 5-14

The query after deleting nonessential columns

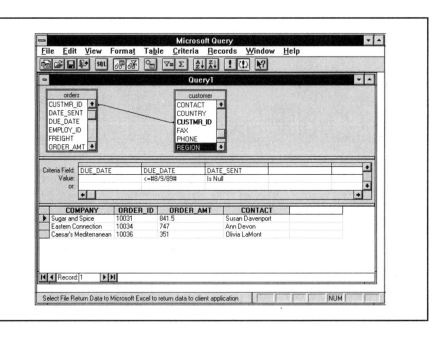

Sorting Results

Once you have created a query, you might need the results sorted in a different sequence. Of course, many client applications (Excel and Word, for instance) have sorting capabilities themselves. However, you might be creating a query to assist inexperienced users in performing a routine procedure in the client application. In such cases, it's better to have the query sort the records than to rely on the users to sort them in the client application.

To sort the result set on any field, simply click anywhere in that field in the data pane. Then on the toolbar click either the Sort Ascending or Sort Descending button, shown here:

You can sort on more than one field (that is, sort values in one column within groups of identical values in another column). To illustrate, suppose your result set contains sales information by country and region. Follow these steps to sort the current result set by state within region:

1. Click anywhere in the Country column.
2. Click the Sort Ascending button.
3. Click anywhere in the Region column.
4. Hold down the CTRL key while clicking the Sort Ascending button. (Holding down CTRL tells Query that the selected field is a secondary sort key.)

Query keeps the result set sorted by country, but within each group of records for a single country, it sorts the records by region. If you had not held down CTRL, Query would have resorted the result set by region code.

You might want to sort on a field that is not displayed in the data pane. For example, you might be accustomed to seeing lists of customers sorted by salesperson. To sort by a nondisplayed field, follow these steps:

1. Choose Records, then Sort. This brings up the Sort dialog box.

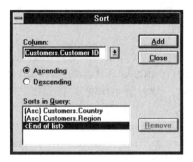

2. Enter the name of the column you want to sort on in the Column box. (You won't be able to select the name from the pull-down list; it lists only unsorted columns in the result set.)

3. Select the desired ordering option (Ascending or Descending).

Notice that if you have previously sorted the result set, the previous sorts appear in the Sorts in Query list. The (Asc) notations indicate the sorts were in ascending order.

Returning Data from Microsoft Query

Because you started Query from Excel, Query understands that its mission is to send the result set to Excel. To copy the result set to the active Excel worksheet, simply click the Return Data to Excel button, shown here:

This brings up the following dialog box:

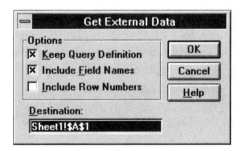

(You can also choose the Return Data to Microsoft Excel command from the File menu to display the dialog box.)

The Destination box refers to the cell that was active when you chose the Get External Data command in Excel. This cell will become the upper-right corner of the range that will receive the results set from Query. You can enter or click on another cell to change the destination.

The following table explains the other options in the Get External Data dialog box:

Option	Explanation
Keep Query Definition	Stores the query information in Excel, allowing you to run the query and refresh results from within Excel.
Include Field Names	Pastes the field names from the column headings in the data pane.
Include Row Numbers	Assigns sequential numbers to the records pasted into the worksheet and enters them in the first column of the pasted range.

When you are satisfied with the options you have selected in the dialog box, choose OK. Excel pastes the query results into a worksheet as text. Figure 5-15 shows the result set after returning it to Excel.

note *In this example, you started Query from within Excel. If you had started Query in its stand-alone mode (by clicking the Query icon in the Program Manager), the Return Data to Microsoft Excel menu option would not have been available. You would have had to select the records in the data pane and copy them into Excel.*

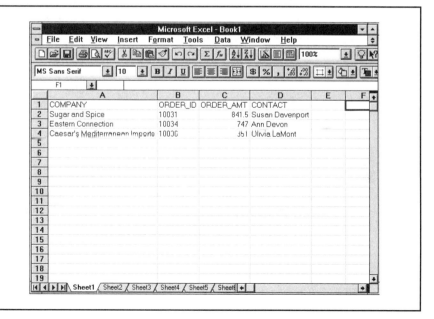

FIGURE 5-15

The list of unfilled orders, with customer contact information, returned by Query to an Excel worksheet

Updating Query Results

You might have occasion to return data from a given query to Excel several times as you revise your worksheet. The data in the data source could change in the meantime. If you selected the Keep Query Definition option when you returned the result set to Excel, you can update your query from within Excel. Choose the Refresh Data command from the Data menu. Excel will start or activate Query. Next, Query will perform the query again to obtain the most recent data and return the updated result set to the worksheet, replacing the old query results.

Copying Data from Microsoft Query

You can copy a result set, or selected rows or columns from a result set, into another application. To do this, you use the typical method for copying and pasting between applications. (That is, copy the selection in Query, and then paste it into the other application.) Copying is useful when

- You have started Query from the Program Manager and the Return Data to option is not available on the File menu.
- You want to send only part of the result set to the other application.

After copying data from Query and activating the other application, you can plain-paste or paste-link the data. Paste-linking, however, is generally not a good idea, because it creates a DDE link to specific rows or columns in the result set. Consequently, it is not nearly as "intelligent" as storing a query definition in Excel. If you paste-link from a result set, simply inserting a new field in the data pane might change paste-linked dollar values to text descriptions, producing nonsensical results in the client application.

Saving and Opening Queries

To save your query, click the Save File button on the toolbar or choose the Save command from the File menu. This displays the following dialog box:

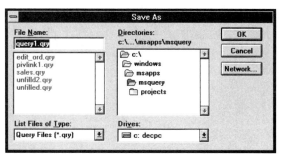

Enter or select the name for the query file and choose OK. (Query files carry the extension QRY.)

To open a previously saved query, click the Open Query button or choose the Open Query command on the File menu.

Editing a Data Source

In some cases, you can edit data in Query's data pane and change the data in the data source. The Allow Editing command in the Records menu must be selected before you can edit data. (A check next to the command indicates that editing is allowed.) Changes you make to records in the data pane are automatically saved to the data source when you select another record or close the Query.

caution *It's very dangerous to edit data in Microsoft Query, because Query does not offer proper safeguards against deleting critical data. Query will allow you to delete data that is vital to the structure of the database without warning. You should leave the Allow Editing feature off when working in Query. Turn editing on only when you need to correct an entry in a field, then turn it off immediately afterward.*

Conclusion

As you saw from the examples in the chapter, Query is enormously useful in bringing data into Excel. Query can provide data to Word, too. You'll see how this works in Chapter 8. In the next chapter you will learn some of the basic operations of Microsoft Access, including query capabilities that Microsoft Query does not have.

CHAPTER 6

An Introduction to Microsoft Access

In Chapter 5, you learned to extract information from databases with Microsoft Query. At times, however, you will need to do more than extract. You might want to add new records or change existing ones. You might want to create detailed reports from your data. You might even want to automate some of your analysis and reporting activities with macros or a programming language. Or maybe you *do* want to extract data, but you want to pull data together from multiple data sources—something you cannot do with Query.

Microsoft Access can perform all of these functions because, unlike Query, it is a complete database management program. Access is included with the Professional Edition of Microsoft Office.

This chapter alone cannot possibly give you a complete guide to using the Access program. Access, after all, contains extensive database programming tools and has the ability to recognize a wide variety of data formats. However, it has become a very popular database since its introduction, and increasing numbers of users are called upon to enter important data into the program. Moreover, Access (true to its name) can be used to tap into large-scale databases; it offers more sophisticated data extraction tools than does Microsoft Query. In short, Access is a very effective conduit between corporate data (whether on your hard disk or on a mainframe) and the desktop analysis and productivity tools in Excel, Word, and PowerPoint.

This chapter will teach you:

- How to view and edit data in Access *forms*

- How to create complex queries that Microsoft Query cannot handle (such as a query to more than one data source)

- What ODBC is and how you can use it to access data from different sources

- How to create structured database reports

For more detailed information on using Access, consult a more complete treatment of the subject, such as *The Microsoft Access Handbook,* by Mary Campbell (Osborne/McGraw-Hill).

Many Access features look and act like Microsoft Query features, though they may have different names in Access. To minimize repetition, this chapter occasionally refers you to Chapter 5 for a complete explanation of some of these similar features.

Opening Access Files

Access maintains all data relating to a particular database in a single file. Access database files (which use the extension MDB) store not only the tables, but also all queries and specifications for other design elements such as forms and reports. Forms and reports will be explained later in this chapter.

Before you can do anything in Access, you have to open a database. Opening an Access database is analogous to specifying a data source in Query. In its execution, however, the procedure is more like opening a file in any application program. (Databases are called *data sources* in the documentation for Microsoft Query because the presumption is that Query users are simply extracting information.)

Follow these steps to open the sample Northwind Traders database:

1. From the File menu, choose Open Database.
2. Select the SAMPAPPS directory in the Directories list.
3. Select NWIND.MDB in the File Name box.
4. Choose OK.

To create a new database, you would choose New Database from the File menu. That opens a dialog box where you would enter or select the file and path for the database files.

Once you have opened or created a database, Access opens a dialog box, shown on the following page, called the Database window. (If you opened a new database, no tables will be listed.)

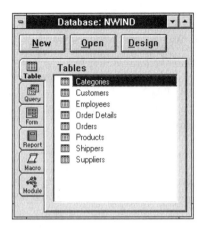

From the Database window, you can go directly to all major database activities such as data entry, querying, and reporting. The important elements of the database, such as tables and queries, are shown on tabs along the left side of the window. These elements are called *database objects* in Microsoft's documentation for Access. To work with any particular type of object, you click the corresponding tab in the Database window. To create or modify a query, for instance, you would click the Query tab.

Viewing and Editing Data

To gain an understanding of how Access works, it's vital to understand how databases are constructed. For the examples in this chapter, you will use the sample Northwind Traders database that you opened a few minutes ago.

Viewing Tables

As you may remember, the basic containing structure for data in a database management system (DBMS) is the table. With Microsoft Query, you can't view data unless you create a query. In Access, however, you can browse through tables in a database just as you can scroll through an Excel worksheet.

To open a table from the Database window, follow these steps:

1. Click the Table tab in the Database window. This displays a list of tables in the database.

2. Click on the name of the desired table.

3. Choose the Open button.

Access now displays the table in *datasheet* view, as shown in Figure 6-1. (There is another way to view a table, called a *form*, that will be explained later in this chapter.)

Editing Data in Tables

Though a datasheet looks much like a spreadsheet, you don't have the same freedom to enter data and formulas as you do in an Excel worksheet. Each field (column) in the table is set up to contain a certain type of data, such as text, dates, or numbers. Certain fields might be defined as *required* fields, meaning they cannot be blank. A number of restrictions might apply to what kind of data can reside in specific fields or records in the table. For example, in a table containing information on product orders and shipments, the shipping date should never precede the order date. As a full-function DBMS, Access provides tools to specify these rules.

Incorporating these rules into a database is the responsibility of the database programmer or application designer. (This chapter assumes you are a database user, not a designer.) Database programs include programming languages and tools so that qualified individuals can design *database applications*. A database application is a custom-designed solution created within a DBMS such as Access or dBase. Usually, a database application includes tables, data-entry forms, and automated procedures.

FIGURE 6-1

A table displayed in datasheet view

Order ID	Customer ID	Employee ID	Ship Name	Ship Address	
10000	FRANS	6	Franchi S.p.A.	Via Monte Bianco 34	To
10001	MEREP	8	Mère Paillarde	43 rue St. Laurent	Mc
10002	FOLKO	3	Folk och fä HB	Åkergatan 24	Brä
10003	SIMOB	8	Simons bistro	Vinbæltet 34	Kø
10004	VAFFE	3	Vaffeljernet	Smagsløget 45	Årh
10005	WARTH	5	Wartian Herkku	Torikatu 38	Ou
10006	FRANS	8	Franchi S.p.A.	Via Monte Bianco 34	To
10007	MORGK	4	Morgenstern Gesundkost	Heerstr. 22	Lei
10008	FURIB	3	Furia Bacalhau e Frutos do Mar	Jardim das rosas n. 32	Lis
10009	SEVES	8	Seven Seas Imports	90 Wadhurst Rd.	Lor
10010	SIMOB	8	Simons bistro	Vinbæltet 34	Kø
10011	WELLI	6	Wellington Importadora	Rua do Mercado, 12	Re
10012	LINOD	6	LINO-Delicateses	Ave. 5 de Mayo Porlamar	I. d
10013	RICSU	3	Richter Supermarkt	Starenweg 5	Ge
10014	GROSR	4	GROSELLA-Restaurante	5ª Ave. Los Palos Grandes	Ca
10015	PICCO	6	Piccolo und mehr	Geislweg 14	Sa
10016	FOLIG	3	Folies gourmandes	184, chaussée de Tournai	Lill
10017	BLONP	4	Blondel père et fils	24, place Kléber	Str
10018	RATTC	4	Rattlesnake Canyon Grocery	2817 Milton Dr.	Alb
10019	MAGAA	6	Magazzini Alimentari Riuniti	Via Ludovico il Moro 22	Re

Record: 1 of 1078

The database programmer might be an outside consultant or someone who works for your organization. You can also purchase database applications that are sold as prepackaged software.

As a user, be aware that whenever you are prevented from altering data in an Access datasheet, there is probably a reason for it. Most likely, the person who designed the database application decided that you should not be allowed to change the data—at least not in the datasheet view. Notwithstanding the slight bruise to your ego, this gives you some assurance that your database designers are diligently protecting important data.

Assuming that the database application allows you access, and you don't violate any of the restrictive data rules in the table, you can make changes as you would in a spreadsheet. To select a record for editing, click the gray box next to that record (known as the *record selector*) on the left border of the datasheet window. When you move the mouse pointer over the record selector area, it changes to a small black arrow shape (circled below):

Order ID	Customer ID	Employee ID	Ship Name	Ship Address	S
10000	FRANS	6	Franchi S.p.A.	Via Monte Bianco 34	To
10001	MEREP	8	Mère Paillarde	43 rue St. Laurent	Mo
10002	FOLKO	3	Folk och fä HB	Åkergatan 24	Brä
10003	SIMOB	8	Simons bistro	Vinbæltet 34	Kø
10004	VAFFE	3	Vaffeljernet	Smagsløget 45	År

- To *add* a record to a datasheet, select the last row in the datasheet, which is marked with an asterisk (*). Enter all the necessary values in the record's fields. To save the new record and update the file on the disk, select another record in the datasheet. Alternatively, you can press the TAB key until you go past the last field in the record.

- To *change a value* in a record, select the field within the desired record and edit the entry or enter a new value. Select another record in the datasheet to save the change(s) to the current record.

- To *delete* a record, select the record, and then press the DEL key. Choose OK to confirm the deletion.

Note: When you change data in datasheet view, each change to a record is automatically saved to disk.

If you are working in a database application designed in Access, you might not be allowed to make changes directly to a table in this manner. Imagine the problems you might cause if, for example, you were to delete an employee from the master employee table while the person was still working for the company. Access has built-in safeguards to prevent such gaffes; additionally, database designers can use password security to provide additional assurance against errors or unauthorized access to sensitive data.

In the event that that you *do* have the ability to modify data in datasheet view, it might be due to an oversight. To be on the safe side, you should avoid using the datasheet view to make changes. Instead, you should work with the data in form view to make use of whatever error-trapping measures have been installed.

Working with Forms

If you are using a database application created in Access, you will typically perform all operations from forms. Forms can be used to edit data in tables, execute queries, and run reports. Forms can also display information normally not available by simply viewing a table. For example, a form could contain a chart showing sales trends by product, region, or sales manager.

Again, however, forms are customized items that are typically created by a database programmer. Forms are a vital part of most database applications.

Opening a Form

To open a form, click the Form tab in the Database window. The Form tab, shown here, displays a list of forms in the database:

In the Forms list, simply click the form you want to open, and then choose the Open button to open the form. Click Customers and Orders. The Customers and Orders form (Figure 6-2) displays product and price information in customer orders.

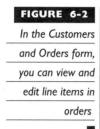

FIGURE 6-2

In the Customers and Orders form, you can view and edit line items in orders

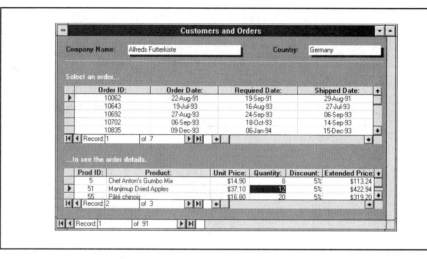

How Forms Enhance Accuracy

Think back to the example in Chapter 5, where you used Query to produce a list of customers whose orders were due to be shipped by a certain date. In order to combine data on orders, products, and customers in a query, you had to open several tables. The Customers and Orders form likewise pulls a few selected data items from one or more tables in the Access sample database. By selectively limiting users' ability to view fields, this form prevents you from inadvertently editing the wrong field.

Usually the form fields you see in a form are *enabled*, meaning you can select them and enter or change data in them. To move through all the enabled fields in a form in sequence, press the TAB key repeatedly. (Note, however, that the application designer can override the conventional top-left-to-bottom-right tabbing sequence.) What happens when you press TAB after selecting the last field in sequence depends on how the form was designed. In many cases, it saves whatever changes you made to the record and displays the next record.

You can also select any enabled field with the mouse.

Sometimes the form displays fields that are not enabled so that you can view the information but not change it. You cannot select a field that is not enabled.

note *You can be prevented from making changes to an enabled field. This can happen when the field you want to change "belongs" to a file that another user has opened on the network.*

Changing data in a field is simply a matter of selecting the field and entering the new or revised data. In Figure 6-2, the Quantity field in one of the records has been selected. At this point, you can enter a different number. However, you might not be able to enter just *any* number.

In many cases, the application designer attaches *validation rules* to form fields. Validation rules ensure that the entered data is valid; that is, that it makes sense. It would not make sense, for instance, to enter a letter or a negative number into the Quantity field. In many cases, fractional amounts would be invalid. Most likely, a Quantity field in any order entry form will allow you to enter only positive, non-zero whole numbers.

A form might include other accuracy-enhancing tools. The Orders by Customer form in the Northwind Traders database includes a drop-down list to help you select the region. Database application designers can also purchase other controls, such as scroll bars, from independent software developers, and incorporate the controls into forms. (These controls are called OLE custom controls, or OCXs.)

Saving Changes to the Data

Once you've made your changes in the form, you need to save the changes to the database. You accomplish this by doing any of the following:

- Select another record with the mouse.
- Tab past the last enabled field in the record.
- Close the form.

note *It is possible for application designers to change the effects of any of these actions.*

Close a form in the same way you close any window: by double-clicking the Close box in the upper-left corner, or by clicking the box once and choosing Close from the menu that appears.

Now that you know a little about entering data into Access, it's time to move on to weightier matters. Often, you will use Access to get at data in corporate databases or accounting systems. That's where Access lives up to its name.

Accessing Data in Other Database Programs

A moment ago, you learned that opening an Access database is similar to specifying a data source in Query. That's only partially true. In Access, you can open not only native Access databases, but also database files created in Paradox, dBase, or Oracle. The process of opening a table in an external database is called *attaching*. The key to this is Microsoft's Open Database Connectivity Standard, or ODBC.

What Is ODBC?

When Microsoft released the first version of Access, it also released ODBC, which is a set of specifications for describing the nature of data contained in a database. Following the ODBC standard, database vendors or independent third parties can create ODBC *drivers*. These are programs that, running in conjunction with any Microsoft Office application, translate external data to a form readable by Access and Query, and vice versa.

You'll learn more about ODBC and drivers later in this chapter.

Attaching Tables

Follow these steps to attach a table in a foreign database to a currently open Access database:

1. From the File menu, choose Attach Table. This brings up the Attach dialog box, which lists all the types of data sources Access can attach to.

2. In the Data Source list, select the desired data source type (Paradox 4.*x*, for instance) and choose OK. This brings up the Select File dialog box:

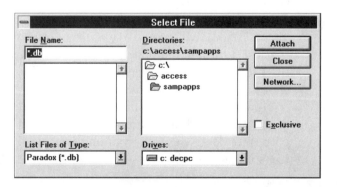

3. Select the name of the desired file, browsing through directories as necessary, then choose OK.

4. If Access is successful in attaching the table, it displays a message to that effect. Choose OK.

5. Repeat steps 3 and 4 until you are finished attaching, then close the Select File dialog box.

You can now use the attached table as you would any other table in the Access database you are currently working with.

note *If Access cannot attach to a table, it displays an error message in a dialog box after you perform step 4. For instance, the file you selected might not be in the database format you selected. Choose Help in this dialog box for information on solving the problem.*

The subject of ODBC drivers might seem arcane and a bit daunting. Normally, however, you will be blissfully unaware of the presence of ODBC drivers when you attach to an external data source. The attachment process is completely transparent, as long as the ODBC driver for that particular data source is installed on your PC. If it isn't, however, you will have to fiddle around "under the hood" by running a separate installation routine.

Installing ODBC Drivers

Microsoft Office ships with the ODBC drivers for Access, Paradox, dBase, and other common database formats. These drivers are automatically installed along with the Access program. Many database formats, however, are not supported. Many drivers for other formats are available from independent vendors such as Q+E Software. Microsoft also sells a set of ODBC drivers that are not included with Office. To obtain a list of ODBC drivers provided by Microsoft and other vendors, you can access the Microsoft Knowledge Base on CompuServe (GO MSKB).

caution *If you work in a large organization and are connected to a network, contact your network administrator before installing new ODBC drivers. It's conceivable that you could install an updated version of a driver over an old one, even while other application programs still need the older version to be installed. See the README file that's included on your ODBC driver disk for more information.*

The following steps illustrate the procedure for installing additional ODBC drivers, using the Microsoft ODBC Drivers as an example:

1. Insert the Microsoft ODBC Drivers disk labeled Disk 1 - Setup in your floppy disk drive.

2. From the File menu in the Windows Program Manager, choose Run. Windows displays the Run dialog box.

3. Enter **a:setup** in the Command Line box. The setup program starts up and displays the Install Drivers dialog box, shown here:

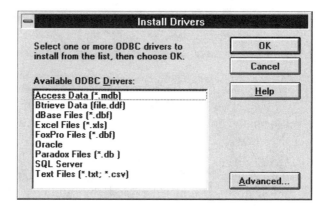

4. In the Available ODBC Drivers list, select the driver(s) you want to install, then choose OK.

5. Follow the setup program's instructions to insert disks containing the needed program files. After the setup program installs the driver software from the floppy disks, it displays the Data Sources dialog box, shown here:

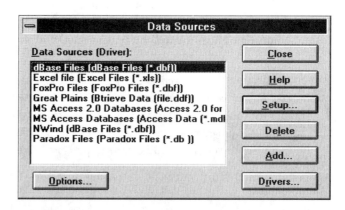

6. Choose Close. The setup program displays a message that the new drivers were successfully installed.

7. Choose OK.

Once you have set up Access to attach to all potentially useful data sources, you're ready to learn how to build queries to get the particular data you need.

Creating Queries

You can create queries in Microsoft Access in much the same manner as you would in Microsoft Query. The two programs' query windows look and act similarly, with a few exceptions.

When you create a query in either Access or Query, the program translates your selections into actual Structured Query Language (SQL) code behind the scenes. It is actually SQL, the standard database language for most relational databases, that queries the data source(s). SQL is based on a standard maintained by the American National Standards Institute (ANSI). It is possible to edit the SQL code generated by Access or Query, but the details are well beyond the scope of this book.

As in Microsoft Query, creating a query involves two basic steps:

- Specifying which fields in which table(s) you are interested in
- Specifying criteria to select the particular records you are interested in

Adding Fields

To create a new query and add fields in Access, follow these steps:

1. Display the Query tab in the database window.
2. Choose New to display the New Query dialog box.
3. Select the New Query button.

New Query

Access opens a Select Query window and (on top of the Query window) the Add Table dialog box.

4. From the Table/Query list in the Add Table dialog box, select the table(s) on which you want to base your query.

5. Close the Add Table dialog box.

Figure 6-3 shows a query window after selecting the Orders and Order Details tables. The line connecting the two tables is called the *join line*. Near the Orders field list, you see a small "1" above the point of connection. On the Order Details side, you see a small infinity sign (∞). That is to indicate the direction of the *one-to-many* relationship between the two tables. In this example, one-to-many means that one order might contain many order details (line items). Each Order ID is unique in the Orders table, but there can be many records with the same Order ID in the Order Details table.

note *Remember, the reason tables containing related data need to be joined is to identify the common fields so that Access can pull all the data together in the query.*

The Access query window is organized a bit differently from that of Microsoft Query. The latter divides the query window into three panes: table, criteria, and data. The upper area of the Access query window, on the

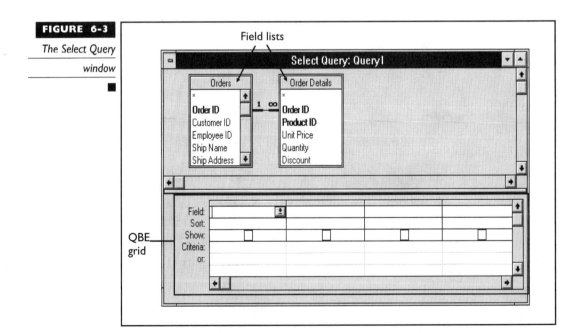

FIGURE 6-3

The Select Query window

other hand, is the equivalent of the Query table pane. Access does not display a data pane; the result set, which is called a *dynaset* in Access, does not appear in the query window. Access' QBE grid combines information on criteria and fields selected for display—information that in Microsoft Query is divided between the criteria pane and the data pane.

You might not always see a join line between two tables in a query window. In that event, you must join the tables yourself. (Access will attempt to join tables based on column names common to the tables in the query.) To define a join, drag the column name from one table to the related column in a second table, as you would in the Microsoft Query table pane. (See the section, "Joining Tables Manually," in Chapter 5 for a description of this procedure.)

Select the columns you want in your query by either dragging them from the table to the fields row in the QBE grid or by double-clicking the column name in the table definition.

Adding Fields and Criteria

You add fields to the Select Query window as you would in Query: by double-clicking the field names or by dragging the names down to columns in the QBE grid. As in Query, you can add all fields to a query by double-clicking (or dragging) the asterisk in the appropriate field list.

The last crucial step in creating the query is to specify criteria. The QBE grid provides a Criteria row that works like the rows in the criteria pane in Query. You specify criteria in one of two ways: by typing the expression (such as >**10022**) or by clicking the Build button in the toolbar to use the Expression Builder.

Build

The Access Expression Builder, shown next, is a beefed-up version of the Add Criteria dialog box you saw in Chapter 5. A full demonstration of the Expression Builder is well beyond the scope of this book. However, the point-and-click operation of the dialog box is intuitive, and the online help is fairly complete.

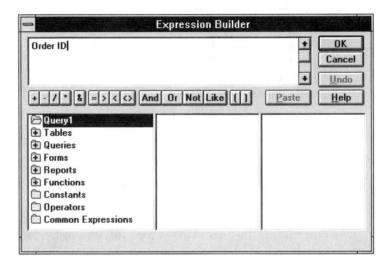

Using Query Wizards

Access offers a range of more complex query procedures such as Crosstab, Find Duplicate Records, Find Unmatched Records, or Archive Queries. You can create these queries by clicking the Query Wizards button, shown here:

Query Wizards provide informative screens and prompts for creating common types of queries in point-and-click fashion.

Using Functions

The query design window in Figure 6-4 shows a fairly typical query. The query joins two related tables, Orders and Order Details, which are joined on the common Order ID field. Note also the value in the last field (on the right). This field is a calculated value of the number of units multiplied by the price per unit less the discount. Access provides an extra element of automation compared to the query engine in Microsoft Query.

The expression is actually part of an Access *intrinsic function*. Intrinsic functions are built-in Access functions that are similar to Excel functions. In the example, the **Ccur** function converts the results of the multiplication to a Currency data type.

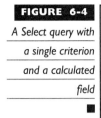

FIGURE 6-4

A Select query with a single criterion and a calculated field

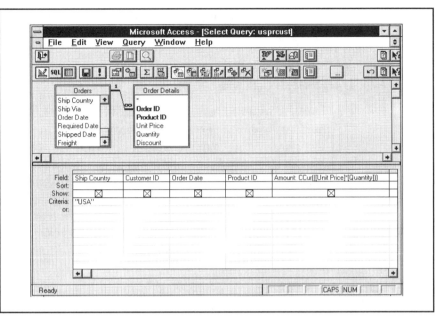

You can also create user-defined functions using the Access Basic programming language included with Access—a subject beyond the scope of this book.

Managing the Query Window

You can perform various housekeeping tasks in the query window using the same methods described in Chapter 5 for Query, as summarized here:

ACTION	METHOD
Changing column width	Drag the right border of the column to the desired width.
Moving fields	Select the field, and then drag it to the desired position.
Deleting fields	Select the field, and then press the DEL key.
Inserting fields in a particular location	Drag the field from the field list to the desired location.
Changing column headings	Click the top of the column and type the new heading.

You control the sort order of records in datasheet view in the QBE grid's Sort row. The Sort row is located below the Field row. To sort query results by a specific field, follow these steps:

1. Select the box within the sort field in the Sort row.

2. Click the arrow that appears within the box.

3. Select the desired option (Ascending, Descending, or Not Sorted).

Querying Multiple Data Sources

One important Access capability that is not available in Microsoft Query is the ability to create queries from more than one data source. As you learned at the start of the chapter, Access can attach to tables created in other database programs. Access' ability to tap multiple databases in carrying out a single query is an extension of its attaching capability.

Suppose for a minute that the Orders table in Figure 6-4 is an Access table, and the Order Details table is an attached table from an Oracle database. After the tables are attached, creating the query is exactly the same regardless of the actual source of the data.

caution *Queries that join tables from multiple data sources can execute extremely slowly. Certain operations can cause the query to perform less than optimally in a multi-user environment. Using Access functions (whether intrinsic or user-defined) can slow things down. Additionally, you should avoid using Access-specific extensions to SQL, such as crosstab queries, when using multiple sources. These queries will run slowly because they must be executed on the client PC rather than the server.*

Creating Queries from Other Queries

Another feature in Access that you won't find in Query is the ability to use a previous query as a table in a new query. Earlier in the chapter, you saw that the list in the Add Table dialog box was named Table/Query. That's because the ODBC driver for Access allows you to create a "query on a query." This can be very helpful when you are trying to create a complex query, because it allows you to use simpler queries as building blocks for higher-level queries.

Saving Queries

As you might expect, you can save and open Access queries. You open a saved query (also known as *executing* the query), much as you would open a table or form:

1. Display the Query tab in the Database window.

2. Select the query you want to open.

3. Click the Open button.

Access then opens your query and displays it in datasheet view, which contains the query results. The datasheet view of the query in Figure 6-4 displays the query results shown here:

Ship Country	Customer ID	Order Date	Product ID	Amount
USA	RATTC	10-Jun-91	11	$980.00
USA	RATTC	10-Jun-91	50	$113.00
USA	RATTC	19-Jun-91	43	$320.00
USA	RATTC	19-Jun-91	53	$343.50
USA	RATTC	19-Jun-91	56	$1,560.00
USA	RATTC	21-Jun-91	16	$122.00
USA	RATTC	21-Jun-91	28	$63.80
USA	OLDWO	12-Jul-91	29	$346.40
USA	OLDWO	12-Jul-91	36	$104.00
USA	OLDWO	12-Jul-91	57	$390.00
USA	OLDWO	12-Jul-91	76	$108.00
USA	WHITC	17-Jul-91	30	$1,080.00
USA	WHITC	17-Jul-91	56	$910.00
USA	SAVEA	06-Aug-91	16	$244.00
USA	SAVEA	06-Aug-91	60	$2,070.00
USA	SAVEA	06-Aug-91	75	$486.00
USA	THECR	14-Aug-91	58	$27.00
USA	THECR	14-Aug-91	74	$28.00
USA	SAVEA	28-Aug-91	1	$693.00
USA	SAVEA	28-Aug-91	15	$100.00
USA	SAVEA	28-Aug-91	19	$252.00
USA	RATTC	15-Oct-91	8	$980.00
USA	RATTC	15-Oct-91	13	$117.60
USA	RATTC	15-Oct-91	10	$224.00

You're now familiar with the Access query engine and know how to obtain the data that you want.

Moving Access Data to the Other Office Applications

Recognizing that many users will want to manipulate Access objects in Excel or Word, Microsoft provided some useful toolbar buttons for quickly transferring data out of Access. Now you'll learn to move that data elsewhere for processing.

Access offers convenient toolbar buttons that can move Access data directly into Excel worksheets and Word documents. Before you learn to use these buttons, however, you need to understand what the Access manual means by the term *recordset*.

Understanding Recordsets

A *recordset* is simply a collection of database records; it's roughly equivalent to a range in Excel. Unlike an Excel range, though, recordsets can be manifested in many different forms. The following items are all considered to be recordsets:

- An entire table
- The results of a query
- A set of records that supply data to a form or report
- A subset of any of the above defined by a selection (made by dragging the mouse across record selectors or column heads)

You might wonder whether a recordset is the same as a *dynaset*. (Dynaset is a term used frequently in Microsoft's documentation for Access.) A dynaset is an updatable form of a recordset. Some types of recordsets in Access, such as the results of crosstab queries, are not updatable.

Using the Access Exporting Buttons

The Access Print Preview bar contains two buttons (shown below) that offer immediate gratification when you want to export the selected recordset to Word or Excel:

Publish It and Analyze It

Simply select the desired object (a table, query or report, for instance) in the Database window, then press the Publish It or Analyze It button. This will start the appropriate program (Word or Excel, respectively) and export the selected recordset.

Pressing the Publish It button starts Word and opens a Rich Text Format (RTF) document. It copies and plain-pastes the data in the current recordset into the RTF document as a table. If you want to put the data into an existing Word document, you must copy it from the RTF document. Pressing the Analyze It button starts Excel, opens a new Excel worksheet, and copies the data in the current recordset to the worksheet.

FIGURE 6-5

Data copied to Excel by pressing the Analyze It button

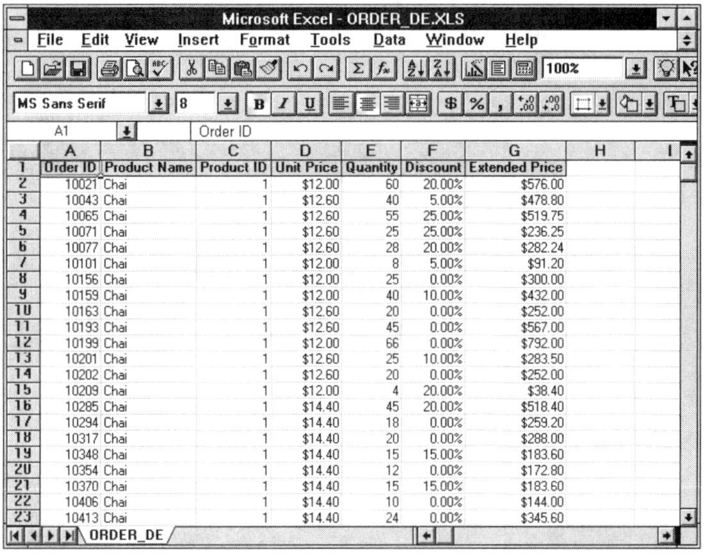

[Figure 6-5: Screenshot of Microsoft Excel - ORDER_DE.XLS showing columns Order ID, Product Name, Product ID, Unit Price, Quantity, Discount, Extended Price with sample Chai order data]

Figure 6-5 shows how the Order Details Extended query in the Northwind Traders database would look after it is copied to Excel by the Analyze It button.

note *The Analyze It button creates an Excel 3.0-format worksheet; this is for compatibility purposes. Be sure to save the new worksheet in the current file format.*

Using the Merge It Button

It's easy to use the data in your Access database to generate mass mailings. Click the Merge It button in the Database toolbar (shown here) to start the Microsoft Word Mail Merge Wizard.

Merge It

The Mail Merge Wizard, shown next, offers you the choice of linking the data in the selected recordset to an existing Word document or to a new document.

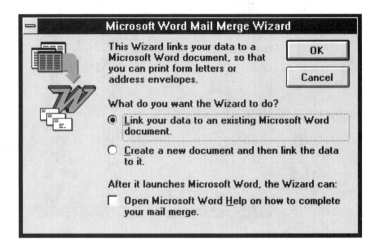

If you select the former, a dialog box will appear so you can select the form letter document you want to use. Selecting the second option starts Word, opens a form letter document, and displays the Mail Merge toolbar. Simply insert the merge fields and draft the rest of the document. (See Chapter 9 for information on using the Mail Merge toolbar.)

Customizing the Access Toolbar

If you frequently transfer Access data to Word or Excel, you might want to streamline the process further by adding the Analyze It or Publish It buttons to the Database toolbar. Follow these steps:

1. Click anywhere on a toolbar with the right mouse button.

2. In the Shortcut menu that appears, choose Customize. This displays the Customize dialog box.

3. Drag the button icons from the Customize dialog box up to the Database toolbar.

You're now familiar with Access' query engine, and how to return query results to Excel and Word. But Access, as a fully functional database program, can also generate its own reports.

Creating Reports

Sometimes you simply want to print or present query results rather than copy them to Excel or Word. Access provides a report writer to help you make the data easier to read and understand. When you want to create a detailed listing of information in the database, Access' full-featured database reporting tool will be much faster than the formatting tools in, for instance, Word.

Reports can provide important statistical data or transaction listings. They can incorporate graphs alongside tabular data. They can also be automatically converted into Rich Text Format files and incorporated into Microsoft Mail messages.

You open a report much as you would open an Access table or query: Select the Reports tab in the Database window, select a report from the list, and choose Preview. Usually, database applications include predesigned reports.

Follow these steps to generate a report listing Northwind sales transactions, with totals by date, for March 1994:

1. Display the Report tab in the Database window.
2. Select the Sales by Date report from the list.
3. Choose Preview. Access displays a Parameter Value dialog box asking you for the beginning date of the range.
4. Enter 3-1-94 and choose OK. A second Parameter Value dialog box prompts you for the last date of the range.
5. Enter 3-31-94 and choose OK.

You see the results in Figure 6-6. You can now print the report in its current form. You can also display the Report Design toolbar and make changes to the report format. (The topic of designing reports is beyond the scope of this book.)

note *You might notice some delay while a report is opening. All reports are based on queries, and Access executes the query before displaying the report. Depending on the complexity of the query, this delay could be a second, or it could be several minutes.*

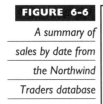

FIGURE 6-6

A summary of sales by date from the Northwind Traders database

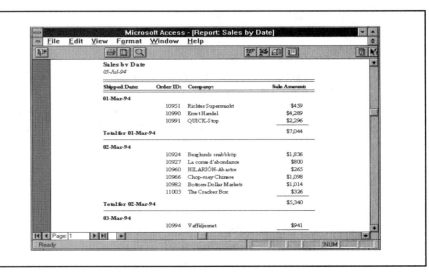

Conclusion

By now, having completed this and the previous chapter, you have become fairly proficient at finding and extracting data for analysis purposes. You will use Microsoft Query primarily as a tool to place data from a single data source into Excel and Word. You will use Access when you need full database features such as a forms-based interface or sophisticated database reports, or need to join data from multiple data sources.

In the next chapter, you'll change gears. You'll learn how to use various forms of graphical data in Word, Excel, and Access, and how to determine what type of graphical data is appropriate in which circumstances.

CHAPTER 7

Working with Graphical Data

We absorb pictorial information more readily than we do information in the form of text. As a result, when we look at a printed page our eyes unconsciously gravitate toward the pictures or diagrams before we concentrate on the printed text.

As computers continue to deliver more processing power for a given amount of money, the sophistication of graphic images will grow, and it will become increasingly important to master the art of graphic persuasion. By making use of graphics and drawings in your documents, you can communicate better and make your work product more effective.

Naturally, graphic images are quite different creatures from the numbers and alphanumeric characters that have traditionally constituted the raw material of most business computing tasks. Graphic objects are wonderfully expressive compared to alphanumeric characters; they do, however, have their quirks.

In this chapter you will learn

- How to create graphic objects with an application's own drawing tools
- How to position graphics effectively in documents, using the graphics and text layers of the client application
- The advantages of using various types of graphic objects, such as drawings, pictures, clip art, and ordinary OLE objects

This chapter is not meant to be a complete guide to designing documents containing graphics. Its purpose is to familiarize the business-oriented user with the basic techniques for exploiting the graphics-handling technology in Office and OLE 2. You will find practical examples of incorporating graphics into documents in Chapter 8.

Drawing Graphic Objects in the Client Application

To this point, this book has focused primarily on linked and embedded OLE objects. However, all the applications in the Office suite (except for Mail) contain drawing tools of their own. With the aid of Word's drawing toolbar (shown here), for instance, you can draw lines, boxes, curves and other shapes in documents.

Using the Drawing Toolbar

The Office applications provide varying degrees of drawing capability. Excel does not contain all the drawing tools found in Word and PowerPoint, although its chart formatting tools are extensive. Access has very little drawing capability; the only graphic objects you will find there have been created in another application.

Table 7-1 describes the shape-creating tools in Microsoft Word's Drawing toolbar. (Display this toolbar by clicking the right mouse button on any toolbar, then selecting Drawing from the submenu that appears.)

Button	Shape	Ordinary Mouse Drag Results	Shift+Drag Results
	Line	Straight line between the beginning and end points of your mouse-drag movement	Straight line oriented at 0, 45, 60, or 90 degrees or equivalent angle.
	Rectangle	Rectangle	Square
	Ellipse	Oval (elliptical) shape	Circle
	Arc	Quarter section of an oval	Quarter section of a circle
	Freeform	Irregular shape	Irregular shape

TABLE 7-1 *Shapes You Can Create with Word's Drawing Tools* ∎

To create a shape, follow these steps:

1. Click the button on the Drawing toolbar for the shape you want to create.

2. Move the mouse pointer to where you want the upper-left corner of the shape to be located.

3. Press and drag the mouse pointer down and to the right to define the dimensions of the object. As you do so, the shape appears on the screen and expands or contracts as you move the mouse.

4. Release the mouse button when the shape is the right size.

Note   *In Chapters 3 and 4, you learned how to put objects into a client application by copying them from a server application into the client application, or by inserting them from with client application's commands. This chapter adds another basic method for creating graphics: creating graphics by using the inherent drawing capabilities of client applications.*

Understanding Drawn Objects

Drawn objects differ from OLE objects and pictures in that they reside in the *graphics layer* of a displayed document. This means that drawn objects in Word document can overlap text, and vice versa.

The main layer of a document is the *text layer*; in Word, the text layer contains, unsurprisingly, text. In Excel, the text layer contains the worksheet grid and the values displayed in the cells.

The graphics layer in Excel and Word floats on top of the text layer. In a document containing no graphic objects, the graphics layer is transparent and unnoticed. In Excel, all graphic objects, including those created with Excel's drawing tools, reside in the graphics layer. In Word, by contrast, OLE objects and pictures reside in the text layer. As a result, when you insert, embed, or link an OLE object or a picture in Word, it "elbows aside" the text to make room for itself.

Drawn objects can be moved around Word or Excel documents without disturbing anything in the text layer. They might, however, obscure the text by covering it up. Figure 7-1 depicts the graphics and text layers in a Word document.

You can insert an OLE graphic object into the graphics layer by putting it inside a picture object. See the last section of this chapter for more information.

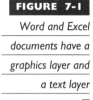

FIGURE 7-1

Word and Excel documents have a graphics layer and a text layer

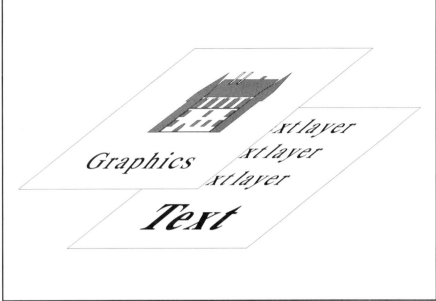

Layering Drawn Objects

In the graphics layer, newly created objects are layered on top of previously existing objects. Figure 7-2 shows five objects that were created with the help of the Drawing toolbar in the following sequence:

- An ellipse (circular)
- An arc
- A rectangle
- A free-form shape
- A line

This sequence is also the sequence (bottom to top) in which the objects are layered in the document. You can change the layering position of a given object with regard to other objects (or with regard to text). Simply select the object and select one of the Drawing toolbar buttons described in Table 7-2.

The preceding examples and tables have only touched the surface of what you can do with the drawing tools. Not covered, for instance, are the techniques for changing the line weights and fill colors that were used in

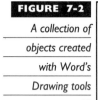

FIGURE 7-2

A collection of objects created with Word's Drawing tools

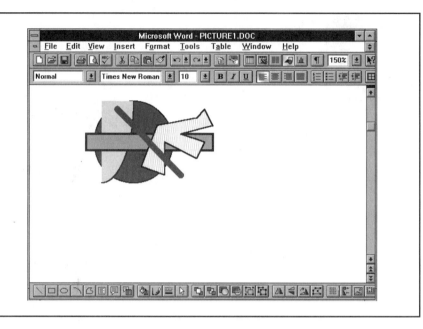

creating Figure 7-2. For more detailed coverage of Word's drawing capabilities, please refer to *Microsoft Word for Windows: The Complete Reference*, by Mary Campbell (Osborne/McGraw-Hill).

In normal circumstances, naturally, you will not concern yourself with the more arcane aspects of drawing. Most of your graphics are likely to be simple ones like that in Figure 7-3.

Button	Action	Result
	Bring to front	Places the object in front (on top of the "pile" of objects)
	Send to back	Pushes the object to the back (to the bottom of the pile)
	Bring in front of text	Places the object in front of the text layer
	Send behind text	Pushes the object behind the text layer

TABLE 7-2   *Effects of Positioning Buttons on the Drawing Toolbar on a Selected Object*

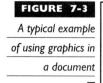

FIGURE 7-3

A typical example of using graphics in a document

Putting Objects into Client Applications

Naturally, simple shapes and lines won't always fill the bill, and relatively few of us have both the talent and available time required to create detailed images with Word's drawing tools. Often you will need to use a server application as a source for a graphic image. That server application might be another Office application (such as when you create an Excel chart object) or a third-party application (such as Adobe Illustrator or CorelDRAW). The server application could also be one of the embedding applications (such as Microsoft Graph or WordArt) included with Word.

Creating Objects with the Embedding Applications

Together, the Windows operating environment and the individual applications in the Office suite provide several *embedding applications* that can create numerous types of graphic objects. They are called embedding applications because their sole purpose is to create objects for embedding into productivity applications such as Excel, Access, and Word. Other commonly used names for these small programs are *applets* and *OLE servers*.

When you display the Object dialog box, you see several object types that are created by embedding applications included in the Office suite. Some examples are listed here:

- WordArt
- Equation Editor
- Microsoft Graph
- Microsoft Organization Chart

The programs that create the first three of the object types listed above are included with Microsoft Word. The Microsoft Organization Chart program is part of PowerPoint.

You will see examples using WordArt and Microsoft Graph in Chapter 8.

Note *Using the Windows Paintbrush program, you can create bitmap drawings that you can copy, embed, or link into documents. (You can see examples of bitmap images used in an application by viewing the Categories form in the Northwind Traders database in Access.) Keep in mind though, that pictures created in Word use less memory and disk space than the bitmaps created in Paintbrush.*

Inserting Objects

Because of differences in the main menus among the Office applications, the command sequences for inserting OLE objects in client applications are not the same. In Word, Excel, and PowerPoint, displaying the Insert menu and choosing Object brings up the Object dialog box. In Access and Mail, you must choose the Insert Object command from the Edit menu. Here's a summary of the command sequences that insert an object in the Office applications:

Client Application	Menu	Command
Word, Excel, and PowerPoint	Insert	Object
Access and Mail	Edit	Insert Object

These sequences each display the Object dialog box in the application, with the Create New tab displayed (Figure 7-4). Though the command sequence might vary, this chapter refers to both variations of this procedure collectively as "inserting an object."

After displaying the Object dialog box, select the type of object you want to insert and choose OK. This brings up the editing "environment"

FIGURE 7-4

The Object dialog box

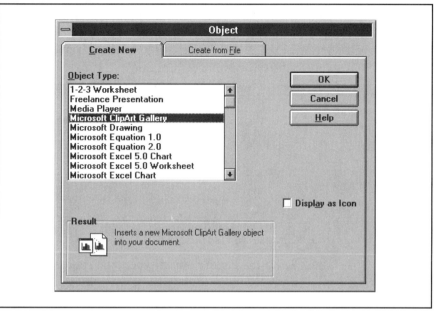

corresponding to the object type you select. For instance, if you select the Microsoft Excel 5.0 Chart object type, Excel starts. On the other hand, if Word is the active application and you select Word Picture Object 6.0 in the Object dialog box, Word simply opens its own picture-editing environment (which includes the Picture and Drawing toolbars).

The action you take to return to the client application varies depending on the particular editing environment. If you've created a Word picture object, click the Close Picture button on the Picture toolbar. (This toolbar appears automatically when you create a picture object.) If a server application was started, display the File menu and look for an Exit & Return command at the bottom.

Using Third-Party Drawing Programs

On some occasions, Word's drawing tools won't be sophisticated enough to create the image you want. In that case, you will have to create the image in a third-party graphics program and import it (or embed or link it) into the client application.

One example of a picture that would be difficult to create with Word's drawing tools is a flowchart. Although you can create a flowchart in Word, it would be extremely time-consuming. Every time you moved, say, a box in the chart, you would have to move the lines that are connected to it.

Visio, from Shapeware Corporation, is a drawing program that can keep track of objects that are connected to other objects. Version 2 of Visio supports OLE 2; it's a good example of a third-party program that can add value to the Office suite of programs.

To insert a Visio flowchart in a Word document, follow these steps:

1. Start Visio and open (or create) the flowchart.
2. Select the entire flowchart.
3. Choose Edit, Copy.
4. Start Word and activate the document into which you want to insert the flowchart.
5. Choose Edit, Paste Special.
6. Select the Picture object type, then choose OK.

The result will look something like Figure 7-5.

Incidentally, the Visio program comes in two flavors: the full program and a less powerful version, specifically designed for Microsoft Office users, called Visio Express. The latter version has been certified as an "Office-compatible" program. Microsoft certifies programs as Office-compatible if they meet certain standards such as similarity of toolbar and menu structure and other features.

FIGURE 7-5

A Visio flowchart embedded in Word

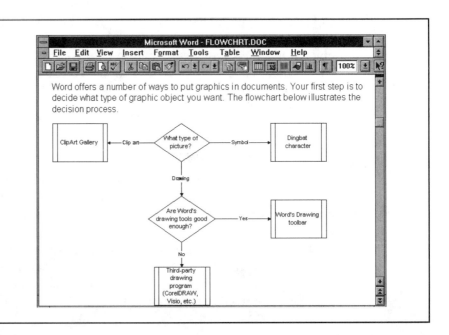

Note *You don't have to start a third-party graphics program in order to insert an object from that application. Simply choose Insert, then Picture and select the desired object type from the Insert Picture dialog box that appears.*

Using Graphics in Access Tables

You can store graphic data in Access, too. Generally, graphic images are stored in Access tables when it's important to have a photographic image of an item or a person.

To see how graphics can be useful in a personnel-related application, follow these steps:

1. In Access, open the Northwind Traders database (NWIND on the SAMPAPPS directory).

2. Display the Form tab.

3. Select the Employees form and choose Open.

In addition to the conventional demographic information you would expect in a personnel-related document (such as ID number, name, and title), the form displays photographic images of the employees. Scroll through the records in the form, and watch the employee images change.

Later in the chapter, you'll learn how to use clip art in an Access field.

Inserting Pictures

As you learned in Chapter 3, linked or embedded OLE objects are not suitable for some purposes—when you have to send a document in final form (in electronic format) to a typesetter or print shop, for instance. In such cases, you can use picture objects instead of OLE objects.

As you learned in Chapter 3, you can link or embed objects as unconverted OLE objects, as text, or as pictures. (You do this by selecting the Picture option in the Paste Special dialog box after you've copied the object.) For example, an Excel range embedded as an OLE object (the Excel 5.0 Worksheet type) retains its "Excel" character, because you can still use the Excel program to edit it. If, on the other hand, you select the Picture object type before linking or embedding the object, it will no longer be an Excel object, and you will not be able to edit it with the Excel program. The same goes for PowerPoint slides, Visio drawings, and bitmap images created in Paintbrush.

As you learned in Chapter 3, pictures are mathematically defined objects, so they are "slimmer" than more robust objects like Excel charts and Visio drawings. As a result, they occupy less space on disk and in your computer's memory. That allows documents containing only pictures to update faster than documents containing an equivalent number of OLE objects.

In earlier chapters, you learned how to link and embed objects as unconverted OLE objects, text, or pictures. One technique that has not yet been demonstrated, though, is how to create a picture from an existing file that was created by a server application.

Suppose, for instance, that you want to insert an OLE object into a Word document as a picture, and that you know the name and location of the graphics file containing the object. Follow these steps to insert the graphic object and simultaneously convert it to a picture:

1. From the Insert menu, choose Picture. This brings up the following dialog box:

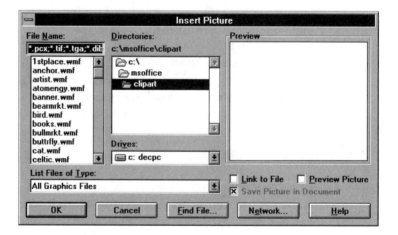

2. To view a small representation of the graphic object (called a *thumbnail*), choose Preview Picture.

3. Select the file containing the picture, then choose OK. Word inserts the picture into the file you selected.

Note   *The process of converting the object into a Word picture is performed not by OLE 2, but by a graphics conversion utility included with the Word program. Thus you can insert a picture in this manner even if the server application does not support OLE 2–as long as the appropriate Word for Windows conversion utility program is installed.*

If Word cannot convert the file you selected, you might have to rely on the drawing program's exporting capability. Most graphics programs can export to a file format Word can recognize.

Caution   *Keep in mind that converting an object to a picture means you cannot subsequently use the original server application to edit the object; you can only use Word's picture editing tools.*

Using Clip Art

On occasion, for presentation purposes, you may want to include some bold or fanciful images. Because creating computer-drawn images is very exacting work, consider using *clip art*—graphic images and drawings provided on disk by independent vendors for this purpose. Most of the leading drawing programs such as Adobe Illustrator, CorelDRAW, and Harvard Draw include extensive clip art collections.

Using the Microsoft ClipArt Gallery

If you have no other source of clip art, you can use one of the clip art images in the Microsoft ClipArt Gallery, which is included with the Office package. Follow these steps to use the ClipArt Gallery:

1. From the Insert menu, choose Object.

2. In the Object dialog box, select the Microsoft ClipArt Gallery object type. This brings up the ClipArt Gallery, shown in Figure 7-6.

   The Gallery provides subject matter groupings called *categories*. Business, People, and Technology are some of the categories of clip art Microsoft provides with Office. It's much easier to find the image you are looking for if you limit the Gallery display to a single subject area.

3. Select a subject from the category list at the top of the dialog box.

4. Select the image you want from the large grid, then choose OK.

The clip art image you selected is inserted in the client application, as shown in Figure 7-7.

You can insert clip art in any of the Office applications. Access, however, restricts where you can insert them.

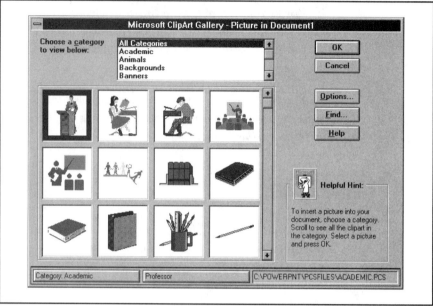

FIGURE 7-6

The Microsoft ClipArt Gallery

Using Clip Art in Access

The Employees form in the Access sample database, which you looked at just a few minutes ago, provides another example of how you can use clip

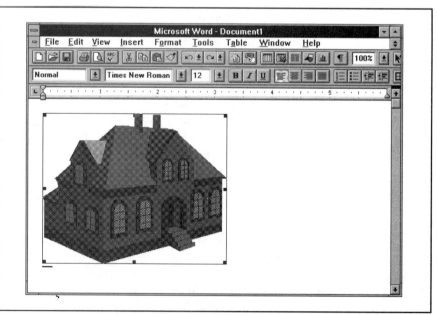

FIGURE 7-7

A Word document after inserting an object from the Microsoft ClipArt Gallery

art. In this example, you will replace an employee's picture with an image from the ClipArt Gallery. Follow these steps:

1. In the Employees form, display Justin Brid's record.
2. Click the photographic image in the Employees form to select it.
3. Choose Edit, Insert Object.
4. In the Insert Object dialog box, select the Microsoft ClipArt Gallery object type, then choose OK. This brings up the ClipArt Gallery (see Figure 7-6).
5. Display the Cartoons category.
6. Select one of the images, then choose OK.

Figure 7-8 shows Justin Brid's employee form with the picture replaced by the first Cartoons image displayed in the ClipArt Gallery.

Note *Clip art images are usually collections of graphic objects grouped together as one whole object. You cannot edit specific portions of clip art images unless you first ungroup, or break apart, the objects that comprise the entire image. The ClipArt Gallery does not provide any editing tools to ungroup images; its sole function is to provide a selection of image files. Accordingly, double-clicking a clip art image does not bring up an editing environment.*

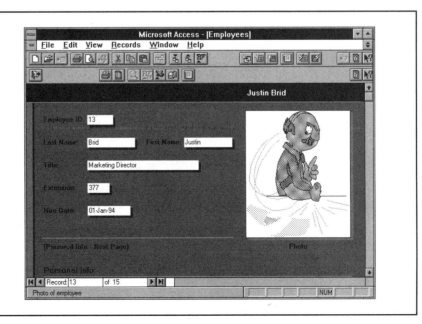

FIGURE 7-8

This employee's picture was replaced by a clip art image

Creating Picture Charts in Excel

To add some zest, you can use graphic images in place of plain column markers in Excel charts. To see how this works, open an Excel workbook containing a chart. Then follow these steps:

1. Display the ClipArt Gallery.
2. Select the clip art image you want. (The example will use the first image in the Electronics category, which is a squarish television set.)
3. Choose OK. The image will be embedded into the Excel worksheet.
4. With the image selected, choose Edit, Copy.
5. Double-click the chart to activate it.
6. Click one of the data series markers.
7. Choose Edit, Paste.

This replaces the columns with stretched versions of the clip art image you copied. To change the stretched images to smaller, stacked images, follow these steps:

1. Double-click the chart to activate it.
2. Click one of the data series markers.
3. Choose Format, Selected Data Series. This brings up the Format Data Series dialog box:

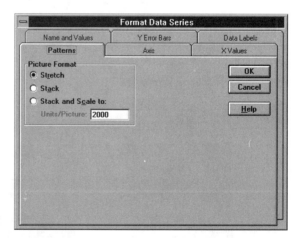

4. Display the Patterns tab.

5. Under Picture Format, select Stack.

The markers are now made up of stacked images, as shown in Figure 7-9.

Some Techniques for Using Graphics in Word

So far you've learned quite a bit about pasting, linking, and embedding graphic information into Word documents. Now you need to know more about what you can do with that graphic information once it's in the document. If you really want to use graphics effectively in Word, you at least have to begin exploring some of Word's desktop publishing features.

Putting Embedded Graphics into Frames

You can acquire more freedom to move an embedded object within a Word document by putting it into a frame. Follow these steps to frame a graphic object:

1. Click the object to select it.

2. Choose Insert, then Frame.

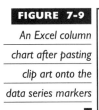

FIGURE 7-9

An Excel column chart after pasting clip art onto the data series markers

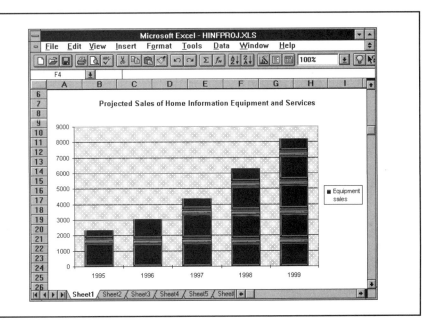

Word surrounds the object with a shaded border. Now that the object is in a frame, its location is not tied to a paragraph, and you can move it around the document more freely. You can even move it into the margin.

You'll learn more about the advantages of framed objects in Chapter 8.

Putting Graphics in Text Boxes

Even after you put an object in a frame, it is still in the text layer. To be able to move an object in front of (or behind) text, you have to move it to the graphics layer. You can do that by inserting the object into a text box. Follow these steps:

1. In Word, display the Drawing toolbar.

2. Click the Text Box tool:

Text Box

3. Draw the outline of the text box in the document by dragging the mouse button, as you would to draw a rectangle.

4. Use any of the procedures you have learned in this chapter to place a graphic object into the text box. (For instance, you can display the Object dialog box and create a Paintbrush or CorelDRAW object, or you can select an image from the ClipArt Gallery.)

Figure 7-10 shows a text box containing a graphics image (the brick wall) placed underneath some text.

Using Graphics in Tables

Sometimes you want a graphic image to remain in a fixed position in relation to certain text. This would be the case, for instance, if you were creating letterhead containing a logo graphic and an address consisting of Word text.

The best way to "chain" text and graphics together for this purpose is to create a two-column table with the graphic in one cell and the text in the other. The following steps illustrate how you would insert a CorelDRAW image into a cell in a table:

1. In Word, use the Insert Table button to define a table of one row by two columns.
2. Start CorelDRAW and open the file containing the logo image you want to use.
3. With the logo image selected, choose Edit, then Copy.
4. Activate Word and position the insertion point in the cell that is to contain the logo image.
5. Choose Edit, then Paste Special.
6. Select the desired options in the Paste Special dialog box, then choose OK.

Now you can enter the address information in the adjoining cell. Figure 7-11 shows an example of such a table.

You can put this letterhead data at the top of a document or in a header to create a letterhead template document.

Using *Dingbats* Instead of Graphics

Don't get so mesmerized by OLE's graphics capabilities that you ignore simpler means of accomplishing the same result. You can put graphics in a Word document without importing or embedding graphic files.

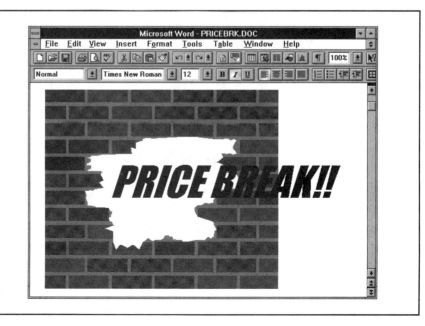

FIGURE 7-10

The brick wall background was placed in a text box so the text could be layered on top of it

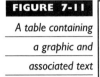

FIGURE 7-11

A table containing a graphic and associated text

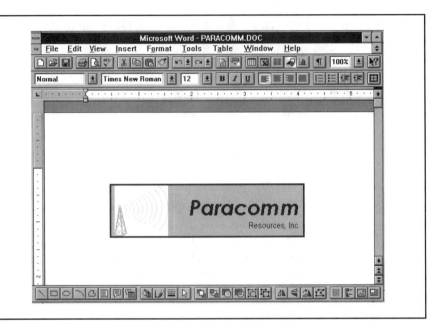

Windows provides a set of special characters called *symbols*, or *dingbats*, that can substitute for embedded graphics at a much lower cost to memory and performance.

Figure 7-12 shows a seminar announcement, created in Word, that contains only one embedded graphic image. All of the other "graphics" are actually special characters created with Windows 3.11's Wingdings font and the ITC ZapfDingbats font that comes with the Hewlett-Packard LaserJet 4 printer.

To insert a Wingdings character in a Word document, follow these steps:

1. Choose Insert, Symbol. This brings up the Symbol dialog box.

2. From the Font drop-down list, select Wingdings. The Symbol dialog box now looks like this:

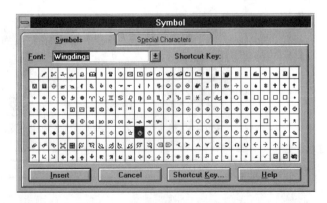

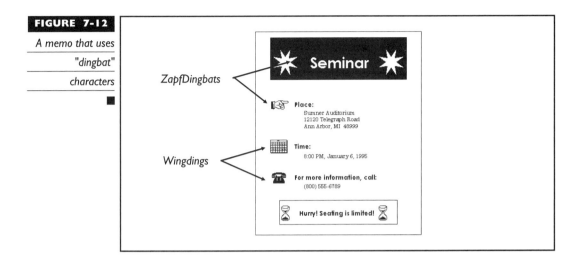

FIGURE 7-12

A memo that uses "dingbat" characters

3. Select the Wingdings character you want. When you click one of the characters, a magnified image of the character pops up.

4. Choose Insert.

Conclusion

This chapter has provided a useful introduction to the world of graphic objects. The next chapter will show you how to integrate graphics and other OLE objects into a newsletter document. You'll also learn how to create an Excel macro that helps you create monthly reports reflecting the most current data.

Part II

Putting Office to Work

CHAPTER 8

Creating Publication-Quality Reports

IN evaluating a document's credibility, many readers will assign considerable weight to the document's overall appearance. Because of this, you must not overlook the tools for giving a professional look to your reports. Besides the impressive editing and presentation capability of Word for Windows itself, the Office suite provides many other powerful tools. This chapter will introduce a number of these tools and techniques.

Most business-oriented reports contain numbers—numbers that might be generated and changed in Excel but which are presented in text documents. As you learned in earlier chapters, manually entering data into both Excel and Word is inefficient. OLE linking can ensure that changes you make to an Excel worksheet will be incorporated automatically into business reports you create in Word.

In this chapter, you will learn to

- Create a logo with the WordArt application.
- Add "drop caps" to Word documents.
- Create a Visual Basic module to update monthly numbers within Excel automatically.
- Add visual interest with reverse type.
- Add a chart to a document by embedding a Microsoft Graph.

The Scenario: The Monthly Mutual Fund Report

In this chapter, you'll pretend you're in charge of shareholder communications for IMF Funds, a mutual fund company. Each month you prepare a report describing the performance of a number of your company's mutual funds for upper management. Once approved, your report is incorporated into a newsletter sent to shareholders and potential shareholders. This report shows the fund's performance for the past three months, along with a chart presenting performance for other time periods.

Your monthly reports integrate data from several sources, and you must take care to present accurate information. Additionally, since the report is a marketing vehicle, you want to present the material in an interesting way. Word offers numerous ways to improve the appearance of documents.

Creating the Body of the Report

The report usually starts out with some encouraging news about the advantages of mutual fund investing or a glowing report on how IMF's funds have performed. Figure 8-1 contains a representative example. To create a file you can use with the examples, enter this text (or something of your own creation) into a Word document.

Using WordArt to Create a Company Logo

After you enter the text, it's time to consider some basic enhancements. First you need to add the company logo to the top of your document. The logo you will create uses a number of features in both Word and in WordArt. As you learned in Chapter 7, WordArt is one of the embedding applications included with Microsoft Word. WordArt's objects are placed in Word (or

The narrative text in the report

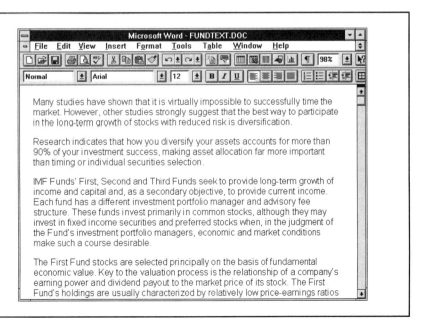

other applications) using OLE. With WordArt you can add interesting and enhancements such as 3D effects and unusual alignments. For example, you might choose to add shading and borders to the text, or to stretch and flip it.

Inserting a WordArt Object

To create the company logo, you have to insert a WordArt object. Follow these steps to create and insert a new object:

1. Place the cursor near the top of the report where you want the company logo to appear.

2. Choose Insert, Object.

3. In the Create New tab of the Object dialog box, select Microsoft WordArt 2.0, then choose OK. This displays the following dialog box:

4. Type the text **IMF**, and choose Update Display.

A basic IMF logo appears in the document. Notice also that a special WordArt toolbar is displayed. These tools help you fine-tune the logo. Table 8-1 describes the WordArt toolbar buttons you will use in the upcoming example.

Formatting with WordArt

WordArt can rotate and reshape text; it can also add shadowing and other formatting not available in Word. Though it's impractical to cover all the possibilities in this chapter, performing the following steps will demonstrate the formatting process in general:

1. Select a font from the Font drop-down list. (The font displayed in the ensuing figures is Book Antiqua.)

2. Click the arrow in the Line and Shape box (at the extreme left of the toolbar) to display the drop-down grid.

Button	Name	Description
	Stretch	Causes the size of the WordArt text to adjust proportionately when the dimensions of the object change
	Special Effects	Rotates text and adjusts shapes
	Shading	Adds shading
	Shadow	Adds shadow effects to text
	Border	Adds borders

TABLE 8-1   *Effects of Buttons in the WordArt Toolbar*

3. Select the Stop Sign shape from the grid, as illustrated next. (The selected item is the second item from the right, in the second row of the grid.)

4. Click the Stretch tool. (This causes the text to size with the frame when you resize it in Word.)

5. Click the Border tool, which displays the Border dialog box:

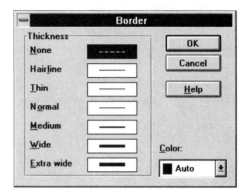

6. Under Thickness, select the Normal option.
7. Under Color, select Black, and then choose OK.
8. Click the Shading tool, which displays the following dialog box:

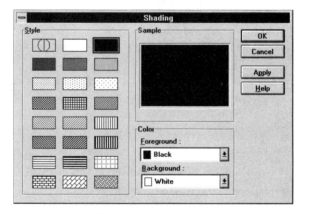

9. From the Foreground Color drop-down list, select Teal, then choose OK.
10. Click the Shadow tool to display the Shadow dialog box, shown here:

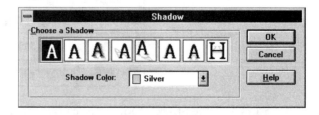

11. Select the third shadow from the left, and then choose OK.

12. Select the Special Effects tool. This displays the Special Effects dialog box, shown here:

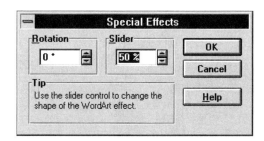

13. Increase the Slider value to 75%, and choose OK. The Slider changes the shape of the WordArt effect. In this case, the value makes a crisper border.

14. Click outside the WordArt object to return to Word.

At this point your logo looks like this:

Adding Borders in Word

Next, you will put the finishing touches on your company logo in Word. Follow these steps:

1. Click the logo to select it. (Incidentally, double-clicking the logo brings up the WordArt editing environment.)

2. Resize the logo as desired.

3. Center the logo on the page.

4. Choose Format, Borders, and then Shading to display the Picture Borders dialog box:

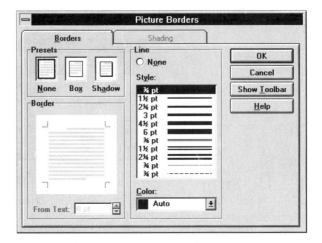

5. Select the Shadow option.
6. Select Dk Blue from the Color drop-down list.
7. Select a Line Style of 1 1/2 Pt, and choose OK.

Your final product should now look similar to Figure 8-2.
As you can see, it is a relatively simple task to create striking special effects using WordArt and Word tools.

FIGURE 8-2

Your logo in final form

Using Drop Caps

Adding *drop caps* is a simple enhancement that gives your documents a polished, professional look. Drop caps are one or more letters that are larger than the remaining text of the sentence and around which the remaining text might wrap. In general, drop caps are used sparingly—for example, at the beginning of an article or book chapter. To create a dropped cap letter for the first paragraph of your report, follow these steps:

1. Position the insertion point in the paragraph that will contain the drop caps. (For a single-letter drop cap, position the insertion point anywhere in the paragraph. To drop-cap the first word in the paragraph, select that word.)

2. Choose Format, Drop Cap. This displays the following dialog box:

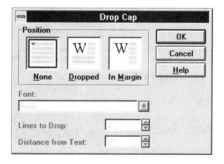

3. In the Position area, select Dropped.

4. In the Lines to Drop box, enter 2.

5. In the Distance from Text list, select 0.1", and then choose OK.

6. If the document is displayed in Normal view, Word will display the dialog box shown next. If so, choose Yes. (If the document is already in Page Layout view, Word simply applies the drop-cap formatting.)

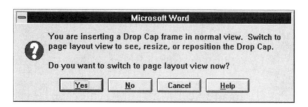

The beginning of your report will now look like Figure 8-3.

FIGURE 8-3

The heading and first paragraph of your report with the logo and drop caps added

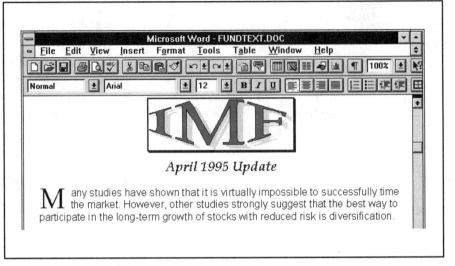

note *You must display a document in Page Layout view or Print Preview to see drop caps as they will be printed.*

Creating the Worksheet That Calculates the Return to Investors

You want to include in your report a table showing the annualized percentage of return of your three stock fund portfolios for the past three months. It will also calculate the average return over the three-month period for each portfolio as well as the average for the combined portfolios. Each month you need to update this spreadsheet, but you don't want to have to re-enter figures from previous months into Word. Instead, you will create an Excel worksheet (Figure 8-4) and link the figures to the Word document.

Creating the Worksheet

To set up your spreadsheet, follow these steps:

1. In an Excel work sheet, enter the labels and percentages shown in cells A1:D6 in Figure 8-4. (In reality, the cells B4:D6 would contain formulas to compute the annualize yield. Creating such formulas is a fairly straightforward Excel operation, but for now you will enter "dummy" constants in these cells. This will permit

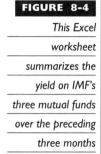

FIGURE 8-4

This Excel worksheet summarizes the yield on IMF's three mutual funds over the preceding three months

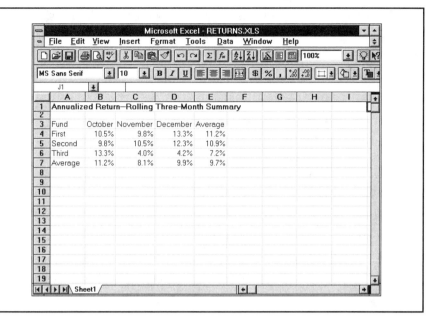

the example to focus on the procedure for automatically updating the figures each month.)

2. In cell E4, enter the formula =**AVERAGE(B4:D4)**.

3. With cell E4 selected, double-click the fill handle. This will copy the formula to cells E5:E6.

4. In cell B7, enter the formula =**AVERAGE(B4:B6)**.

5. With cell B7 selected, drag the fill handle to cell E7. This will copy the formula to cells C7:E7.

6. Select the range B4:E7, and then click the Percent tool on the Formatting toolbar, shown here:

Percent

7. Click the Increase Decimals tool on the Formatting toolbar, shown here:

Increase Decimals

Now that the worksheet is completed, you will automate the monthly updating process by recording a Visual Basic macro.

Recording a Visual Basic Macro to Update the Figures

The report in this example is typical of many business-oriented reports that must be prepared at regular intervals. Such repetitive tasks can often be automated. In this case, you can create a macro in Excel that prepares the worksheet to receive the new figures each month.

If you have not yet worked with Visual Basic for Applications (VBA), the prospect of creating a macro in this new programming language might seem a bit daunting. However, the updating of the monthly investment results provides an excellent example of how to automate a task without writing programming code.

Version 5 of Excel includes two programming languages: the "traditional" Excel 4.0 macro language and VBA. Generally, aim to use the Visual Basic language when you record a macro; VBA is the "wave of the future" in automating Microsoft Office operations. Because the Excel 4.0 macro language usually executes faster, though, you might prefer it in tasks requiring intensive calculations.

Before you begin recording your actions, it's best to outline the steps involved in your task. Think: What is it that I want to automate? Looking at Figure 8-4, you realize that each month you must do the following:

- Copy cells C3:D6 to B3. (You must copy, not move, the figures; copying would mess up your averaging formulas).

- Clear cells D3:D6.

- Enter the most recent month in cell D3.

To record a macro that will perform these operations, follow these steps:

1. Choose Tools, Record Macro.

2. Choose Record New Macro from the submenu that appears. This displays the Record New Macro dialog box, shown here:

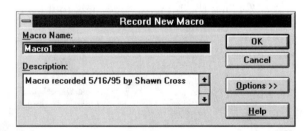

3. Type **MonthlyRoll** in the Macro Name box, and choose OK. Notice that a new macro sheet, Module1, has been added to your workbook and that Excel is in the Recording mode as indicated on the Status bar.

4. Copy the range C3:D6 to cell B3. This moves the data for the "surviving" two months over to the beginning of the period.

5. Delete the formulas in cells D3:D6.

6. Select cell C3 and drag the fill handle to cell D3. This creates a header for the most recent month.

7. Click the Stop Recording button, shown here:

note *By default, Excel version 5 records macros in Visual Basic. To record an Excel 4.0 macro instead, choose Options in the Record New Macro dialog box in step 3, and then select the MS Excel 4.0 Macro option under Language.*

Assigning the Macro to a Button

To make running the macro a snap, you will add a button to the spreadsheet. Then you only need to click the button to run the macro each month.

To assign the macro to a button, follow these steps:

1. Display Excel's Drawing toolbar.

2. Click the Create Button button on the Drawing toolbar, shown here:

Create Button

3. With the mouse, press and drag to define the rectangular area in the spreadsheet where you want the button. Releasing the mouse button displays the following Assign Macro dialog box:

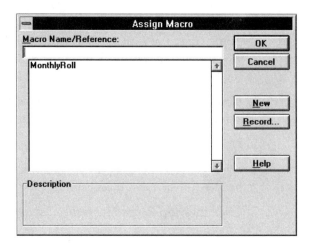

4. In the Macro Name/Reference list, click MonthlyRoll, and then choose OK.

5. Drag the mouse through the default name on the button (Button1), and type **Roll Over Prior Months**.

6. Click the worksheet outside the button object.

Now, to update your figures every month, you only need to press the Roll Over Prior Months button, and then enter the current month's three percentages in cells D4:D6.

Bringing the Excel Worksheet into Word

Before you copy the Excel computations into Word, it's a good idea to apply an AutoFormat. (Choose Format, AutoFormat, and then select an AutoFormat such as Colorful 2 from the Table Format list in the AutoFormat dialog box.)

The next step is to copy the range A3:E7 and paste-link it to the Word document as a Microsoft Excel 5.0 Worksheet Object. Press ENTER to put the linked object into its own paragraph. Your document will look like Figure 8-5.

Integrating the OLE Objects with the Text

If you want your documents to look professional, you must place OLE objects in the text with a certain degree of sensitivity. You can't just plop

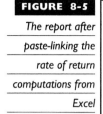

FIGURE 8-5

The report after paste-linking the rate of return computations from Excel

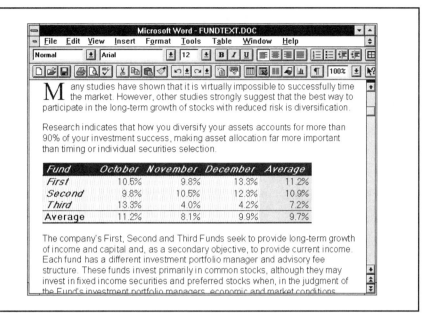

them anywhere. Sometimes, of course, you have to balance aesthetics with the practical necessity of keeping the objects in close proximity to related text. Frames and descriptive captions can help resolve these problems.

Using Frames

In Chapter 7, you learned that OLE objects reside in Word's text layer. That means they must obey the same rules as ordinary text. (For instance, OLE objects must fit within the document's margins.) You also learned that *frames* are containers into which you can place objects.

Putting an OLE object into a frame frees the object from some restrictions that apply to ordinary text. Text can be made to flow around the contents of a frame. You can position frames anywhere in a document, even placing framed items into the margins.

One simple way to embellish your document is to "outdent" the linked Excel object in your document and have the text flow around it. Follow these steps:

1. Select the linked Excel object.
2. Choose Insert, Frame.

   If you are not viewing the document in Page Layout view, you will be asked if you wish to switch to it. Choose Yes. (You must be in

Page Layout view to see the formatting changes resulting from moving the frame.)

3. Move the mouse pointer toward any edge of the object.

4. When the mouse pointer moves directly over the edge of the object, a four-headed arrow appears in the pointer. Press the mouse button and drag the object a bit to the left, so the left edge of the object extends into the margin. Then release the button.

Figure 8-6 shows the results.

Adding Captions to Objects

Inserting captions to explain the purpose of tables and illustrations helps the reader follow your line of thinking. To insert a caption for the linked Excel object, follow these steps:

1. Select the Excel object.

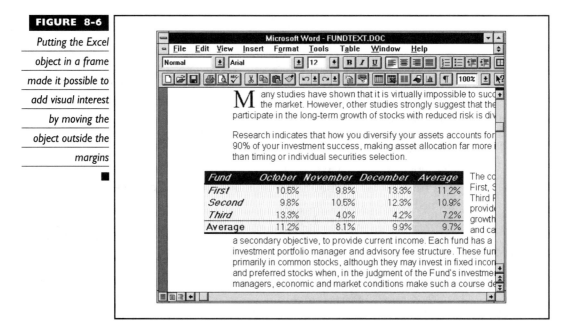

FIGURE 8-6

Putting the Excel object in a frame made it possible to add visual interest by moving the object outside the margins

2. Choose Insert, then Caption. This brings up the following Caption dialog box:

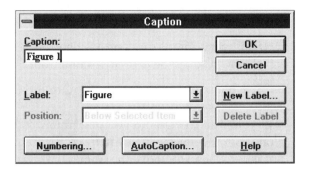

3. In the Caption box, type a colon, then a space, then **IMF Funds' Rate of Return for Prior Three Months.**

4. Choose OK.

The caption you typed will appear beneath the object.

After you insert a caption, the insertion point is still in the caption. Press ENTER to start a new paragraph of normal text.

You can tell Word to automatically create captions every time you insert an object. Follow these steps:

1. Choose Insert, then Caption.

2. In the Caption dialog box, choose AutoCaption. This brings up the following AutoCaption dialog box:

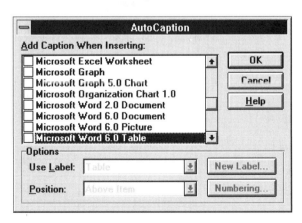

3. In the Add Caption When Inserting list, select the type of object for which you want to automatically generate captions.

4. To change the generic text label to something other than Figure, select a different option from the Label drop-down list. If nothing on the list suits you, choose New Label, type your own label, and then choose OK.

5. If you want the captions positioned in a location other than below the object, select the desired position from the Position drop-down list.

6. Choose OK to close the AutoCaption dialog box.

If you want to put an object in a frame, make sure you select the caption along with the object when you insert the frame. Otherwise the caption will not move when you move the frame.

Using Reverse Type

Reverse type (that is, light type on a dark background) is a great attention-getter when used appropriately. It's especially effective for page numbers and labels. Follow these steps to display the caption you just added in reverse type:

1. Select the caption text.

2. From the Format menu, choose Borders and Shading. This displays the Borders and Shading dialog box.

3. Display the Shading tab, shown here:

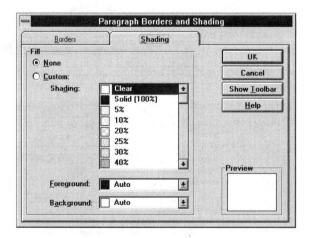

4. From the Shading list, select Solid.

5. Choose OK.

As Word applies the dark background it also changes the font color to white, as shown in Figure 8-7.

tip *Remember, you can use a table, instead of captions, to position text near related objects. You can also put a table inside a frame.*

Using Microsoft Graph

As you learned earlier in this book, you can create charts with the Microsoft Graph embedding application as an alternative to creating them in Excel. Charts created in Graph can be helpful when your destination document contains other linked objects, which can slow down processing. Graph objects also take up less memory and disk space than embedded Excel charts.

To create a chart using Microsoft Graph, follow these steps:

1. Position the insertion point where you want the chart, and then

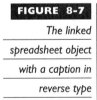

FIGURE 8-7

The linked spreadsheet object with a caption in reverse type

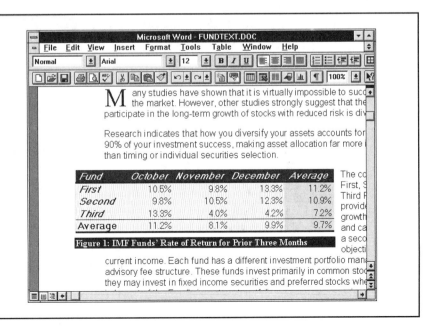

click the Insert Chart button, shown here:

Insert Chart

This starts Graph in Datasheet view, as shown next. The datasheet is where you enter the text labels and values for the chart. When you first start Graph, the datasheet displays dummy data.

		A 1st Qtr	B 2nd Qtr	C 3rd Qtr	D 4th Qtr
1	East	20.4	27.4	90	20.4
2	West	30.6	38.6	34.6	31.6
3	North	45.9	46.9	45	43.9
4					

Document1 - Datasheet

2. Click the upper-left square in the datasheet. This selects all the cells.

3. Press DEL to delete the dummy data.

4. Enter your data. The dialog box shown next contains some data comparing year-end values of one of IMF's funds to those of a fictitious market index.

C:\!WINWORD\08\FUNDTEX2.DOC - Datasheet

		A	B	C	D
		1991	1992	1993	1994
1	Wystar Index	11317	12499	12856	13213
2	First Fund	12064	14357	16403	18980
3					
4					

5. Choose View, Datasheet to exit the Datasheet view and display the chart.

6. Format the chart to your liking. The Graph's editing environment is very similar to its counterpart in Excel. You can, for instance, change the axis scaling, the number formatting of the axis labels, and the font size in the legend using the same command sequences as in Excel. All of these formatting changes are reflected in the chart shown here:

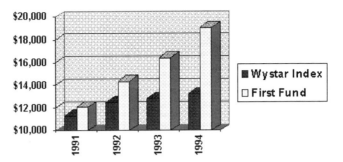

When you are done formatting, click outside the chart. You will return to Word.

Conclusion

The techniques you have learned in this chapter should put you more at ease in the new world of the compound document. You can see that Office provides numerous tools to enhance quality and efficiency in creating publication-quality reports. You've learned to create visual interest in a document, without overwhelming the information in the document with too-busy formatting.

In the next two chapters, you will learn how to link Word documents to data sources (first Excel, then Access). The examples will show you how to combine Word's document processing power with sophisticated analytical and data management tools.

CHAPTER 9

Creating a Form Letter Using a Mailing List in Excel

ONE of the most time-honored principles of business success is staying in contact with customers and others who can help you sell your product or service. Microsoft Word for Windows (and before that, Word for DOS) has always been adept at handling form letters, but version 6 of Word for Windows offers something new: direct access to Excel worksheets as data sources for form letters. Excel works wonderfully as a flat-file database. Many people use it for storing names and addresses because it makes entering, viewing, and sorting records so easy.

This chapter will show you how easily you can improve your visibility with key people in your industry. The practice exercises will demonstrate the extremely close cooperation between the two flagship programs in the Office suite: Excel and Word.

The Scenario: Sending Out a Press Release

In this chapter, you will play the role of a public relations specialist. One of your clients, UltimaSoft, is preparing to announce a major new product. Your firm considers the product such a blockbuster that you're going to send out a teaser press release. In effect, you will announce the announcement. By sending out two releases, you hope to build excitement for the new product launch to a fever pitch by the time it ships.

You will mail your "pre-announcement" to a list of computer magazine editors who you think might be interested in running a news story about UltimaSoft's new product. Figure 9-1 shows the Excel worksheet that contains the mailing list. To prepare for the example, create a worksheet similar to this one. Although six records are shown in the figure, three will be sufficient to demonstrate the steps in the example.

If you already have an Excel worksheet containing a list of names and addresses, you can use that list. However, if the worksheet contains data other

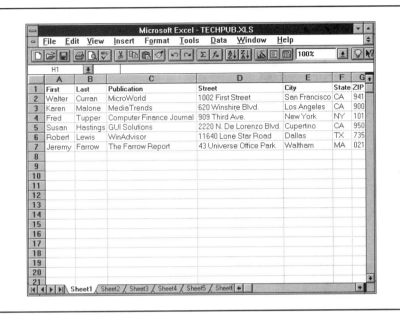

FIGURE 9-1
This Excel worksheet contains addresses of the people who will receive your announcement

than the name and address list, you should assign a name to the range that contains the list. (To assign a name to an Excel range, select the range, then enter the name in the Name box, which is at the extreme left of the formula bar.) You'll soon see why it's helpful to assign a name to the list in Excel.

Creating the Main Document

Once your mailing list is all ready, the first step in sending your announcements is to create the form letter itself. Draft a document similar to the one in Figure 9-2. You will use this as your *main document*. A main document is the same as a form letter, except that the former term encompasses other document types such as mailing labels.

This is obviously a very terse letter, but a short document makes it easier to illustrate how Word merges address data with main documents. Note also that nonprinting characters such as linefeeds and paragraph marks are displayed. This is so you can see where the address information will go.

Save the file as EVTEAS1.DOC. At this point, your announcement is no different from an ordinary Word document. To transform it into a main document, choose the MailMerge command from the Tools menu.

FIGURE 9-2

This is the wording of your main document (form letter)

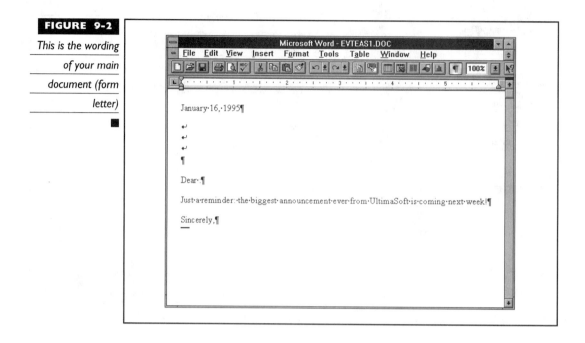

In the Mail Merge Helper dialog box, you can complete any or all of the three basic steps involved in creating a form letter. The box looks like this:

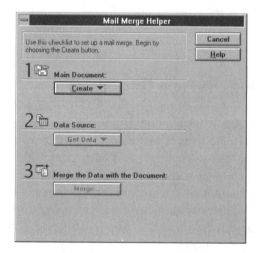

To designate EVTEAS1.DOC as the main document, follow these steps:

1. Click the Create button.

2. Select Form Letters from the drop-down menu that appears. This brings up the following dialog box, from which you can either make the active document the main document, or create a main document from scratch:

3. Choose the Active Window button to use EVTEAS1.DOC. Word brings you back to the Mail Merge Helper.

Specifying the Data Source

Under section 1, the Mail Merge Helper now reflects the choices you made in creating the main document:

The next step is to designate the data source (the Excel worksheet with the names and addresses of your press contacts). Follow these steps:

1. Under the section 2 (Data Source) of the Mail Merge Helper, click the Get Data button.

2. Choose Open Data Source from the drop-down menu that appears. Word displays the Open Data Source dialog box:

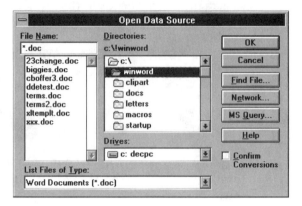

3. Enter or select the name of the file that will provide the names and addresses to your main document, browsing through the directories as required. (Naturally, if you want to view filenames with any extension—rather than just those with a DOC extension—you will have to select All Files option from the List Files of Type drop-down list.) When the file you select is an Excel data file the following dialog box will appear:

4. Choose OK. (If the source document contains named ranges, the ranges will be shown in the list box. If the address data is contained in a named range, you would select the range name from the list box.) Word will display the following dialog box:

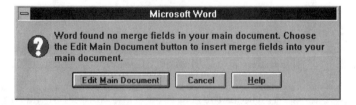

5. Choose the Edit Main Document button.

You're now ready to add merge fields in the main document. Merge fields point to specific fields (columns) in the data source, telling Word exactly where to put the data items from the Excel mailing list.

Merging the Name and Address Data

The final phase of your form letter project, naturally, is to merge the data with the main document. In the process, Word helps you locate problems that could generate errors in the printed documents.

Using the MailMerge Toolbar

The Mail Merge toolbar, which Word displayed after you specified the data source, the main document, has all the buttons you need to finish the job. Here's how the toolbar looks:

The Insert Merge Field and Insert Word Field buttons are for inserting, respectively, merge fields and other kinds of Word fields. You'll also use most of the toolbar buttons in producing your announcements. Here's a summary of the other buttons on the Mail Merge Toolbar:

Button	Name	Effect
« » ABC	View Merged Data	Allows you to preview the merged documents
⏮ ◀ 1 ▶ ⏭	Scrolling Controls	Used in conjunction with the View Merged Data button, allow you to find individual merged documents. Clicking the arrow buttons move backward or forward either one at a time (inner buttons) or all the way to the beginning or end (outer buttons). To view a specific document, enter the record number in the middle box
	Mail Merge Helper	Displays the Mail Merge Helper dialog box
	Check for Errors	Checks for errors such as mismatches between field names in the data source and merge fields in the main document

Button	Name	Effect
	Merge to New Document	Puts the merged letters into a single document; individual letters are separated by page breaks
	Merge to Printer	Prints the merged letters
	Mail Merge	Displays the Merge dialog box, which offers a variety of options such as selecting a range of records to be merged
	Find Record	Allows you to preview records meeting specified parameters, such as all products priced over $500 or all employees living in a certain ZIP code
	Edit Data Source	Displays data records in the Data Form dialog box for convenient editing

Adding Merge Fields to the Main Document

The Mail Merge toolbar makes adding the merge fields to a main document a breeze. Follow these steps to add the addressee's name:

1. Move the insertion point to the beginning of the first paragraph following the date.

2. Choose the Insert Merge Field button. This displays a list of the fields in the source Excel worksheet:

3. Double-click First.

4. Press the space bar to insert a space between the first and last names.

5. Double-click Last. As you insert each field, Word inserts a placeholder for the field. You can move or copy the placeholders as you would any text in a document.

6. Select the First placeholder in the document and copy it to the salutation.

Insert the remaining merge fields (Publication, Street, City, State, and ZIP) in the appropriate places in the document. Insert spaces or punctuation between merge fields as needed. When you have finished, your document should look like that shown in Figure 9-3.

Checking for Errors

Viewing the Merged Data in the Document

By default, Word displays the generic main document with its merge field placeholders. You can view the individual letters, complete with merged data, by clicking the View Merged Data button, shown here:

View Merged Data

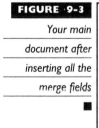

FIGURE 9-3

Your main document after inserting all the merge fields

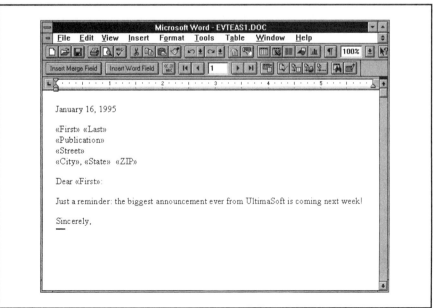

With the merged data displayed, you can browse through the individual letters. Clicking the View Merged Data button again displays the placeholders.

Searching for All Errors

When your mailing list is lengthy—500 names, let's say—browsing through the entire merged document is too cumbersome. In that case, check the data source for errors (for instance, illegal field names). Follow these steps to have Word complete the merge and display messages as errors occur:

1. Click the Check Errors button on the Mail Merge toolbar.

Check Errors

This brings up the Checking and Reporting Errors dialog box:

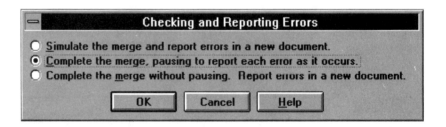

2. Select the second option (the default). Complete the merge, pausing to report each error as it occurs.

3. Word checks the document for a number of potential errors. For instance, if the number of field names in the main document and the data source are not the same, or if all records do not contain the same number of fields, Word will display an error message. If the merge is completed without any errors, Word will display a message to that effect.

The Invalid Merge Field dialog box, shown next, advises you that something is wrong with a field name in the data source. This a very common merge error message.

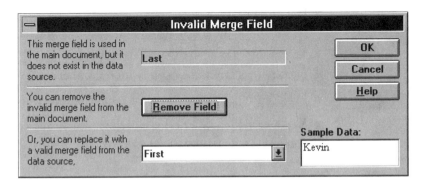

The dialog box gives you several choices:

- Choose OK to clear the dialog box and continue with the merge.
- Choose Cancel to halt the merge.
- Choose Help to view information that might help you correct the problem.
- Choose Remove Field to remove the field from the main document.
- Select another valid field as a replacement from the drop-down list in the bottom section of the dialog box. (The drop-down list contains all valid fields Word can find in the data source.)

If you see that the field shown in the top section of the dialog box doesn't belong in the document in the first place, you can simply choose the Remove Field button. If you need to replace the invalid field name with a valid field name, you can select it from the drop-down list.

If removing or replacing the field doesn't solve the problem, you have to do a little more research. Canceling the merge and examining the entire source document might shed some light on the problem. On the other hand, you might learn more about the problem by continuing with the merge and seeing how many errors there are. (Just make sure you delete the merged document when you have finished. Sending out erroneous letters to clients or customers can be costly to your professional image.)

Avoiding Errors

If you created the Excel worksheet shown in Figure 9-1, the merge should not generate any errors. However, be sure to follow these guidelines to prevent problems:

- Field names must not contain certain characters. The most common illegal character is a space. Most special characters, such as dollar signs and percentage signs, are illegal.
- Field names must not *begin* with a number.
- Make sure field names are not duplicated in your data source.
- Make sure there are no blank cells in the header row (the top row, containing the field names) of your list.

Printing the Letters

After you've checked for errors (and corrected any that were uncovered), you're ready to print the announcements. First, make sure you have selected the proper printer and that the printer has appropriate paper (letterhead, for instance) loaded. If you are sure you want to send out identical announcements to all recipients, click the Merge to Printer button, shown here:

Merge to Printer

Merging to a Document

Rather than merge directly to the printer, you might prefer to merge to a new document. This can give you a little extra assurance that your printed documents will look exactly as you intended. Printing to a document is also a very convenient way of making changes to certain selected documents if you want to customize some of them for special recipients.

Merge to New Document

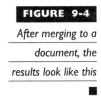

FIGURE 9-4

After merging to a document, the results look like this

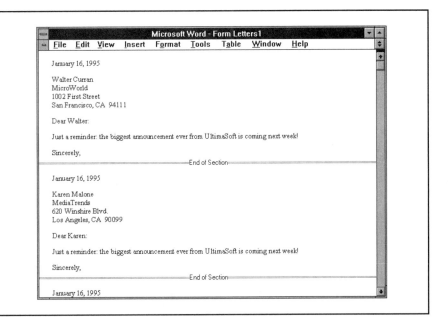

To merge to a form letter document, click the Merge to Document button, shown above. Figure 9-4 shows a merged form letter document. (Word is displayed at 75% scaling so you can see more of the merged document.)

Once you have made any necessary changes and are satisfied with the condition of the merged document, simply click the Print icon on Word's Standard toolbar, or choose the Print command from the File menu, to print the form letters.

Creating Mailing Labels

After printing the letters, it's time to address the envelopes. Your practice is to print mailing labels from Word, by creating a main document and then printing the labels on self-adhesive or other stock. Before you create a mailing label main document, determine which label type you are using according to Avery's numbering system. Word uses Avery product number codes to tell Word how to set up the merged document. (If you are not using Avery labels, use the Avery product number for the same-size label.) For purposes of this example, assume you are using Avery 5160 labels.

To create mailing labels for the announcement, follow these steps:

1. Click the Mail Merge Helper button (shown below) to display the Mail Merge Helper dialog box again.

Mail Merge Helper

2. Choose the Create button in section 1 of the dialog box and select Mailing Labels from the menu that appears. This brings up the dialog box shown here:

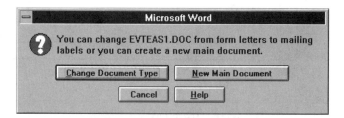

3. Choose New Main Document. The Mail Merge Helper reappears.

4. In section 2 of the Mail Merge Helper, choose Get Data, and then select Open Data Source from the submenu that appears.

5. In the Open Data Source dialog box, select the source worksheet as you did earlier when you created the form letter announcement. Word displays the following dialog box:

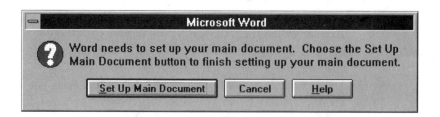

6. Choose Set Up Main Document.

7. The Label Options dialog box appears.

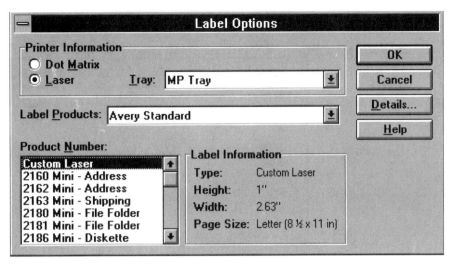

Click **5160 - Address** in the Product Number list, then choose OK.

8. The Create Labels dialog box appears. Use the Insert Merge Field button to put merge fields into the Sample Mailing Label area of the dialog box as you did when you created the form letter main document. When you have finished, your Create Labels dialog box will look like the one shown next. Choose OK.

9. In the Mail Merge Helper dialog box, choose Merge. Word displays the Merge dialog box.

10. In the Merge dialog box, you can specify a number of options that are also available in the Mail Merge toolbar. (You will learn more about the operation of the Merge dialog box in later chapters.) In this case, choose Merge.

11. Close the Mail Merge Helper dialog box.

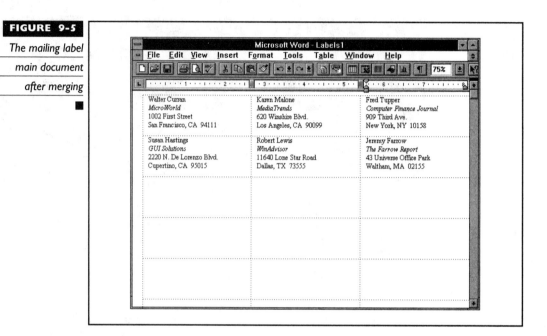

FIGURE 9-5

The mailing label main document after merging

Figure 9-5 shows the mailing label main document. Word inserted merge fields in six cells—one for each record in the data source. If you want to print actual envelopes for form letters rather than labels, see Chapter 10 for more instructions.

Conclusion

As you learned in this chapter, Microsoft has designed Excel and Word to work quite closely together, with Excel serving up source data and Word generating complete documents based on that data. Word can also make use of source data created in Microsoft Access. You will see an example of this in the next chapter, which will also show you how to mail to a selected subset of the mailing list.

CHAPTER 10

Generating Sales Activity Reports

To hold on to your valued customers, you have to keep in regular touch with them. After all, your competitors might be in touch with them, too. Tracking customer order activity helps you keep your finger on your customers' collective pulse. A drop-off in orders from a particular customer, for instance, might prompt an informal inquiry into the reasons behind it.

One fairly innocuous way to begin such an inquiry would be to send letters to customers whose buying patterns have recently changed. Word's mail merging and database linking features support targeted mailing. You can combine Access' query engine and Word's automated document production capabilities to create an effective promotional machine.

In this chapter, you will create a customized mailing to your customers. In the process, you will

- Gain a basic understanding of crosstab queries in Access
- Learn to use Word's mail merge function to generate a mailing that uses accounting data from an Access database
- Learn to make computations in a Word document
- Learn to generate letters for certain selected records based on criteria you specify in Word

The Scenario: Informing Customers About Their Buying Activity

In this chapter, you will play the role of a sales manager for the fictitious Northwind Traders company in the Access sample database. You want to send a letter to customers whose purchasing activity has been declining recently.

Your purpose in creating this document is to determine whether these customers are buying less because of problems with service or quality. If so, you intend to find out what the problems are, so you can make improvements. Your secondary objective is to boost sales by making sure that your customers are fully aware of the benefits of your full line of products. Once they are so informed, you hope to encourage them to increase their orders.

Creating the Main Document

With all of this in mind, you draft a letter similar to the one in Figure 10-1 that lays the groundwork for you to contact these customers personally.

This document will be the main document as you create your mass mailing. As you remember from Chapter 9, you must also specify a data source. The data source (in this example, the Northwind Traders sample database included with the Access program) will provide the name, address, and other customer data that will appear in the form letter. Though you will not have to create the data source yourself, you will have to modify one of the sample queries in the Northwind database to obtain all the required customer data.

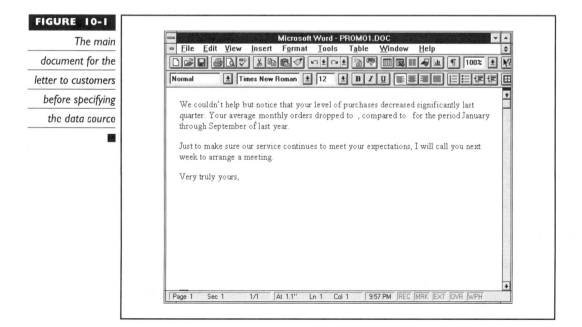

FIGURE 10-1

The main document for the letter to customers before specifying the data source

Finding the Data You Need

To find or create a data source for a Word main document, you have to know a little bit about how a database is organized. Naturally, if your organization employs a database analyst or other technical resource person, that person can help you find the right query or table for your purpose. Otherwise, you will have to start Access and browse through queries and tables yourself.

The Northwind Traders database includes a query that, with some modifications, can supply all the data needed for your customer letter. To open the query, follow these steps:

1. Start Access.
2. Display the Query tab in the Database window.
3. Select the Quarterly Orders by Product (Crosstab) query from the list, and then choose OK.

The datasheet view of the Quarterly Orders by Product (Crosstab) query looks like Figure 10-2.

Understanding Crosstab Queries

As you can tell from the name, the Quarterly Orders by Product (Crosstab) query is a *crosstab* query. You need to understand a few things about

FIGURE 10-2

This query in the Access sample database is the basis for your data source

Crosstab Query: Quarterly Orders by Product (Crosstab)

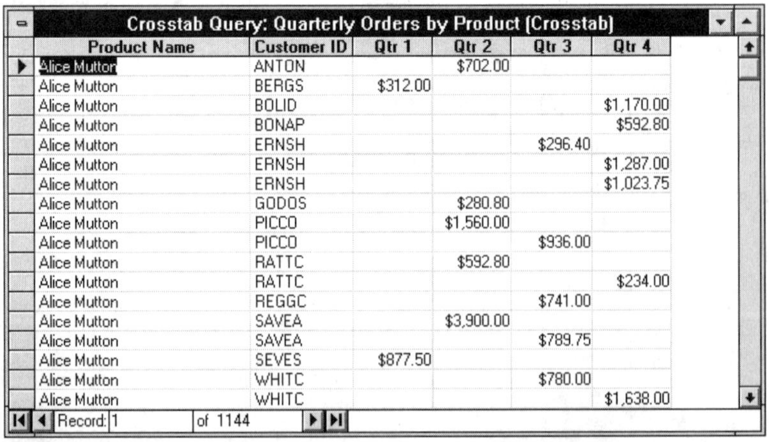

Product Name	Customer ID	Qtr 1	Qtr 2	Qtr 3	Qtr 4
Alice Mutton	ANTON		$702.00		
Alice Mutton	BERGS	$312.00			
Alice Mutton	BOLID				$1,170.00
Alice Mutton	BONAP				$592.80
Alice Mutton	ERNSH			$296.40	
Alice Mutton	ERNSH				$1,287.00
Alice Mutton	ERNSH				$1,023.75
Alice Mutton	GODOS		$280.80		
Alice Mutton	PICCO		$1,560.00		
Alice Mutton	PICCO			$936.00	
Alice Mutton	RATTC		$592.80		
Alice Mutton	RATTC				$234.00
Alice Mutton	REGGC			$741.00	
Alice Mutton	SAVEA		$3,900.00		
Alice Mutton	SAVEA			$789.75	
Alice Mutton	SEVES	$877.50			
Alice Mutton	WHITC			$780.00	
Alice Mutton	WHITC				$1,638.00

Record: 1 of 1144

crosstab queries to understand why the more conventional Select query (which was demonstrated in Chapter 6) would not provide the data you need for this letter.

Crosstab queries differ from Select queries in the way they present data in columns. Look carefully at the last four columns in Figure 10-2. These columns display order amounts (expressed in dollars) for a twelve-month period, divided into four quarters. The totals are computed by an expression in the QBE grid. (It is not necessary to explain the nuances of this particular expression for purposes of this example. You can, however, examine the expression in the QBE grid if you're curious.)

In effect, a single field has been split into four columns. That is the distinguishing characteristic of crosstab queries. In the QBE grid of a crosstab query, you identify a *column heading* field, one or more *row heading* fields, and a *value* field. The value field is the one that is "divvied up" among multiple columns. The precise manner in which this is done is controlled by an expression in the column heading field (the third column in the QBE grid shown next).

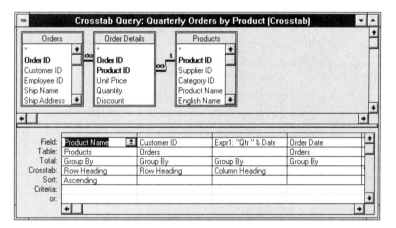

Again, it is not necessary for you to study the intricacies of this rather arcane expression. It is sufficient for you to understand in principle that the purpose of this expression is to determine how the crosstab table computes values appearing in the columns labeled "Qtr 1" through "Qtr 4."

The first two fields in the QBE grid are *row heading* fields. Row headings with "Group By" entries in the Total row control how totals are aggregated in the *rows* of the crosstab. A crosstab query can have multiple row fields.

Figure 10-3 illustrates the relationships between the row, column, and value fields, as specified in the QBE grid, and the result in the datasheet view. The value field specifies the data item being summarized. In this case, an expression (which is truncated in the figure) defines the value as the sum of the order amounts. The expression in the column field specifies how these values are aggregated into columns—by calendar quarter, in this case. The row field, Customer Name, tells Access to aggregate order totals for each customer. (The Group By value in the Total row causes the order amounts to be summed by customer.) As a result, the datasheet view displays a single record per customer.

It is the crosstab query's ability to divide a single field and display the component amounts that makes it valuable for your customer letter. You want to be able to compute changes in order volume for specific customers over several time periods. A Select query would restrict you to computing total orders for a *single* span of time. Only a crosstab query can divide a time period up into segments.

For more information on crosstab queries, please refer to *The Microsoft Access Handbook* from Osborne/McGraw-Hill, or to the Microsoft Access documentation.

Modifying the Quarterly Orders by Product Query

You need to make some changes to the query design before you connect it to your customer letter. First, to preserve the existing query in its current form, save the query under a different name, such as **Customer Order Trend**, then follow these steps:

1. Display the Design window of the query.

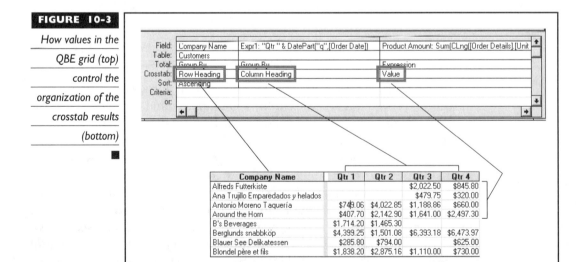

FIGURE 10-3

How values in the QBE grid (top) control the organization of the crosstab results (bottom)

2. Delete the Product Name field. (You are only interested in total sales by customer, so this field is extraneous.)

3. Delete the Products table from the query. (That is, select the Products field list in the upper part of the screen and press DEL.)

4. Delete the Order Date field containing the "Group By" entry in the Total row (the row in the QBE grid indicated by the "Total" label at left). If this field were to remain in the grid, it would cause the query to create a record for each separate order.

5. Add the Customers table to the query.

6. Add the following fields from the Customers table to the QBE grid:

    Company Name
    Contact Name
    Address
    City
    Region
    Postal Code

7. For each of the fields you added in the previous step, click the extreme right of the Crosstab row (the row in the QBE grid indicated by the "Crosstab" label at left) to display the drop-down list, then select Row Heading. This will include the field in the query results.

8. Delete the Customer ID field from the query.

9. Specify an ascending sort for the Customer Name field.

When you display the query in datasheet view, it should look like the screen shown in Figure 10-4. This query contains all the address and financial data you need for your main document.

Using an Access Query as a Data Source

To use the Customer Order Trend query as a data source for the form letter, start Word and open the main document. Then follow these steps:

1. Choose the MailMerge command from the Tools menu. This brings up the Mail Merge Helper dialog box (shown next), reviewed in depth in Chapter 9.

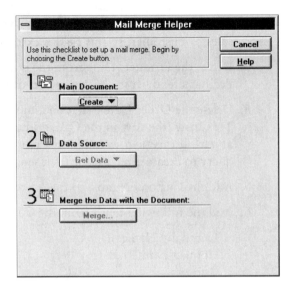

2. Choose Create.
3. Select Form Letters from the drop-down menu.
4. In the dialog box that appears, choose Active Window to use the current document.

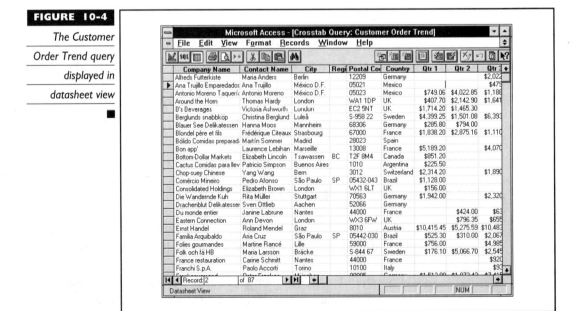

FIGURE 10-4

The Customer Order Trend query displayed in datasheet view

Word brings you back to the Mail Merge Helper. The next step is to specify the data source for the document.

Connecting to Access with the Mail Merge Wizard

To specify the Customer Order Trend query as the data source for your letter, follow these steps:

1. In the Mail Merge Helper, choose Get Data.
2. Choose Open Data Source from the drop-down menu that appears. Word displays the Open Data Source dialog box.
3. Select the NWIND.MDB file on the SAMPAPPS subdirectory and choose OK.
4. In the dialog box that appears, display the Queries tab.
5. Select the Customer Order Trend query from the Queries in NWIND.MDB list, then choose OK.
6. Word then displays a message telling you that it found no merge fields in the main document. Choose Edit Main Document.

Word brings you back to the document. The Mail Merge toolbar is now displayed.

Adding the Merge Fields

Now it's time to insert the name and address fields. Use the Insert Merge field button as you did in Chapter 9 to insert the company name and address fields, properly spaced, in the main document.

If you followed the steps outlined so far, selecting the Northwind Traders database and the Customer Order Trend query, your document should look like Figure 10-5.

Note that the address shown is an international address. You'll add the Country merge field later on in the example.

Merging from Access

You can also start the merge process from the Access program. Both of the following procedures produce the same result as starting the Mail Merge Wizard from Word.

FIGURE 10-5

The main document after inserting company name and address fields

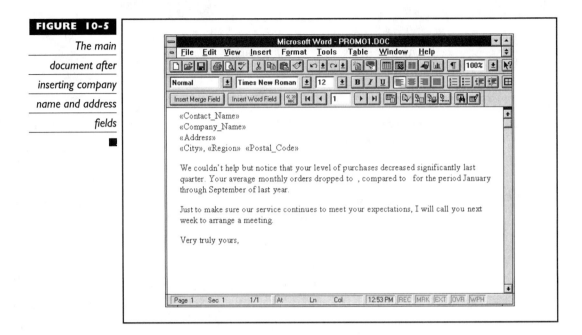

Merging with Access' New Report Wizard

With the database that contains the desired table open in Access, follow these steps:

1. Click the Auto Report button (shown next) on the Standard toolbar.

Auto Report

2. In the New Report dialog box, click the Report Wizards button. This brings up the following dialog box:

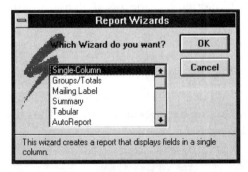

3. Select MS Word Mail Merge from the list (it's the last item), then choose OK.

This starts the Word Mail Merge Wizard.

Merging with the Merge It Button

You can also initiate a merge by clicking the Merge It button:

Merge It

Though this button does not appear on Access' Standard toolbar, it can be added from the File category in the Customize Toolbars dialog box, as explained in Chapter 6.

Performing Computations in Word

Now you need to put the dollar amounts into the document. The data in the Customer Order Trend query, however, isn't quite what you want to see in the letter. You want each letter to contain average monthly sales amounts for two different time periods (the first nine months and the last three months of the year).

If you are extremely proficient in Access, you can design a query that will perform these computations. However, you might not be that experienced with Access; or you might not have access to the entire financial database, as you do with the Northwind Traders sample database. You can still perform computations by using formulas (called *expression fields*) in Word.

Computing the Base Period Order Level

To compute the desired monthly averages, you first need to insert merge fields to bring the intermediate figures (the quarterly totals) into the main document. Follow these steps:

1. Insert the merge fields for each of the first three quarterly totals in a new paragraph above the address. For visual clarity, separate the merge fields with some white space (that is, tabs or spaces). The fields and white space will be hidden later.

2. Select the three merge fields you just inserted and assign the bookmark **BasePeriod** to the selection.

Your document should now look like this:

«Qtr_1» «Qtr_2» «Qtr_3»
«Contact_Name»
«Company_Name»
«Address»
«City», «Region» «Postal_Code»

We couldn't help but notice that your level of purchases decreased significantly last quarter. Your average monthly orders dropped to , compared to   for the period January through September of last year.

Just to make sure our service continues to meet your expectations, I will call you next week to arrange a meeting.

Very truly yours,

Computing the Base Period Average

With the figures for the January-to-September "base period" in the main document, you can now enter an expression field to compute the base period monthly average. Follow these steps:

1. Position the insertion point in the correct location (in the second sentence between "compared to" and "for the period").

2. Choose Insert, then Field. This brings up the Field dialog box.

3. Click the Field Code box. (You can skip past the two list boxes at the top because the expression field name, shown as = (**Formula**), is the default selection in the Field Names list. Normally, you would have to select a field in the Field Names list.)

4. Type **BasePeriod**, followed by **/9**. This expression divides the total sales for the first three quarters by nine to arrive at the monthly average.

5. Type a space, followed by the numeric picture switch **\# $#,###.00** (it controls how the dollar amounts are formatted in the text).

6. Turn off the Preserve Formatting During Updates option.

7. Choose OK.

Don't worry that the field returns an error result; that's because View Merged Data is turned off.

tip *Another way to insert an expression field is to press* CTRL+SHIFT+F9, *and then type the expression.*

The expression field you created will divide the sum of the three quarterly totals by nine, yielding the monthly average order level for the January-to-September period. To see the result for the first record, click the View Merged Data button. It should return the amount $224.72.

Hiding the Computations

When you turned in your high school algebra homework, "showing your work" was a good practice; you do not intend, however, to carry on that practice in this letter. To prevent the order amounts above the address from printing, format them as hidden text. Follow these steps:

1. Select the entire paragraph containing the amounts.
2. Choose Format, then Font.
3. Display the Font tab of the Font dialog box.
4. Under Effects, select the Hidden option, and then choose OK.

By default, Word displays hidden text on the screen, so you can still view the computations as you continue to work with the document. If by some chance your hidden text has disappeared from view, you can display it by following these steps:

1. Choose Tools, then Options.
2. Display the View tab of the Options dialog box.
3. Under Nonprinting Characters, select the Hidden Text option.

Computing the Current Sales Level

Now you want to insert the other sales amount (the monthly average for the last three quarters of the year). With View Merged Data not selected, follow these steps:

1. Insert the **Qtr_4** merge field in the correct location (between the word "to" and the comma).

2. Position the insertion point just to the right of the merge field's closing angle brackets.

3. Type **/3**.

4. Press ALT+F9 to display field codes.

5. Select the entire expression, as shown in the following representation of the paragraph on the screen:

> We couldn't help but notice that your level of purchases decreased significantly last quarter. Your average monthly orders dropped to { MERGEFIELD Qtr_4 }/3, compared to { = BasePeriod/9 \# $#,###.00 } for the period January through September of last year.

6. Press CTRL+F9.

7. The insertion point is now just to the left of the merge field. Type an equal sign (=), then a space.

8. Enter the numeric picture switch **\# $#,###.00** at the end of the expression field.

This expression returns the monthly average of the last quarter's sales for the displayed record.

Viewing the Computations

To see the computed amounts in the letter, click the View Merged Data button and press ALT+F9 to display field results. This produces a disconcerting result: the name and address information disappears. Don't worry, though; that's because the first record in the query contains blanks in one of the result fields. You'll solve this problem later. For now, display record number 3. Your screen should look like Figure 10-6.

Allowing for International Addresses

The last line of the address in Figure 10-6 is incomplete, because the customer is located outside the United States. To provide for both domestic and foreign address formats in the same main document, you must use an IF field.

FIGURE 10-6

The letter for the third customer record

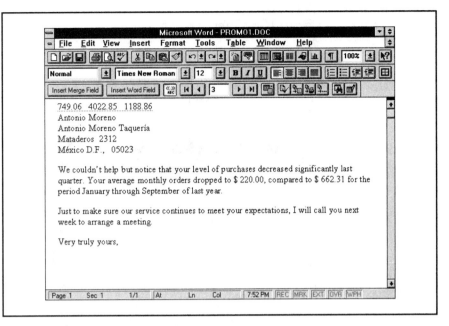

To "internationalize" the address fields in the main document, follow these steps:

1. Select the Region merge field in the last address line.
2. Press CTRL+F9 to enclose these two fields within a new field.
3. Type **if**, followed by a space.
4. Insert the Country merge field.
5. Type <>"USA", followed by a space.
6. Insert the Country merge field, followed by a space.

Your address merge fields will now look like this when viewing field codes:

{ MERGEFIELD Qtr_1 } { MERGEFIELD Qtr_2 } { MERGEFIELD Qtr_3 }

{ MERGEFIELD Contact_Name }
{ MERGEFIELD Company_Name }
{ MERGEFIELD Address }
{ MERGEFIELD City }, { if { MERGEFIELD Country }<>"USA" { MERGEFIELD Country } { MERGEFIELD Region } } { MERGEFIELD Postal_Code }

Selecting Specific Customers

Word packs quite a punch when it comes to selecting records based on criteria. In the Mail Merge Helper's Query Options dialog box (shown next), you can enter multiple comparison criteria to limit the records included in the merged document.

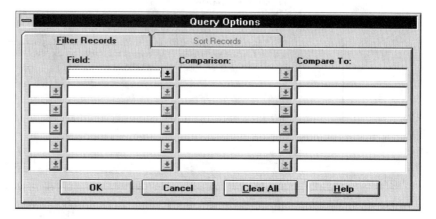

In this case, you don't want to send letters to customers whose activity is minimal. To eliminate customers whose purchases were less than $500 in each of the first three quarters, follow these steps:

1. Display the Mail Merge Helper.
2. Choose the Query Options button. This displays the Filter Records tab of the Query Options dialog box.
3. In the Field box of the first row, select Qtr_1 from the drop-down list.
4. In the Comparison box of the first row, select Greater than from the drop-down list.
5. In the Compare to box of the first row, type **500**.
6. For each of the next two rows, repeat steps 3 through 5 above, except for the Field box, where you will select Qtr_2 and Qtr_3, respectively, in the second and third rows. Your Query Options dialog box now looks like this:

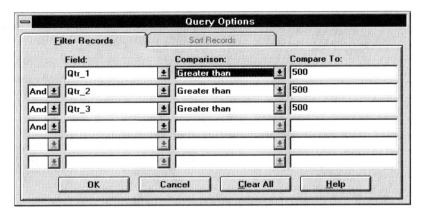

7. Choose OK.
8. In the Mail Merge Helper, choose Close.

Now only customers meeting your selection criteria (that is, those who have ordered at least $500 of goods in each of the first three quarters of the year) will be merged with the main document. Adding the criteria also eliminated the error results you encountered when you first clicked the View Merged Data button—errors that were caused by records with blanks in some of the quarterly totals.

note *By default, Word assumes that criteria you add to the Query Options dialog box are "and" criteria. You can, however, add "or" criteria by selecting Or from the boxes at the extreme left of the dialog box.*

Selecting Records with SKIPIF Fields

If you scroll through the records and look carefully at the computed dollar amounts in the first paragraph of the letter, you'll see that some of the customers *increased* their orders in the last quarter. The letter you are creating does not apply to those customers, so you need to filter out their records.

Unfortunately, the Query Options dialog box is no help to you, because it can only filter on field values, not on computed amounts in the document. You will have to use a SKIPIF field, which causes Word to bypass records based on a condition.

To eliminate the unwanted records with a SKIPIF field, follow these steps:

1. Position the insertion point at the end of the document.
2. Press CTRL+F9.
3. Type **skipif**, then a space.
4. Insert the Qtr_4 merge field.
5. Type a space, then the greater-than operator (>), then another space.
6. Copy the expression field for the average sales for the fourth quarter to the right of the greater-than operator.
7. Position the insertion point just to the left of the BasePeriod/9 expression.
8. Type **2***.

The formula compares the total orders for the fourth quarter to the monthly average for the first three quarters times two. When you merge, any customers whose average for the fourth quarter is more than two-thirds of the base period average will be skipped. In other words, Word will generate a letter for each customer whose monthly average for the last quarter has declined by more than one-third from the level in the first three quarters.

note *The Word manual says that SKIPIF fields can't do anything that the Query Options dialog box can't do, but this is incorrect. The Query Options dialog box can only compare merge field values, whereas the SKIPIF field can compare bookmarks and computed values in addition to merge field values.*

Merging the Records

Click the Merge to New Document button (shown next) to create the merged document.

Merge to New Document

The SKIPIF field eliminates 9 of the 17 records, leaving the 8 customers you want to reach.

Printing Envelopes

In Chapter 9, you learned to print mailing labels for your form letters. In this case, you want to avoid the "mass-produced" impression that computer-printed labels give, so you will use Word to print the addresses on the envelopes.

Creating envelopes for your form letters is very similar to creating mailing labels. Follow these steps to create an envelope main document for your customer mailing:

1. Save your main document, then save it again under a new name. (You will change the new file into an envelope main document.)

2. Select the entire address area of the document, from Contact Name through Postal Code and choose Edit, then Copy. (You'll see why in a moment.)

3. Click the Mail Merge Helper button.

4. Choose Create, and select Envelopes from the menu that appears.

5. In the dialog box that appears, choose Change Document Type.

6. Choose Setup. This brings up the Envelope Options dialog box.

7. In the Envelope Options dialog box, you can describe the envelope dimensions and specify certain parameters such as the tray that will feed the envelopes to the printer. Choose OK when you are done. This displays the following dialog box:

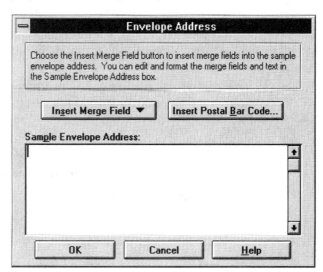

Normally, you would insert the address merge fields into this dialog box. In this case, however, the address data contains an IF field, so you must choose OK.

8. A dialog box appears asking if you want to replace the text in the document. Choose OK.

9. Close the Mail Merge Helper. You are now looking at a blank envelope document.

10. Click in the center of the envelope document. A rectangular border appears, indicating the address block.

11. Choose Edit, then Paste. Your envelope document should now look something like this:

```
{ MERGEFIELD Contact_Name }
{ MERGEFIELD Company_Name }
{ MERGEFIELD Address }
{ MERGEFIELD City }, { if { MERGEFIELD Country }<>"USA" {
MERGEFIELD Country } { MERGEFIELD Region } } { MERGEFIELD
Postal_Code }
```

12. If necessary, drag the address block to the correct location in the envelope document.

You are not home free yet. Unfortunately, the selection criteria you created in the letter document do not carry over to the envelope document. Follow these steps:

1. Display the Query Options dialog box and re-enter the selection criteria you used in the letter document.

2. Copy all bookmarks and expression fields from the letter document into the envelope document.

3. Copy the SKIPIF field to the envelope document.

4. Format all the copied text as hidden text.

Now click the Merge to Document button, shown here:

Merge to New Document

The merged document will include a record for each customer in the merged letter document. Load envelopes into the printer and click the Merge to Printer button (shown next) to print the envelopes.

Merge to Pointer

note *As mentioned earlier, someone experienced at building queries in Access could have performed the subtotaling and averaging computations (performed by Word in the example) in Access by stringing together multiple queries.*

Conclusion

Having completed this chapter, you now have a very thorough grounding in the subject of integrating the Office productivity applications (Access, Excel, and Word). In the next chapter, you will learn to transmit your work product in electronic form with Microsoft Mail.

CHAPTER 11

Mailing, Routing, and Faxing Documents

A LONG with its formidable array of application programs, the Office suite includes a user license for Microsoft Mail. If your PC is connected to a network or a workgroup running Windows for Workgroups, you can exchange electronic messages with your co-workers. Compared to leaving a message with a receptionist or on an answering system, electronic mail allows you to provide much richer information in your message. It's also a much faster way of transmitting documents and files than regular or express mail.

It's usually easier, too, to prioritize incoming electronic mail than phone calls and letters. Microsoft Mail, like most E-mail systems, allows you to respond immediately to messages, or to store them in folders for later response. All told, electronic mail systems such as Microsoft Mail can be vital to the timely completion of work projects.

You might use Microsoft Mail to send a message as simple as, "I'll get back to you Tuesday." Or you might send a message with embedded graphics and an attached Excel workbook.

You can send and receive ordinary Mail messages only if you are connected to a Microsoft Mail *post office*. A post office is a directory on a server that stores information about a group of Mail users. The server might be a file server on a Novell network or a PC you are connected to via Windows for Workgroups. This chapter assumes you have an account on a post office and that you have been assigned your password. (See your network administrator for information on how to connect to a Mail post office.)

Using Mail, you can also send messages by fax. This requires use of a computer fax board connected to your PC or to the network. Your fax messages can be received by ordinary fax machines or by fax boards connected to another computer network. If the recipient has Mail and Office installed, you can even attach fully functional documents (binary files) that he or she can save and edit.

The Mail software does not actually ship with the Office program suite; it's included with the Windows for Workgroups software. Purchasing Office gives you the legal right to run Mail on your system and connect to a post office. Because Mail integrates so well with the Office applications, you need to master it to realize the full benefits of Office applications. This chapter teaches the basics of using Mail, including

- How to send Mail messages to individuals and groups
- How to attach documents and OLE objects to messages
- How to route documents to a series of recipients and track their progress
- How to send messages to, and receive messages from, fax machines
- How to transmit binary files using the Microsoft At Work PC Fax program in Windows for Workgroups 3.11.

Sending Messages

The first time you start Mail during a Windows session, you are greeted by the Mail Sign In dialog box, shown here:

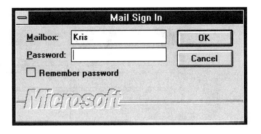

Enter your password and choose OK.

note *If you have not yet logged in to the network when you first start Mail, you will first see a message reminding you to do so.*

Mail starts and displays the Inbox window, shown here:

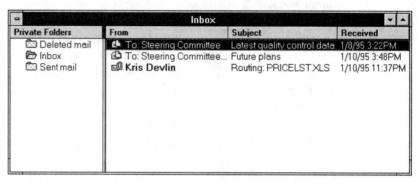

It's a good practice to read any new messages when you sign in. You'll learn about reading messages later in the chapter. Now, let's review how to create and send messages. The process requires only a few simple steps.

Composing a Message

To compose a message, follow these steps:

1. Click the Compose button on the toolbar. This brings up the dialog box shown in Figure 11-1.

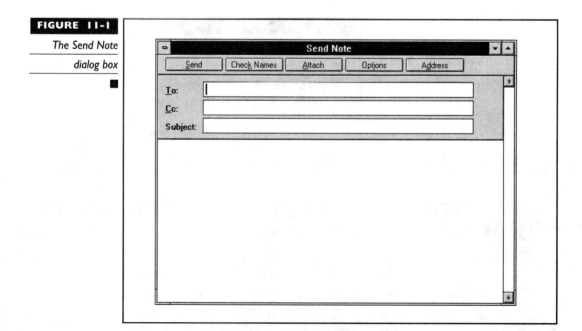

FIGURE 11-1

The Send Note dialog box

2. In the To box, you can type the names of the recipients, separating the names with semicolons. For the sake of accuracy and convenience, however, it is usually better to click the Address button, which displays a dialog box like the following:

3. To add a recipient to the To box, double-click the recipient name in the Directory list. When you finish adding recipients, choose OK.

4. In the Subject box of the Send Note window, enter a brief description of the subject or content of the message.

5. In the message area (the large blank area at the bottom), type your message.

6. Choose Send to send the message.

Creating a Personal Address Book

By default, the Address window lists all names in the post office. The post office contains all the administrative data relating to Mail, including names, addresses, and passwords of all authorized Mail users for the server PC on which the post office resides.

If your post office contains dozens of names, finding a particular name might become unwieldy. However, if you send most of your mail to a relatively small number of recipients, create a *personal address book*—a customized subset of the post office list.

To copy an address from the post office to your personal address book, follow these steps:

1. From the Mail menu, choose Address Book. This displays the Address Book dialog box.

2. Select the name(s) you want to copy to your personal address book. You can select multiple names (as shown next) by holding down the CTRL key as you click additional names.

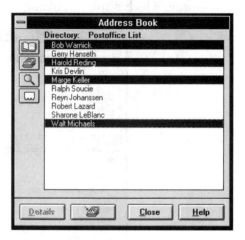

3. When you finish selecting names, click the Copy to Address Book icon. (Don't confuse this icon with the Open Personal Address Book icon. The Copy to Address Book icon, which contains a small arrow, is shown next. It is located at the bottom of the dialog box.)

Copy to Address Book

Sending a Note to a Group of Recipients

If you regularly send messages to the same group of recipients, you can create a *personal group,* which is a list of recipients you treat as a single address. To create a group, follow these steps:

1. From the Mail menu, choose Personal Groups.

2. In the Personal Groups dialog box, choose New. This displays the New Group dialog box.

3. In the New group name box, type a name for the group, and then choose Create. This brings up the following dialog box:

4. Double-click the name of each person in the Directory box you want to include in the group. When you finish, choose OK.

5. Choose Close.

The next time you display the Personal Address Book in the Address window, the group will be listed in bold type, as illustrated by Steering Committee group in the Address Book window shown here:

Attaching Files and Objects to a Message

Mail is perfect for sending plain vanilla messages such as, "Can you still make our 1:30 tee time?" You can also send weightier messages containing embedded objects and pictures.

Attaching a File

Mail provides an excellent delivery mechanism for your work. Let's say you have traditionally drafted reports and sent them to your manager via interoffice or U.S. mail. If your manager's PC is linked to your workgroup, you can send out the report faster via Microsoft Mail. You do this by attaching the file(s) that comprise your work product to a Mail message.

To attach a file to a message, follow these steps:

1. Display the Send Note window.

2. Choose the Attach button on the Send Note toolbar. This brings up the following dialog box:

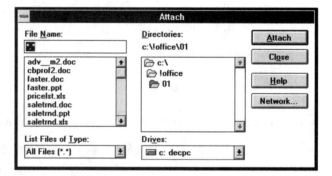

3. Enter the path and name of the file you want to attach.

4. Choose Attach.

An icon appears in the message area (Figure 11-2) to indicate the file has been attached.

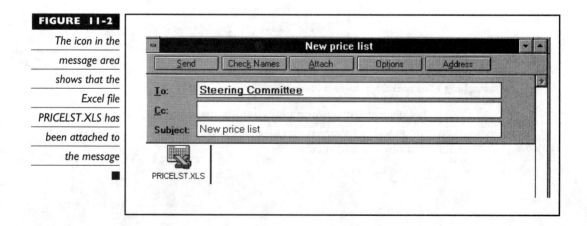

FIGURE 11-2
The icon in the message area shows that the Excel file PRICELST.XLS has been attached to the message

Pasting an Object as Text

Sometimes you don't need to send an entire file, but you want to incorporate some external data in a message. To paste the data as plain text into the message, follow these steps:

1. Copy the object in the server application.

2. Activate Mail and position the insertion point in the desired location in the message area.

3. From the Edit menu, choose Paste.

If you paste text from Word in this manner, it will appear in the message as plain message text. Pasting an Excel range or an Access recordset results in tab-delimited text.

Embedding an Object

Embedding an object in a Mail message yields the same result as embedding an object in a Word document. The recipient can open the object for editing by double-clicking it. (This assumes, of course, that the server application is running on the recipient's PC.)

Follow these steps to embed an object in a Mail message:

1. Copy the object in the server application.

2. Activate Mail and position the insertion point in the desired location in the message area.

3. From the Edit menu, choose Paste Special. This displays a dialog box similar to the one below:

4. Select the object type you would like to paste from the Data Type list.

5. Choose Paste.

Figure 11-3 shows a message with an embedded Excel range.

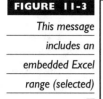

FIGURE 11-3

This message includes an embedded Excel range (selected)

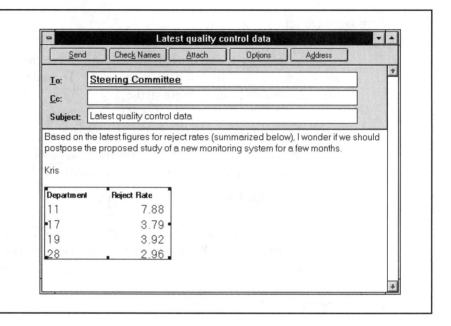

Inserting an Object

Inserting an object is the only way to create objects using an embedding application such as WordArt and the Equation Editor. (Naturally, you can also insert Excel, Word, and PowerPoint objects in this manner.)

To insert an object in a Mail message, display the Edit menu, and choose Insert Object. This displays the Insert Object dialog box, where you can select the type of object you want to insert.

You can insert the contents of ASCII files by choosing Edit, then Insert from File. Then, in the Insert from File dialog box, select the text file. You cannot, however, insert files as OLE objects; you can only attach them to messages.

note *Mail does not provide the option to link objects directly to messages. You can, however, embed a package that contains a linked object. You'll learn how to do this in Chapter 15.*

Sending a Document

When you are working on a document in Word, Excel, or Access, it's very convenient to be able to send the document right from the application rather than start Mail and attach the document. To make it easier to send documents electronically, all the Office applications other than Mail provide a Send Mail command on their File menus. Using an Excel document as an example, follow these steps to mail a document:

1. Open the Excel document you want to send.
2. From the File menu, choose Send Mail. This displays Mail's Sign In screen.
3. Sign in as usual. The Send Note screen appears with the document already attached and iconized, as shown here:

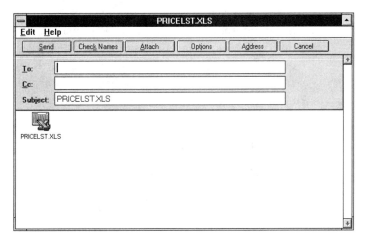

4. Address the message in the usual manner.
5. Add explanatory text in the message area.
6. Choose the Send button.

caution *It is usually not advisable to send extremely large files (1MB or larger) to a long list of recipients. That can bog down the network and increase file storage requirements. Though Mail compresses files before sending them, large objects and long lists are still caution signs. Instead, send a note advising recipients where they can find the file on the network. Another option is to insert a package containing a link object. (You'll learn how to package objects with the Object Packager in Chapter 15.*

Routing Documents

If you're working on a document that requires input from several colleagues, consider using Mail's routing feature when you send the document. You can attach an electronic *routing slip* that moves a message (to which the document is attached) to a sequential series of recipients.

Routing is handy for two reasons. First, it eliminates the possibility of two recipients making simultaneous and conflicting revisions to an attachment. The second recipient will see any revisions made by the first recipient. (Naturally, you will want to specify a routing sequence that moves the document to recipients of progressively higher authority.) Second—as compared with sending the document yourself to Recipient 1, then waiting for the response, then sending it to Recipient 2, and so on—routing saves you time and gets the job finished faster. After Recipient 1 is satisfied with the quality of the document, one click of a button sends it to Recipient 2. You can even have Mail inform you of the document's progress, so you can follow up if a recipient takes too long to respond.

Adding a Routing Slip to a Document

Routing a document is not done in Mail. It is done in the application you use to create the document. To try the following example, then, you must start from a server application. Follow these steps:

1. Open the document to which you want to attach a routing slip.

2. From the File menu, choose Add Routing Slip.

3. If Mail displays the Sign In box, sign in. Mail displays the Routing Slip dialog box, shown in its completed form in Figure 11-4.

4. Click Address to display the Address dialog box, and then select recipients in the order you want them to review the document. Choose OK when you finish.

5. Enter a subject in the Subject box.

6. Enter an introductory or explanatory message in the Message Text box. This text will appear as the message text when recipients view the message. Your routing slip will now look like Figure 11-4.

7. Choose Route.

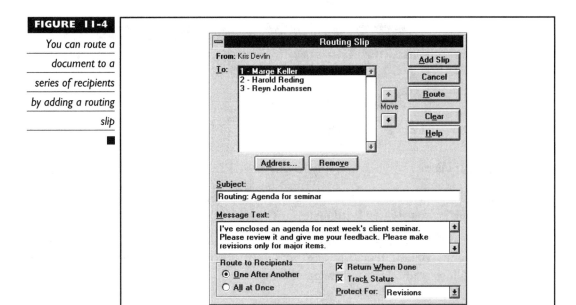

FIGURE 11-4

You can route a document to a series of recipients by adding a routing slip

■

This returns you to the client application. Meanwhile, Mail sends the message and attached document to the first recipient on the list.

By default, the One After Another option in the Route to Recipients area of the dialog box is selected. That routes the document to the recipient list in sequence. If the sequence is not that important and you want to save some time, route the document simultaneously to all recipients by selecting All at Once.

note *Selecting the All at Once option in the Routing Slip dialog box is not quite the same as sending a document via Mail to multiple recipients. The recipients listed on the routing slip must open the attached document in order to route the message, and the document will be returned to you as each recipient routes it.*

The Return When Done and Track Status options are also selected by default. Return When Done returns the document to you when the last recipient on the list sends the document on. When Track Status is selected, you will receive a message like the one shown next whenever one recipient passes the message on to the next recipient in sequence.

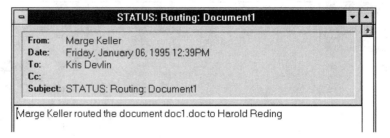

If necessary, you can reply to this as you would any other Mail message.

Responding to a Routed Document

When you read a message that has a routing slip attached, the message will contain text advising you that it contains a routed document, as illustrated by the following message:

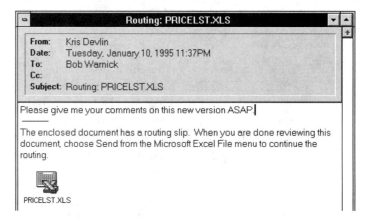

To view the document, double-click the icon. Assuming you have the server application installed on your machine, this action will start that application. After you have viewed the document, you can send it to the next recipient by choosing Send. Before sending it, you might suggest changes by adding to or revising the document. Under the default security options in the routing slip, any changes you make to attached Word documents will be specially marked to indicate the revisions. The types of changes permitted, if any, are determined by the sender in creating the routing slip.

To send a document with a routing slip to its next recipient, choose File, then Send. Mail will display a dialog box. Choose OK to send the document and the routing slip to the next person on the list. The server application will then ask you to confirm the changes you made to the attached document. Choose OK.

Reading Messages

The Inbox, shown next, provides some identifying information about each received message.

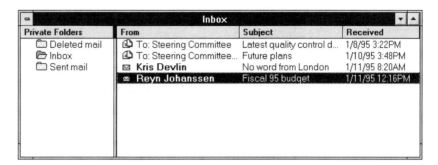

You can widen any of the segments of the information area (for instance, to see more of the subject) by dragging the right border of the segment heading at the top. To view a message, double-click the message under the From heading.

Replying to a Message

To reply to a message, click the Reply button on the toolbar. This creates a new message that is already addressed to the person who sent you the original message. For reference, the original message appears in the lower section of the message area, as illustrated in Figure 11-5. Simply type your reply and choose Send.

Deleting Messages

Common courtesy (along with generally accepted principles of time management) obliges you to respond to messages as soon as possible. Owing to the day-to-day pressures of business, of course, "as soon as possible" does not necessarily mean "immediately."

The Inbox will dutifully store a message until you are able to dispose of it. When you have done so (either by sending a reply, determining that no reply is necessary, or by making a note on your to-do list), don't keep that old message hanging around. Select it in the Inbox, then click Delete on the toolbar.

This removes the message from the Inbox and puts it in the Deleted Mail folder, just in case you change your mind. However, Mail empties the Deleted Mail folder when you quit the program.

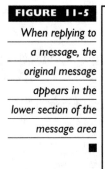

FIGURE 11-5

When replying to a message, the original message appears in the lower section of the message area

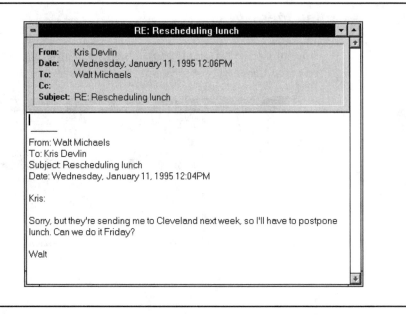

Storing Messages in Folders

As you start using Mail more intensively, you'll find that messages begin to pile up. It's not the unanswered mail that will cause the problem; it's the messages you want to save for later reference. To store these messages in an orderly manner, you will need to add more folders.

Creating a New Folder

You might want to store all old messages relating to a particular topic or project in a separate folder. The Budget and Technical folders in Figure 11-6 are such folders.

To create a new folder, follow these steps:

1. With the Folders list displayed, choose File, then New Folder. This displays the New Folder dialog box.
2. In the Name box, type a name for the folder.
3. Choose OK.

Chapter 11: Mailing, Routing, and Faxing Documents **257**

FIGURE 11-6

The Private Folders list in this window contains the user-created folders Budget and Technical

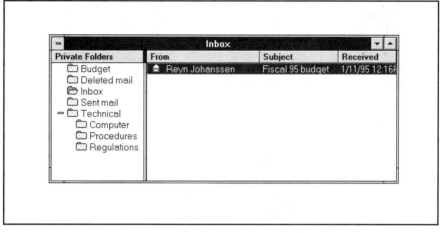

note *You can set up folders on your post office to be shared, meaning multiple users can access it, by selecting the Shared option under Type in the New Folder dialog box.*

The Technical folder in Figure 11-6 contains three subfolders on specific technical topics. Subfolders are analogous to subdirectories on a hard disk.

To create a subfolder, follow these steps:

1. Display the New Folder dialog box.
2. Choose Options. This expands the dialog box, as shown here:

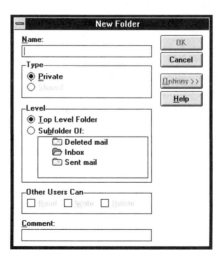

3. In the Name box, type a name for the subfolder.

4. Under Level, select the folder under which you want to create the subfolder.

5. Choose OK.

Saving Messages

To save a message to a specific folder, simply drag it to the desired folder in the folders list.

Rearranging Your Folders

In most respects, the folders list works essentially the same as the Windows File Manager. The folders are like directories and the messages are like files.

MOVING FOLDERS   To move a folder, simply drag it with the mouse as you would a directory in the File Manager.

PROMOTING A FOLDER   To promote a subfolder to a top-level folder, hold down HOME while dragging the folder in the folder list (it doesn't matter where).

EXPANDING AND COLLAPSING FOLDERS   A folder that contains subfolders displays an adjacent plus or minus sign to indicate the folder is collapsed or expanded, respectively. To expand a folder, click the plus sign. To collapse a folder, click the minus sign.

tip   *You can display all folders by pressing* CTRL++ *(plus sign). (That is, hold down* SHIFT *and* CTRL *while pressing the equal sign (=) key, since the plus sign is the shifted character on that key. You can also use the plus sign on the numeric keypad.) To collapse all top-level folders, press* CTRL+- *(minus sign).*

Deleting a Folder

To delete a folder, select the folder in the folders list, then press DEL. Choose Yes in the dialog box that appears to confirm the deletion. Any messages in the folder you deleted will be moved to the Deleted mail folder.

Searching for Messages

You can search for specific messages in your folders by specifying topics, message text, or other criteria. Follow these steps:

1. Choose File, Message Finder. This brings up the following dialog box:

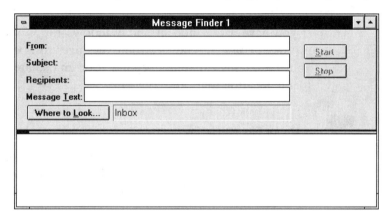

2. Specify your search criteria in one or more of the text boxes labeled From, Subject, or Recipients. To search for a specific text string in message text, enter the text in the Message Text box.

3. By default, Mail searches the Inbox. To search another folder, choose Where to Look, and then select the folder you want to search. You can also search all folders.

4. Choose Start.

Mail searches for messages meeting your criteria, listing the individual messages as it finds them. You can choose the Stop button at any time to end the search.

note *Unlike the File Manager, the Message Finder does not use wildcard characters in searches.*

To read a message in the Message Finder window, double-click the message. You can move messages from the Message Finder window to the Inbox or to other folders by dragging.

caution *Deleting a message from the Message Finder window also deletes it from the folder it's stored in.*

Faxing Messages

If you have a fax modem and Windows for Workgroups 3.11 (not 3.1) installed, you can send electronic messages to fax machines. This extends your messaging capability beyond your immediate network or workgroup to any location that can receive faxes.

Setting Up for Fax Messaging

Windows for Workgroups 3.11 includes version 1.0 of Microsoft At Work PC Fax. PC Fax takes control of your fax modem and uses it to send messages you create in Microsoft Mail over the telephone line. Likewise, your computer can receive faxes sent by ordinary fax machines and other PC Fax users.

PC Fax requires a Class 1 or Class 2 fax modem, or a modem compatible with Intel's Communication Application Specification (CAS). If you have a CAS modem (such as an Intel SatisFaxtion), you must install and start the CAS driver software before you start Windows. Naturally, you will need to follow the directions in the manual for configuring the fax modem.

Most Class 1 or Class 2 fax modems come with driver software to run the modem. Do not use the manufacturer-provided software (other than the driver for CAS modems) when faxing messages. The PC Fax program that comes with Windows for Workgroups 3.11 will control the fax modem.

Configuring the Fax Modem

PC Fax requires you to select some global options before you can send faxes. Follow these steps (which assume you are already connected to a Mail post office):

1. Start the Windows Control Panel.

2. Double-click the Fax icon. This brings up the following dialog box:

Chapter 11: Mailing, Routing, and Faxing Documents

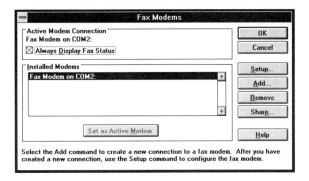

3. Choose Add. The Add Fax Modems dialog box appears:

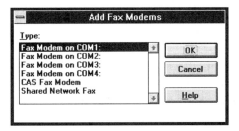

4. In the Type list, select the type of fax modem you have installed and, if applicable, the port to which it is connected. Choose OK.

5. In the Fax Phone Number dialog box, type your fax number, and then choose OK.

6. In the Fax Modems dialog box, choose Setup. This displays a dialog box containing the appropriate options for the fax modem type you specified.

7. Select the desired options. (For an explanation of each of the options, choose the dialog box Help button.) Choose OK when you finish.

8. In the Fax Modems dialog box, choose OK.

note *Once you set up PC Fax and your fax modem, Mail checks for the presence of the fax modem whenever you first sign in. If the fax modem is disconnected from your computer or not turned on, Mail will display an error message.*

Specifying the Active Fax Modem

Because any user, especially one who is connected to a network, might have more than one fax modem available for use, you must specify the active fax modem before you can send faxes. Follow these steps:

1. Close Microsoft Mail.
2. In the Control Panel, double-click the Fax icon.
3. In the Fax Modems dialog box, double-click the modem you want to use.
4. Choose Set As Active Modem, then choose OK.

note *You must restart Mail for the "activation" to take effect. If you try to send, say, an Excel document to a fax with Excel's Send command before the change has taken effect, you will receive an error message.*

Faxing a Message

The procedure for sending a fax with Mail is identical to that for sending an ordinary message. The only difference is in how you address the message. To fax a message to a recipient whose fax address is not in the Address Book, follow these steps:

1. Click Compose on the Mail toolbar.
2. In the To box of the Send Note window, type [**fax:** followed by the recipient name, followed by @, then the fax number followed by], as illustrated in Figure 11-7.
3. Enter the remaining information (such as the subject and the text of the message).
4. Attach a document to the message, if desired.
5. Choose Send.

Microsoft PC Fax sends the message to the phone number in the fax address you entered. If the recipient has a standalone fax machine attached to the line, the message will print as an ordinary fax. If the receiving device is a fax modem connected to a workgroup or a PC running Windows for Workgroups 3.11 and Mail, the message will arrive in the recipient's Mail

FIGURE 11-7

Addressing a fax message

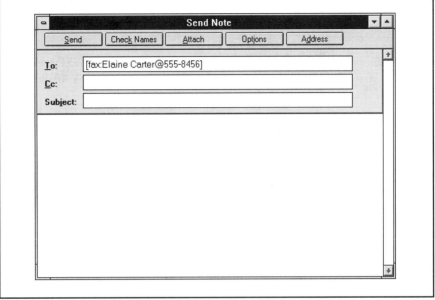

Inbox folder as an ordinary Mail message. Depending on the content, however, reading the message might require a different procedure. You'll learn more about receiving messages sent via PC Fax in a few minutes.

caution *If you don't enclose the fax number in square brackets, Mail will display an error message and refuse to continue if it does not find the address you entered in the Address Book.*

Faxing Documents

You can also use PC Fax to send document from within a server application, such as Word, Excel, or PowerPoint. Follow these steps:

1. Make sure Mail is running. (Even if you have closed the Microsoft Mail window, Mail is still considered "running" if you have not logged off.)

2. Activate the document you want to send.

3. From the File menu, choose Send. This brings up the Send Note window.

4. In the Send Note window, type the fax address in the format shown in Figure 11-7.

5. Change the subject and add text to the message, if desired.

6. Choose Send.

PC Fax converts the document to a bitmapped image, and then sends the fax transmission to the phone number you entered as part of the fax address in step 3.

note *You can also fax a document from within the server application by printing to the fax modem driver. In the Print dialog box, choose Printer Setup, and then select the Microsoft At Work Fax printer driver as the default printer. Then print the document as you normally would to a printer. You will sign in to Mail and see a Send Note window. Just make sure you reselect your normal default printer after you have faxed the document.*

Entering Fax Addresses in Your Personal Address Book

To store fax numbers in your Personal Address Book in Mail, follow these steps:

1. Display the Address Book.

2. Click the following icon:

3. In the New box, select Microsoft At Work Fax. This displays the following dialog box:

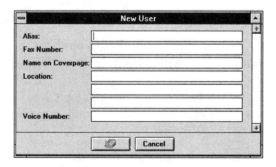

4. In the Alias box, type the name you want to use for the fax address. (If the recipient is already listed in your Address Book, add some text to distinguish the fax address from the person's regular mailbox address.)

5. Enter the fax number and other pertinent data. In the Name on Coverpage box, for instance, you can enter the recipient's proper name for the optional cover page for the fax. The Location and Voice Number entries will expedite physical delivery of a printed fax to the intended recipient.

6. To add the fax address, choose Add. You can then add more fax addresses if you like.

7. When you finish adding addresses, choose Cancel.

Reading Fax Messages

You can receive two basic types of faxed messages in Mail: those that originate from an ordinary fax machine, and those that originate from a sender using Microsoft PC Fax. In either case, the Mail message you receive looks like any other incoming Mail message. However, if the sender uses an ordinary fax machine, the faxed pages are attached as a file with a DCX extension, as illustrated here:

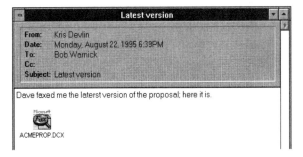

A DCX file, also called a facsimile-format file, is essentially a container for one or more bitmap graphics files—one for each faxed page. Double-clicking the DCX icon opens the Fax Viewer window, shown here:

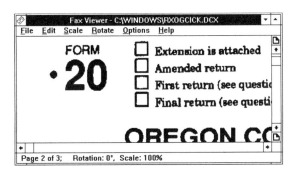

You can scroll through the document to read it, or you can choose File, then Print to print it. To move to the preceding or following page, respectively, click the small page icon at the top or bottom of the scroll bar. You can also save the document in DCX format or convert it to a PCX graphics file. (PCX is a commonly used graphics file format; you can view PCX files with the Windows Paintbrush program.)

Opening Documents Sent via Microsoft PC Fax

PC Fax offers a capability that is truly amazing: the ability to send binary files to a remote PC Fax user. That means you have dial-up messaging and file transfer capability with any other PC running Windows for Workgroups 3.11 or higher as long as it has the right kind of fax modem device. Essentially, by installing Windows for Workgroups 3.11 on your own standalone PC, you can become part of a "super-workgroup" that includes all other Windows for Workgroups 3.11 users who have the required modem hardware!

A message sent and received via PC Fax acts just like any other Mail message. To read an attached document, double-click the icon. This has the same effect as double-clicking an embedded object in a compound document: If the server application is installed on your PC, the application starts, and creates a document with the original filename.

Conclusion

With this chapter, you have mastered the basic tools that Office and Windows for Workgroups provide to deliver your work product electronically. In the next two chapters, you'll focus on using Office to persuade and move people to action. You'll start in the next chapter by creating a written proposal. In Chapter 13, you'll learn how to present that proposal using the remaining Office application that has yet to be covered in this book: PowerPoint.

CHAPTER 12

Automating Sales Proposal Creation

If you work in a service business, you know that the ability to present a comprehensive, insightful proposal is a key factor in obtaining new work. Generating proposals is a demanding, multidisciplinary art. Your proposal needs to represent your expertise and command of the facts. It also needs to demonstrate your sensitivity to client concerns and ability to deal with the human element in business. Finally, the design and appearance of your proposal should reflect a careful attention to detail.

With so much riding on the proposal as a selling tool, you must strive for every possible productivity edge. It's an exhausting job, but if you do it only halfway, you're better off not doing it at all. And since not doing it means no new business, you have no choice but to do it as efficiently as possible.

As you explore the scenario in this chapter, you will learn the following techniques to automate entry of important data in Word documents:

- Using ASK and REF fields
- Using bookmarks
- Using IF fields to insert text conditionally
- Linking Excel ranges to Word tables
- Using DATABASE fields to insert data from Access

The Scenario: The Computer Consulting Proposal

In this chapter, you'll pretend you're a consultant with InfoSense Corporation, and you're trying to sell a consulting engagement for installing a new accounting system. The prospective client, MetroVideo Productions, produces videos for advertising agencies and corporations. You've talked to them at length about their needs, and determined that they need better information from their accounting system. You've also, naturally, described your firm's outstanding qualifications.

Now the client has asked you to deliver a proposal that describes in detail the services you intend to provide, along with an estimate of the cost. In the past, you would have started by opening the last proposal document you prepared and replacing all the outdated information with information relevant to the new prospect. This time, however, things will be different, because you've created a Word template that automates most of the dreariest parts of proposal creation.

This chapter will show you how to create such a template. Along the way, you'll learn techniques for ensuring accuracy while minimizing effort. The template might even make it possible for you to hand most of the work off to a subordinate, leaving you time to prospect for more clients.

Figure 12-1 shows the cover page of the example proposal. You'll see other important parts of the proposal document throughout the chapter. Naturally, much of the effort in creating such a document is in drafting the text itself. This chapter is not a tutorial on effective proposal writing, so it is not necessary to show you the proposal in its entirety. Instead, the example will focus on the areas that demonstrate the automation capabilities of the Office suite.

FIGURE 12-1

The cover page of the consulting proposal

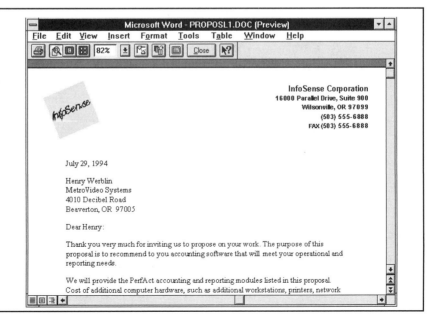

Automating Entry of Client Information

Getting consulting contracts is a game of numbers. If all other factors are held equal, more proposals will generate more business. Word offers a number of features to help you efficiently create such proposals with a high level of quality assurance.

Please note that this chapter is designed to show you how to create the automated proposal system. Along the way, however, it will be necessary to describe what happens during the creation of a specific proposal. In those instances, the text will refer to the "user" of the proposal document—that is, the person responsible for creating a proposal for a specific client.

Prompting for Input with ASK Fields

In preceding chapters, you've seen the power of merge fields to "populate" form letters with data from another document. The purpose of mail merging is to use one data source to generate numerous documents. In this initial phase of the InfoSense example, you'll see a different slant on this theme. In this chapter, the "source" information is contained *in* the document, but it is propagated many times throughout that same document.

Creating ASK Fields

Good quality control obliges you to ensure that a user, when he or she is generating a proposal, provides all the requisite information. The best way to accomplish that is to have the computer program prompt for every bit of information. Word's ASK field, when updated, displays a dialog box that asks for input. After the user responds to the prompt, Word assigns a bookmark to the typed response. (As you might remember, bookmarks are named text blocks—usually a single word, name, or phrase—that can be referred to in other parts of a document.)

Figure 12-2 shows the ASK field codes in the proposal document. The syntax of the ASK field is as follows:

```
{ask bookmark "prompt" }
```

To create an ASK field, follow these steps:

1. After positioning the insertion point in the desired location, press CTRL+F9 to insert a blank field.

2. Type **ask**, then a space, then a name for the bookmark.

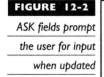

FIGURE 12-2

ASK fields prompt the user for input when updated

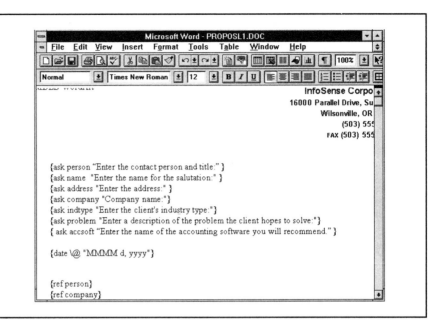

3. Type a space, then type the wording for the prompt, surrounded by quotation marks.

To create an ASK field that will prompt for the name of your contact in the client organization, you would enter some variation on the following:

```
{ask person "Enter the contact person and title:"}
```

Updating ASK Fields

When the document is opened later, the user can select the part of the document containing the ASK fields and press F9 to update the fields. (You can also record a macro that will update the fields automatically. You'll learn how in the section "Adding More Automation" later in this chapter.) When the first ASK field in Figure 12-2 is updated, it displays the following dialog box:

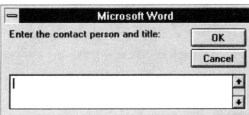

To enter the requested text, type the text, then press TAB, then ENTER,. (If you don't press TAB, you will enter a blank response.) Alternatively, you can click OK after typing the text.

When the F9 key is pressed, each ASK field in the selection displays a dialog box prompt. A bookmark name (the bookmark value in the field code) is assigned to the text the user enters in the dialog box. You'll see in a moment how to use REF fields to place bookmark text elsewhere in the document.

note *If the REF fields are inserted before the corresponding ASK fields in the document, the former will return error results the first time you update all fields in the document, because the fields are updated in the sequence in which they appear in the document. However, all subsequent updates will return the correct values.*

Avoiding Blank Lines in the Document

ASK fields do not take up any "space" in a document. That is, they do not display any results when your document displays field values rather than codes. If you separate the ASK fields with carriage returns (as they are in Figure 12-2), however, the paragraphs will appear in the document, causing unwanted white space.

Of course, putting all the ASK fields in one paragraph would eliminate all but one of the unwanted blank paragraphs in the document. When you display field codes, however, you will see a chaotic jumble of fields, making them awkward to edit.

To keep the fields separated in field view—while avoiding a pileup of blank paragraphs—format the paragraphs as hidden text. First, click the Show/Hide Paragraph tool in the Standard toolbar, shown here:

Show/Hide Paragraph

Word now displays nonprinting characters such as paragraph markers. Now follow these steps for each paragraph containing an ASK field:

1. Select the paragraph marker.

2. Select Format, then Font.

3. In the Effects area, select the Hidden option.

4. Choose OK.

Now that you have formatted the paragraph markers as hidden text, they will not show up in the printed document.

note *You might wonder why you can't simply format the entire group of ASK fields as hidden text. That will be explained momentarily, after you understand how REF fields work.*

Using REF Fields to "Reference" Text

REF fields return bookmark text values, much like an Excel formula returns a value. REF fields take one argument: the name of a bookmark. The field ({ ref company }) is like the Excel formula =A1, which will display the results of cell A1. The REF field will display the text included in the bookmark named Company.

Once you have responded to all the prompts generated by the ASK fields, it's a rather simple matter to use REF fields to place bookmark text in the appropriate places all through the document. (Remember, ASK fields assign bookmarks to whatever text is entered in response to the resulting dialog box prompts.) Figure 12-3 shows two views of the proposal, side by side. The view on the left displays the field codes; the window on the right displays the field values.

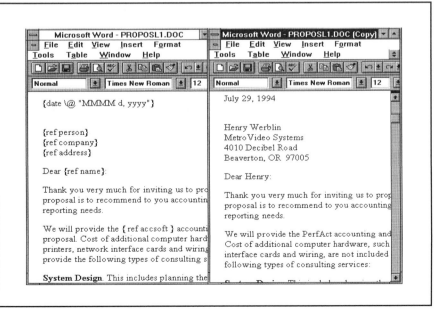

FIGURE 12-3

REF fields (whose codes are displayed on the left) return the bookmark text values on the right

Now you are in a position to understand the reason for hiding the paragraph markers only (rather than the entire group of ASK fields) in the preceding example. When you update a REF field to bookmarked text that has been formatted as hidden, the hidden character format carries through to the REF field result. Hiding the ASK fields themselves, then, would produce REF fields whose results would not print.

tip *To override the automatic copying of text formats from bookmark to REF field, add the * MERGEFORMAT switch at the end of the REF field code. This allows you to apply formatting directly to the field result.*

Adding Intelligence with IF Fields

When you automate a process, there's always a chance of unexpected results in exceptional situations. In some cases, a bookmark value might cause a spelling or grammar error. Consider the following REF field:

```
{ ref company }'s
```

If the company's name is "Microsoft," there is no problem. But if the company is "McDonald's," then this REF field will display "McDonald's's" when updated. In this chapter's example, the company is MetroVideo Systems, which will result in similar punctuation.

One solution is to use an IF field. This field is very much like Excel's IF function. The syntax is similar to Excel's "if-then-else" form, as shown here:

```
{ if expression if_true_text if_false_text }
```

where *expression* is (usually) two values separated by a logical operator such as =, >, or <>.

The following field code will return a company name followed by a single apostrophe (') if the company ends in *s*, and apostrophe-s ('s) otherwise:

```
{ ref company }{ if { ref company } = *s ' 's }
```

note *It's a good practice to use Word's spelling and grammar checking utilities on documents with recently updated fields, to make sure the updates have not caused any new errors.*

Personalizing the Document

Most of us have received form letters that are highly individualized, but in a very insincere way. (For instance: "WE'D LIKE TO DELIVER A CHECK FOR A MILLION DOLLARS RIGHT TO YOUR DOOR IN FARGO, NORTH DAKOTA!")

Naturally, you wouldn't want to present anything that sounds glib to a prospective client. At the same time, you have to produce these proposals efficiently in order to keep the work coming in, so you should not hesitate to use Word's ASK and REF fields for high-value content as well as demographic data. Furthermore, it's best to prompt the user for any information that can vary from one proposal to another. That prevents gaps or irrelevant data carried over from a previous proposal for a different client.

Any proposal worth its salt should state your understanding of what the client hopes to accomplish; the client won't buy if you are not speaking to his or her needs. You can prompt for this information with an ASK field, just as you would for the client's name and address. Figure 12-4 displays the same paragraph in two panes. The upper pane shows field codes; the lower pane displays field results (shaded).

Once you've entered the responses to the ASK fields and updated the REF fields to display your insights, it's usually best to select paragraphs containing high-value content and press CTRL+SHIFT+F9 to replace fields with their results. That does not mean, of course, that you won't revise the wording.

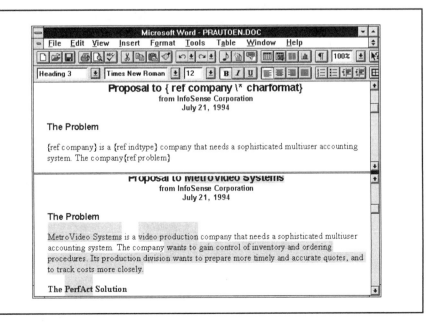

FIGURE 12-4

You can use REF fields to return long text, as shown here for the bookmarks "indtype" and "problem"

Once the user has responded to the prompt, however, the ASK field has served its purpose. It has provided a little bit of structure that can help the user organize his or her thoughts.

Enhancing Accuracy

You've seen how ASK and REF fields can save time in entering addresses, but the major benefit is quality assurance. Both the client's name and the name of your recommended software package will appear many times in any proposal document, as you can see from the excerpt shown in Figure 12-5.

Each time you enter repetitive data in a long document, there is an opportunity to make a mistake in punctuation or spelling. Even if the user creates a new proposal by copying a complete proposal that was created for another client, he or she might miss an occurrence of the old client's company name. (Even the Edit menu's Replace command isn't foolproof, because it could miss abbreviated, alternative, or erroneous spellings of the old client's name.) If, on the other hand, you design your automated proposal process so that the user is required to enter the company name only once, you eliminate a potential source of costly errors.

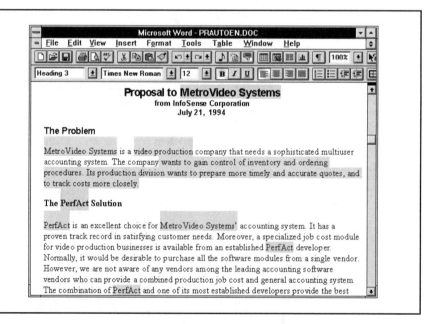

FIGURE 12-5
REF fields are useful for displaying the same information in numerous places in a document, as shown here for client (MetroVideo Systems) and software product (PerfAct)

Linking Computations from Excel

Your prospect will naturally want to see hard numbers for estimated costs and completion dates. The best way to ensure accuracy is to perform these computations in Excel. Figure 12-6 shows low and high estimate computations for the amount of consulting hours required to perform the engagement. (The summary computation is in cells A1:D5. Supporting computations appear in rows 7 and below.) The estimated costs for consulting services shown here are incorporated into a summary schedule in the workbook. The summary schedule, located in a seperate sheet (not shown), rounds the figures to the nearest $100 and includes the cost of the software.

It's usually best to paste-link Excel computations into the proposal as formatted text. That way they will appear in the proposal as Word tables, making it more efficient to format the linked data. After pasting the summary fee computation as formatted text, the document looks like this:

the less common tasks, such as financial statement design and monthly closing. For planning purposes, therefore, we recommend budgeting for the realistic scenario. Naturally, we will only provide as much training and consulting as you request.

Description	Optimistic	Realistic
PerfAct System Manager (for up to ten users), Inventory, Order Entry, Accounts Receivable, Purchase Order, General Ledger and Accounts Payable Modules (including estimated shipping)	$7,900	$7,900
Consulting services	9,300	12,800
	$17,200	$20,700

Suppose you want to include another table in the proposal listing due dates for required progress payments as the work proceeds, as in Figure 12-7. Such a table can be easily created from scratch at the time the proposal is prepared. To guard against errors, however, you (as the designer of the proposal template) want to ensure that the payment schedule always agrees to the cost estimates created in Excel. The best way to do that is to require that all computations relating to fees and prices charged be done in Excel before the proposal is prepared. (The Excel workbook itself can be created from a template document.) The person in charge of selling the engagement estimates the costs. Then the user (the person who creates the word document) copies and paste-links ranges from the workbook into the appropriate places in the Word document.

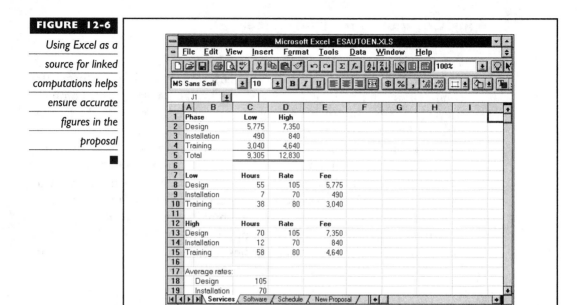

FIGURE 12-6

Using Excel as a source for linked computations helps ensure accurate figures in the proposal

Including the cost information in the Word document is the least automated aspect of the proposal process. It could be automated somewhat by including an ASK field that prompts for the path and name of the source Excel document. As a practical matter, however, most readers will likely find it just as efficient to perform this part of the process manually.

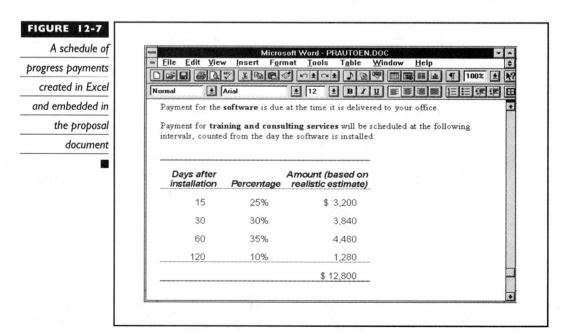

FIGURE 12-7

A schedule of progress payments created in Excel and embedded in the proposal document

note *You might wonder whether you can assign a bookmark to a cell value in a linked table. The answer is yes, but it's not advisable. The bookmark will be wiped out when the table is next updated.*

Linking Rate Information from an Access Database

In Chapters 9 and 10, you learned how to merge Access data into Word form letters to mass-produce numerous documents. Connecting to a database can also be useful when preparing a *single* document. The consulting proposal is a good example. If, for instance, your firm maintains an Access database with billing data, you can insert billing rate information into the proposal template with the Database command on Word's Insert menu.

Inserting a Database

On the surface, "inserting a database" doesn't sound like an especially pleasurable or wise thing to do, but it is not the monumental effort the term might suggest. It would be more accurate to call it "inserting a small table or part of a large table." Even that doesn't tell the whole story, because you can insert other objects, such as query results, providing considerable flexibility.

Suppose your firm has a time and billing database that includes an Access table of rates like the one shown here:

Code	Description	Rate	Long Description
1	Standard	$70	Weekdays until 6 PM
2	Night	$95	Weekdays until 9 PM; Saturdays until 6 PM
3	Sunday/Holiday	$135	All other times, including holidays
0		$0	

This is obviously a simplified example; in most firms, the billing rate will vary depending on the activity, the individual performing the service, and possibly other factors. However, your objective in this situation is not to compute a fee, but to tell your prospective client what to pay on an ongoing basis for ongoing support over the long term. This will obviously be an important factor in the client's purchase decision.

You want to insert your summary of hourly support rates between the two paragraphs shown here:

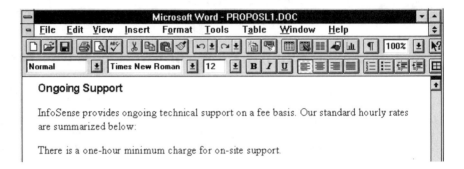

The next steps show you how.

Creating the Query

The first step is to create the query in Access. The steps in the following example assume the existence of a database named BILLING.MDB, and a table in that database named Rates. Though this database is not one of the Access sample databases, you will be able to follow the procedure by substituting any of the tables in the Northwind Traders sample database.

Follow these steps to create the billing rate query:

1. Start Access and open the database that contains the table of billing rates.
2. Click the Query tab in the Database window.
3. Choose New. This brings up the New Query dialog box.
4. Click the New Query button.
5. The Add Table dialog box appears. Double-click Rates in the Table/Query list.
6. Choose Close.
7. In the Rates field list, double-click the Long Description field, and then double-click the Rate field.
8. Click to the left of the field name in the Long Description field, and then type **Description:**.
9. Save the query under the name Billing Rates.
10. Quit Access.

Now you can start Word and use the query as a data source in the proposal document.

Specifying the Data Source

Follow these steps to specify the query you just created as the "database," or data source, to insert in the proposal document:

1. Choose Insert, then Database. This brings up the following dialog box:

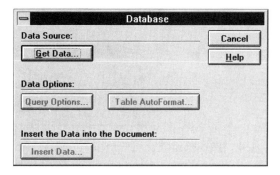

2. Choose Get Data.

3. Word displays the Open Data Source dialog box. Find and select the BILLING.MDB database.

4. Microsoft Access starts up and displays the following dialog box:

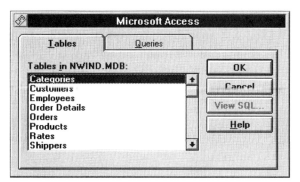

5. Display the Queries tab.

6. Double-click Billing Rates.

Behind the scenes, Access executes the query. Word then displays the Database dialog box. Now all that's left is to return the query results to Word.

Inserting the Query Results in Word

Follow these steps to finish inserting the database:

1. In the Database dialog box, choose the Table AutoFormat button.

2. Word displays the Table AutoFormat dialog box. Select the desired AutoFormat, and then choose OK. It's a good idea to select one universal table AutoFormat for consistency within and among all your proposal documents.

3. Choose the Insert Data button. This brings up the Insert Data dialog box shown here:

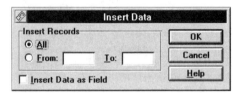

4. If you want to limit the number of records to be displayed, define a range by entering numbers in the From and To boxes.

5. Select the Insert Data as Field option. This will insert the selected data as a field that is linked to the Access database. (If you don't select this option, the table values will be pasted as plain text.)

6. Choose OK.

The inserted database is paste-linked into the Word document as a table. (You will probably have to wait a half-minute or so—perhaps longer—for Access to paste-link the data into Word.) Figure 12-8 shows the Word table resulting from a link to the Access table of rates shown earlier in this section, after applying the same AutoFormat applied to the Excel tables linked earlier.

With the linked rate table in the proposal template, the user does not have to do anything when preparing a specific proposal. Changes entered in Access will automatically flow through when the proposal is created from the template.

note *Inserting an Access "database" does not work as smoothly as paste-linking an Excel range. Dollar amounts from Access, for instance, are usually left-aligned in Word tables. Also, dollar amounts display pennies, even when the field property in the Access table is set to whole dollars. Finally, updating a DATABASE field can also be a slow process. For those reasons, try to use Excel to maintain tabular data that you expect to paste-link into Word.*

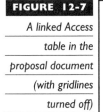

FIGURE 12-7

A linked Access table in the proposal document (with gridlines turned off)

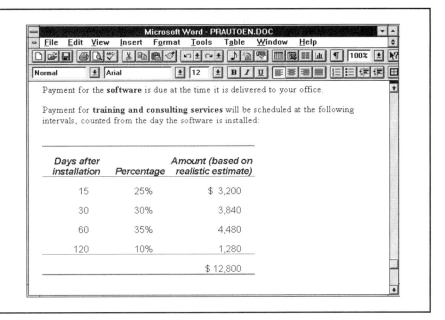

Selecting Fields to Be Inserted

In the preceding example, you created a query that included selected fields from a table. You can also limit the number of fields to be inserted while you are inserting the database.

With the Database dialog box displayed, follow these steps:

1. Choose Query Options. This brings up the Query Options dialog box.

2. Display the Select Fields tab, shown here:

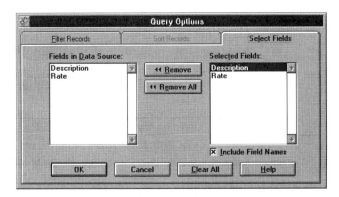

3. Choose Remove All. This removes all fields in the Selected Fields in Data Source list.

4. In the Fields in Data Source list, select the fields you want included.

5. Choose OK. This displays the Database dialog box again.

6. Choose the Insert Data button and finish the procedure as described in the preceding example.

Only the fields you selected in step 4 are included in the inserted database.

caution *Make sure you limit the number of fields and columns whenever possible. Otherwise you might insert a lot of unwanted data, or create more columns than can be displayed on a single page.*

Working with DATABASE Fields

Here's the DATABASE field code resulting from the Access query inserted in the preceding example:

```
{ DATABASE \d "D:\\ACCESS\\BILLING.MDB" \c "QUERY Billing
Rates" \s "SELECT * FROM [Billing Rates]" \l "1" \b "183" \h }
```

An important element is missing from this field code. Unless you add the mergeformat switch (* **MERGEFORMAT**) at the end of the field code, updating the DATABASE field will wipe out any formatting you applied to the table in Word. If, for instance, you changed the font, column width, or horizontal text, the *appearance* will revert to the way it was when you first created the table—even as the *values* are updated to agree with the current data.

The DATABASE field essentially enables you to execute SQL queries from within Word. (The "SELECT FROM [Rates]" parameter is an SQL statement.) You can revise the query by editing the DATABASE field parameters, but that topic is beyond the scope of this chapter.

caution *Updating any cell or row of the linked table will update the entire table. You should be careful, then, not to overtype any values in an inserted table while it is still linked. Before you enter values manually, consider breaking the link so your figures won't be wiped out by a subsequent update. Remember, though, that breaking the link means late changes to the rate schedule in Access won't flow through to the proposal document.*

Adding the Final Touches

There are more ways to generate the "Wow, these guys are serious" reaction, while minimizing the time requirements. You can enhance the level of automation by saving your prototype proposal document as a template. At the same time, you can enhance the sophistication of your document by adding graphics to the headers in the template document.

Adding More Automation

By now your proposal document boasts a number of labor-saving features, but there are a few more ways to automate it still further by combining a template with an AutoOpen macro.

Automating Initial Data Entry

Some of the accuracy-enhancing benefits of bookmarks can be lost if you don't update all the fields in the document. You can ensure this happens by recording a WordBasic macro that automates the updating. Follow these steps:

1. Choose Tools, then Macro.

2. In the Macro dialog box, choose Record.

3. In the Record Macro dialog box (shown next), enter **AutoOpen** in the Record Macro Name box.

4. The dialog box disappears, and the Macro Record toolbar floats in the document. The mouse pointer also has a picture of a cassette tape attached to signify that your actions are being recorded.

5. Press CTRL+A. This selects the entire document.

6. Press F9, then respond appropriately as the dialog boxes corresponding to the ASK fields are displayed. (Your responses will not be recorded as part of the macro, though they will be entered in the document.)

7. When all fields have been updated, position the insertion point at the beginning of the document.

8. Click the Stop button on the Macro Record toolbar to stop recording.

Because you named the macro AutoOpen, the macro will execute automatically whenever the document is opened.

Saving the Document as a Template

When you are satisfied with your prototype proposal document, consider saving it as a template. That way everyone in the organization will know which document is the officially approved master document for creating new proposals.

Putting Your Logo in the Document Header

Because neatness and presentation count, it's always useful to insert a computer graphic image of your company logo in any communications with current or prospective clients. Putting your logo in a header makes it easy to print it on every page of a long document. (Naturally, you might prefer to have the logo preprinted on your stationery. To demonstrate Word's capabilities, however, this example will assume the logo is computer-printed.)

To add a graphic image to a header, follow these steps:

1. Create a graphic logo in WordArt or another drawing program.

2. From the View menu, choose Header and Footer. This displays the document in Page Layout mode and displays the Header and Footer toolbar, shown here:

3. Click the left margin of the document next to the header area (a rectangle with a dashed-line border labeled *Header*).

4. If the header area currently contains any text, press DEL to delete it.

5. Click and drag the Insert Table button on the Standard toolbar and use the drop-down grid to define a table of one row and two columns.

6. Insert the logo graphic into one of the table cells.

7. Adjust the size of the logo, if necessary, so that it doesn't dominate the entire page. (Remember, you want to add a touch of class, not overwhelm the client with your impressive logo. Also note that using a bitmapped logo might create some distortion of the image when you reduce its size.)

8. In the other table cell, type the header text (such as **Proposal for Consulting Services**).

9. Choose the Close button on the Header and Footer toolbar.

The result will look something like this:

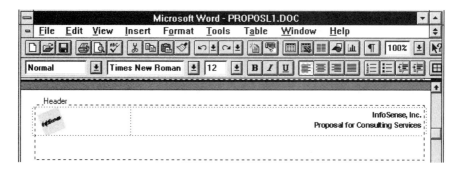

note *The preceding example assumes that your Page Setup options indicate that the first page header is different from the page header for all subsequent pages. Display the Layout tab of the Page Setup dialog box. Then (in the Headers and Footers area) select the Different First Page option, if it is not already selected.*

Conclusion

In this chapter, you've learned how to automate the production of documents with high content value. If you can learn to combine Access's data management features, Excel's computational engine, and Word's presentation features, you can run rings around your competitors.

The next chapter builds on the knowledge you've gained from this chapter. In Chapter 13 you'll learn how use PowerPoint to deliver stand-up presentations that are just as impressive as your printed proposals.

CHAPTER 13

Presenting a Proposal with PowerPoint

THE human mind retains information better when the information is perceived through two or more senses. The traditional stand-up lecture, where one person speaks and the audience listens passively, is usually ineffective. You'll get more of your message across by providing visual stimuli to accompany the auditory message. Visual aids help the audience mentally sort and classify what they hear. Microsoft PowerPoint is a convenient tool for creating the visuals that will drive your points home.

PowerPoint, now in version 4.0, is certainly the least used of all the programs bundled in Microsoft Office, but it is the only one that assists the process of communicating information in person. With PowerPoint, you can quickly prepare a slide show that lets your audience know you are prepared, organized, and professional. Once you start using PowerPoint, you'll likely find it indispensable for creating presentations and supporting material.

This chapter will introduce you to PowerPoint. It assumes you have some experience with Word and Excel, but little or no experience with Power-Point. By the end of this chapter you should be able to

- Create professional-looking presentations in a short period of time
- Include information from other Office sources, such as Word outlines and Excel spreadsheets
- Spruce up a presentation with transitions and audience notes

The Scenario: Presenting a Proposal

In Chapter 12 you created a proposal for a computer consulting engagement with a company called MetroVideo Systems. In this chapter, assume you've been asked to present your proposal at an executive management meeting at the company's headquarters. You will use PowerPoint to create a presentation that highlights the key points of the proposal.

Creating a Presentation

Text documents and stand-up presentations are very different media; to create a presentation from a text document will usually take quite a bit of editing. You'll learn how to do this momentarily. First, though, you'll tell PowerPoint what you want your presentation to look like.

Assigning a Template

When you invoke PowerPoint from the Program Manager, you will see this dialog box:

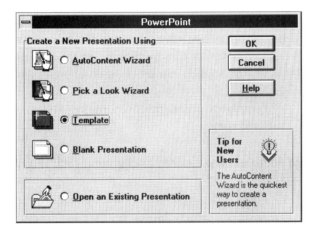

As you can see, there are four ways to create a new presentation. These options are summarized in the following table:

Option	Description
AutoContent Wizard	Creates a presentation with a detailed outline that provides some structure for your content
Pick a Look Wizard	Helps you define features for the appearance of the slides, handouts, notes, and outline
Template	Defines the appearance of the slides only
Blank Presentation	Creates a white presentation on a white background; you must select any options separately

In this case you have a good idea of the content, and you're not ready to concern yourself with ancillary material like handouts and speaker's notes, so it makes sense to choose the Template option. This displays the following dialog box:

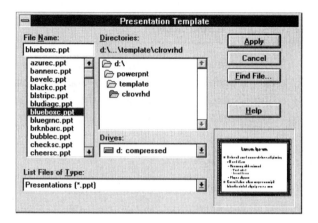

Though the Presentation Template dialog box resembles an Open dialog box, it offers one advantage: the ability to preview files. Browse through the various template files by clicking on the filename or by using the arrow keys. As you do so, you can see thumbnail images in the lower-right corner of the dialog box.

Templates come in three major styles, each located in a different subdirectory.

Colored Features on a Colored Background (SLDSHOW directory)

These styles have some color on every pixel of every slide, so they look great on the screen. However, they lack contrast when printed. They work best when you plan to make your presentation using your computer or on 35mm slides.

Colored Features on a Clear Background (CLROVRHD directory)

The styles with a clear background are a reasonable compromise: they look good on both the monitor and the printed page. Select one of these when you plan to make your presentation using an overhead projector. If you have a suitable printer, you could make professional-looking color overheads.

(For clarity, the figures you will see in this chapter show colored features on a clear background.)

Black-and-white Features on a Clear Background (BWOVRHD directory)

When you are presenting to a large audience and you don't want to spend extra money for color printing, you can use black-and-white slides. However, if you use a color monitor it's still helpful to use color templates as you're creating slides, and then apply the black-and-white template when you're done. It's also advisable to save both color and black-and-white versions of your templates so you'll be ready for a variety of situations.

Once you've found the template you want in the Presentation dialog box, choose Apply. This brings up the New Slide dialog box, shown here.

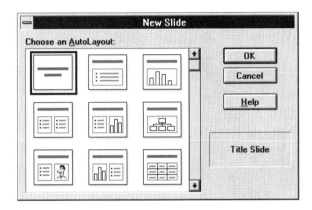

Choosing a Slide Layout

The final design decision before you start creating the substantive part of your presentation is choosing a slide layout. You must select a layout for each slide you include in your presentation. PowerPoint provides 21 different layout options in a scrollable window in the New Slide dialog box.

The purpose of these layouts is to help you make presentations that look consistent from one slide to the next. Choose one that has the kinds of information you want for your first slide. It doesn't have to be exactly right—you can move, remove, or add pieces at will. If you prefer to create slides from scratch, simply choose the last layout, called Blank. For this proposal, since you're trying to sell the capabilities of your firm, most of your slides will probably consist of lists—qualifications, reasons to buy, and so on. Accordingly, you should select the bulleted-list format.

Once you have selected a slide layout, you will see the first slide of your presentation, shown in Figure 13-1. Notice how you add the various elements of a slide—titles, lists, tables, and so on—by simply clicking in the corresponding areas created by PowerPoint.

Creating a new presentation

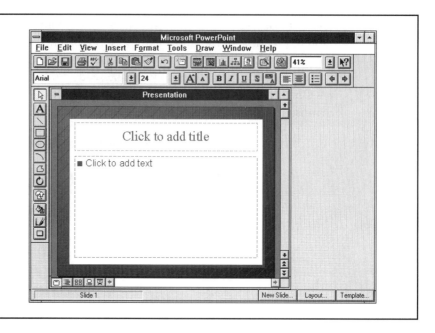

tip *This would be a good time to save your file, even though you haven't entered any data. Working with PowerPoint often involves making small adjustments to perfect the look of a slide, and it is frustrating to have to do that more than once. Save your work early and often, especially when doing more complicated tasks.*

Augmenting Slides with the Pick a Look Wizard

Many people are aware that PowerPoint helps create slides and overheads. In addition, PowerPoint can help you produce other forms of collateral material: handouts, notes, and outlines.

You can use the Pick a Look Wizard at any time during creation or revision of a presentation. It's useful when you start a new presentation because it walks you through the selection of a template, as well as the format of handouts, outlines, and notes. To start the Pick a Look Wizard, click the following button on the Standard toolbar:

In the Notes Options screen of the Pick a Look Wizard, shown next, you determine what information will appear in the header and footer of the notes pages.

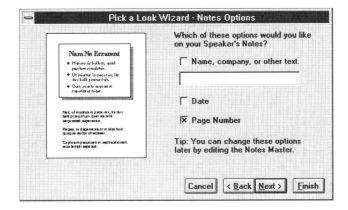

Handouts contain the same material as slides, but you can fit more than one handout on a single page, which makes them a bit easier for the reader to review. Passing out copies of your presentation will give your audience a place to take notes and place them in context. Handouts can also help you as the creator of the slides; you can better see how the presentation flows when you have three or six slides on a page.

Notes provide supplemental material that's helpful to both speaker and audience. Unless you've made the same presentation many times, you'll need speaker's notes to jog your memory about details that do not fit comfortably on the slides. Another benefit, especially helpful for training classes, is that your students can follow along with the notes as you show your slides. Afterward, the students can use the notes as study aids; absentees can also use them as self-training guides.

Outlines can be invaluable while you are developing presentations. Viewing or printing a presentation outline is the best way to see your entire presentation in condensed form. It is also the fastest way to make extensive revisions to bulleted lists; any changes you make to outline text are reflected in the slides.

Using an Outline to Organize the Content

As you prepare for your presentation to MetroVideo Systems, you don't especially have to worry about creating the content of your slides. You've already prepared a proposal document (as described in Chapter 12). Most of what you want to present is contained in that Word document. All you have to do is adapt the material to the medium of the overhead projector.

Revising an Outline for Presentation Purposes

The first step is to create an outline. Typically, you will have to redesign the text document to optimize it for presentation. To transform your proposal document into an acceptable source for a presentation outline, follow these steps:

1. Open your existing proposal document in Word.

2. Choose View, then Outline. The cover page of the consulting proposal document is shown in Outline view in Figure 13-2.

3. Save the document under another name. (You will be making several changes to the document, such as replacing text with headings.)

4. As you read through the proposal, pick out the main points. Delete any text that is extraneous. Use the Promote and Demote buttons to convert the text to the proper levels. Keep in mind that level 1 headings will become slide titles in PowerPoint, and levels 2 and 3 will become bullet lists. Figure 13-3 shows the main points of the cover letter in outline form.

5. Select all text in the document by pressing CTRL-A.

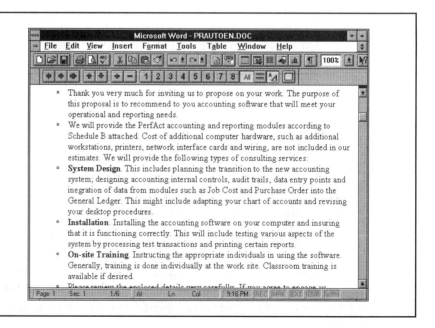

FIGURE 13-2

The first page of the consulting proposal in Outline View

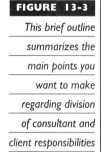

FIGURE 13-3

This brief outline summarizes the main points you want to make regarding division of consultant and client responsibilities

6. Press CTRL+SHIFT+F9 to lock all field results.

7. The Outline view displays all paragraphs, even those that aren't headings. To hide the normal text, click on any of the numbered buttons in the outline toolbar. The numbers correspond to levels in the outline. To display the three highest levels, you would click the button labeled "3."

Your proposal document will now look like Figure 13-4.

FIGURE 13-4

This slide was made from the outline in Figure 13-3

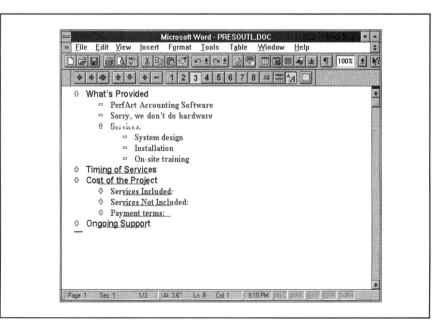

Go through the rest of your proposal document, creating and revising the header paragraphs to optimize them for a hard-hitting presentation. When you are satisfied with the Word outline, save the document. As you will see in a moment, you do not have to delete nonheader text from the document.

Importing an Outline from Word

The next step is to bring the outline into PowerPoint. Follow these steps:

1. Start PowerPoint.
2. Choose Insert, then Slides from Outline. This displays the Insert Outline dialog box, shown here:

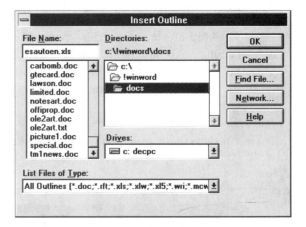

3. Select the path and name of the document containing the outline you will use, and then choose OK.

PowerPoint then imports the outline from the document, displaying a progress indicator as it does so. It imports only the header paragraphs, not text in Normal or other styles. Figure 13-5 shows the proposal document outline as imported into PowerPoint. (Slide 1 reflects the changes shown in Figure 13-4.)

Exporting a Word Outline to PowerPoint

Sometimes you don't have an existing document in a suitable form for creating a presentation outline, so you have to create one from scratch. You can create the entire outline in PowerPoint if you want. You can generally work faster, though, in Word, which has a better set of tools for editing

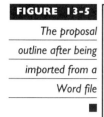

FIGURE 13-5

The proposal outline after being imported from a Word file

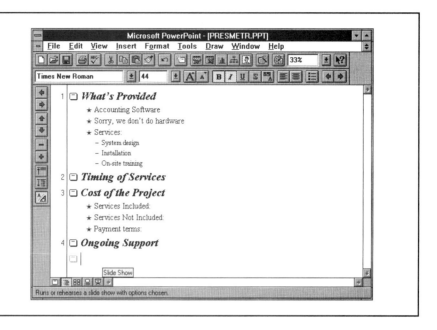

outlines. You can save the outline in Word, load it into PowerPoint, and then change formats and add tables or graphics.

Once you have created your source Word document, follow these steps to export the outline to PowerPoint:

1. In Word, press CTRL+A to select the entire document.

2. Choose Edit, then Copy.

3. In PowerPoint, create a new presentation.

4. Choose View, then Outline.

5. Choose Edit, then Paste Special. This brings up the following dialog box:

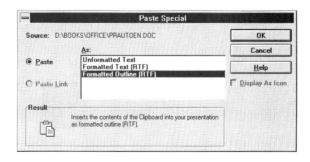

6. Under As, select Formatted Outline (RTF), and then choose OK.

The Word document is copied into the presentation as a PowerPoint outline.

Tips for Creating Effective Slides

Slide creation is an art–it takes practice to create presentations that flow well, provide all pertinent information, and keep the audience involved. Here are a few tips to keep in mind:

- Start your presentation with an agenda or overview slide; give your audience some guidance on where you're headed.
- If the presentation is long, repeat the overview slide at the start of each major section of the presentation. Highlight the name of the section you're about to begin.
- Slides should act only as a guide; do not use long sentences that you simply read during the presentation.

Refining the Presentation

You now know how to create a new presentation, but that only starts the process. You will undoubtedly make changes to the substance of your presentation. Moreover, PowerPoint presentations can include live links to external documents and visual effects to make your presentation interesting.

Reorganizing the Presentation

Rarely will you create a presentation from start to finish without needing to move things around a bit. PowerPoint provides several features to make organizing and reorganizing a little easier.

Changing the Slide Sequence

It's easier to organize your presentation when you can see more than one slide at a time. Outline view is helpful when much of the content is text. (Other objects such as tables and charts don't appear in Outline view.) When you click the Slide Sorter View button (shown next) from the horizontal scroll bar, you'll see a miniature of several slides at once.

Slide Sorter View

A maximized PowerPoint window will display several slides, as shown in Figure 13-6. You can control the number of slides with the Zoom box on the toolbar, which works as it does in Word and Excel.

To move a slide from one position to another, simply drag it to the new location. You should see a gray arrow when you have placed the cursor properly between two other slides. When you release the mouse button the slide will move. To see a slide in Slide view, just double-click the slide.

Scrolling to Specific Slides

The scroll bar at the right of the presentation works a bit differently from the bars in other Microsoft Office products. The up and down arrows at the ends of the scroll bars move the current slide up and down slightly, as you might expect. The "elevator" box in the scroll bar moves you from slide to slide, however, instead of up and down within the slide. To move to a particular slide, click on the elevator and hold the mouse button down. Then drag it up or down to the desired slide. PowerPoint will display the slide number next to the elevator as you drag it, as you can see here:

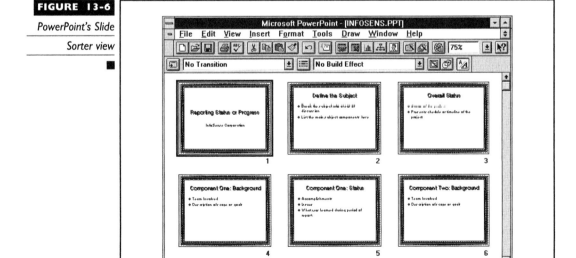

FIGURE 13-6

PowerPoint's Slide Sorter view

If you want to move to the next or previous slide, use the double arrows at the bottom of the scroll bar.

Modifying the Slide Master

If you want to add special global text (such as slide number or date) to all the slides, you must modify the slide master. The slide master controls the look of the slides, the default fonts, the default bullet styles, and text that is placed on all slides.

Suppose you want the date to appear at the bottom of slides. You can do this globally throughout the presentation. Follow these steps:

1. Choose View, then Master.

2. Choose Slide Master from the submenu that appears. Your screen now looks like Figure 13-7.

3. Choose Insert, then Date. PowerPoint will create a placeholder for the date field (a small text box with two slashes in it).

4. Drag the box to the location where you want the date to appear.

5. Select the date field and format it to your satisfaction.

FIGURE 13-7

In Slide Master view, you can specify a design for all slides in the presentation

Linking Slides to Spreadsheets and Tables

PowerPoint gives you several ways to insert a spreadsheet into a slide. You can even create an Excel spreadsheet from scratch (a topic not covered in this chapter).

tip *Though you can create an Excel spreadsheet in PowerPoint, it's usually most efficient to create it in Excel.*

The proposal document in Chapter 12 included a table that was linked from an Excel spreadsheet. You can also link a spreadsheet into a PowerPoint presentation. Follow these steps:

1. In Excel, copy the range you want to appear in your slide.
2. Open your presentation in PowerPoint.
3. Click the New Slide box in the status bar.
4. Scroll to the end of the layout list and select the Title Only layout.
5. Choose Edit, then Paste Special. This displays the Paste Special dialog box.
6. To link the Excel object, select the Paste Link option. (The default Paste option will embed the object.)
7. Choose OK. After a few moments, PowerPoint will display a rather small copy of the selected rows and columns in the center of the slide, as shown in Figure 13-8.
8. Using your mouse, drag the edges of the spreadsheet away from the center of the slide, until the information is readable. Your final slide should look like Figure 13-9.

If, during the presentation, you need to change any of the cell formulas to do some "what-iffing," you can activate the source document by double-clicking the linked Excel object.

If you want to include a table created in Word in your presentation, you can use a similar procedure to link or embed it from Word.

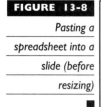

FIGURE 13-8

Pasting a spreadsheet into a slide (before resizing)

Adding Effects

When it comes to keeping the audience interested, you need all the help you can get. That's why it's useful to add visual effects. Even in a serious business presentation, it's probably better to be a bit too glitzy rather than a bit too boring.

FIGURE 13-9

Pasting a spreadsheet into a slide (after resizing)

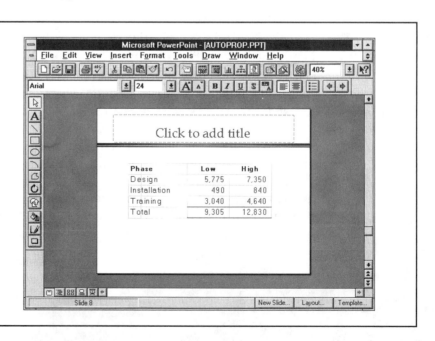

When using your PC as the display mechanism, you can add special effects that animate your presentation. You can add *transitions* that use snazzy effects, such as fading or dissolving, to move from one slide to the next. Additionally, you can use *builds* to display your bulleted items one at a time, which can also help you control when your audience sees each point.

Applying Transition Effects

To modify transitions, click the Slide Sorter view button in the horizontal scroll bar. In addition to displaying multiple slides, the Slide Sorter view includes a special toolbar. To apply a transition effect to a particular slide, select that slide before adding the effect. To apply a transition to all slides in the presentation, choose Edit, then Select All before selecting the transition.

To apply a transition to the selected slide(s), display the Transition drop-down list (which displays No Transition the first time you use it), and select the desired transition effect.

To preview transitions, follow these steps:

1. Display the Transition dialog box by clicking the button to the left of the Transition drop-down list:

2. Select an effect from the Effect drop-down list. The thumbnail image at the lower right of the screen animates the transition effect.

3. Choose OK when you have selected your favorite transition.

Using Builds

A *build* is a way of gradually displaying parts of a slide. Displaying a slide's bulleted items one item at a time creates a minor sense of anticipation in the listener, as he waits to see what you will display next. You can make your bulleted items seem to drop from the sky with the Fly From Top build, or gradually appear with "wipe" or "split" effects.

To apply a build, follow these steps:

1. Click the Slide Sorter View icon.

2. Select one or more slides.

3. Select the desired effect from the Build drop-down list (which displays No Build Effect by default), as shown here:

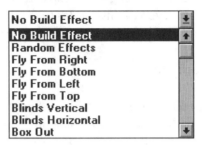

4. Choose OK.

tip *A quick way to jazz up the presentation is to select all slides, and then choose Random Transition and Random Effects from the appropriate pull-down list boxes.*

Rehearsing the Presentation

When you are satisfied with the content of your presentation and the sequence of your slides, you are ready to add a few finishing touches. Resist the temptation to play with special effects before you have finished the content—you might end up with a presentation that looks slick but makes no sense.

The best way to determine if your presentation is well organized is to practice it a few times. Even if you're not going to use your PC as the presentation medium, PowerPoint's Slide Show feature lets you run through your slides without the time and expense of printing or creating overheads.

To start the slide show, click the Slide Show button (shown here) at the lower-left corner of the presentation window.

Slide Show

You can use either the left mouse button or the PGDN key to move from slide to slide. Press ESC if you need to terminate the show.

tip *You can program time intervals into your presentations, so that slides advance automatically. Don't use this when you are presenting, however–the feature doesn't leave room for variation, and will almost certainly trip you up. Instead, use it when you want to use a PC to run an automated presentation–at a convention, for instance.*

Making the Presentation

Now that you've created and rehearsed the best presentation you possibly can, you still have to assemble your physical materials and deliver the presentation personally.

Printing Handout Material

As you learned earlier, you can print all or part of your presentation in the form of slides (with or without speaker's notes) or the presentation outline. Follow these steps:

1. With your presentation open, choose File, then Print.

2. From the Print What drop-down list in the Print dialog box, select what you want to print, according to the following table:

Option	Slides per Page	Other Material Printed
Slides	One	None
Notes pages	One	Notes at the bottom of each page
Handouts	2, 3, or 6	None
Outline	None	Outline view of the presentation

3. Choose OK.

Using a Service Bureau to Print Slides

To produce physical overhead transparencies or 35mm slides you will have to find a service bureau. You will likely find one in your local business directory under such headings as "Audio-Visual Production Services," "Photo-Imagesetting," or "Slides & Film Strips."

PowerPoint also includes software from Genigraphics, a leading service bureau, to capture images from your PowerPoint presentation files. You can then bring the image files to a Genigraphics service center to be transformed into film. You can also send the physical disks or send files via modem to the nearest Genigraphics service center. For details, consult the booklet entitled *Using Microsoft PowerPoint and Genigraphics Presentation Services* included in your PowerPoint documentation.

Running a Presentation from a PC

To run a presentation from your computer, set up all peripheral equipment (such as overhead LCD projection panels). Then follow these steps:

1. In the Windows Program Manager, double-click the PowerPoint Viewer icon:

   PowerPoint Viewer

   It should be located in the window that contains the icons for your other Office applications.

2. In the Microsoft PowerPoint Viewer dialog box, select the PowerPoint file containing your presentation.

3. To advance from one slide to the next, click the left mouse button.

4. To return to the previous slide at any point, click the right mouse button.

5. When you are done with your presentation, press ESC. The Microsoft PowerPoint Viewer dialog box will appear.

6. To resume your presentation, choose Show. To quit, choose Quit.

tip *If you print numbered slides for reference, you'll be able to return to a given slide by using the vertical scroll bar. You can automatically assign sequential numbers to slides in a presentation in the Slide Master (displayed by choosing View, Master, then choosing Slide Master from the submenu).*

Creating Future Presentations

One procedure not yet discussed is opening an existing presentation. As you continue to make presentations, you will often want to modify existing presentation files rather than create new ones all the time.

Opening an Existing Presentation

PowerPoint's initial dialog box offers the option of opening a presentation file. However, it's often faster to simply close that first dialog box, and then choose File. Like the other Office programs, PowerPoint's File menu lists the four most recent files loaded into the program.

note *After a while, you will probably want to disable the initial dialog box by turning off the Show Startup Dialog option in the Options dialog box.*

To create a new presentation based on an existing one, follow these steps:

1. Open the existing presentation.
2. Choose File, then New.
3. Select the Current Presentation Format option. This allows you to apply the template and other layout characteristics from the existing presentation to your new one.

You can now work with the presentation as if you had created it from scratch.

Getting a Head Start with the AutoContent Wizard

When you're really at a loss for how to get started on a presentation that you're creating from scratch, try the AutoContent Wizard.

You can use the AutoContent Wizard before you create your presentation, but when you do that PowerPoint selects a template for you and you might not like the template. The following alternative technique works better for many users:

1. Create a new, blank presentation and save it under an appropriate name.

2. Choose File, then New. (This might seem strange, but it's necessary.)

3. Choose AutoContent Wizard and click OK.

4. Follow the Wizard through its steps. The third panel looks like this:

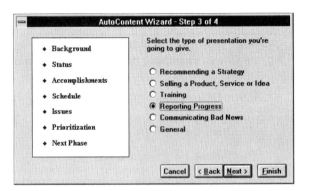

5. Often, the task for your presentation will match one of the choices provided by the Wizard. If not, you'll have to start with the General option. As you select each of the radio buttons, you can see the titles of the five to seven slides supplied by the wizard.

6. When you finish the wizard, two things should happen: (1) a new presentation will appear, in the outline view, and (2) the PowerPoint Cue Cards will appear at the right of the screen. Figure 13-10 shows the screen after the AutoContent Wizard has created a "Reporting Progress" presentation. Close the cue cards for now; you can use them later if you want.

7. Choose Edit, and then Select All, then Copy. This will copy the information supplied by the Wizard into the Clipboard.

8. Choose File, then Close. (Don't save the changes.)

9. Display the presentation in Outline view.

10. Choose Edit, then Paste. The outline generated by the AutoContent Wizard will now be part of your presentation.

FIGURE 13-10

A sample presentation created by the AutoContent Wizard

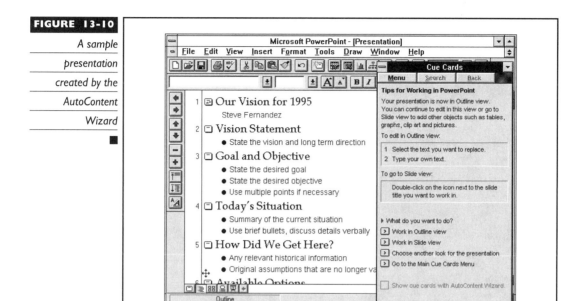

You can now modify the presentation to add detail relevant to your situation, using the headings and items provided by the Wizard to stimulate your thinking.

Conclusion

This chapter described the steps involved in making quality presentations using PowerPoint, including using data from other Office programs to keep the presentations consistent with their sources. You have now learned the essentials of each of the programs in the Microsoft Office suite. In the final section of the book, you will learn how to automate tasks with Visual Basic and OLE Automation. You'll also learn some of OLE 2.0's advanced features.

Part III

Advanced Examples

CHAPTER 14

Building a Rapid Response Interface with Excel

THESE days, everyone in the workplace feels the constant pressure of time. Everything happens quickly: changes in buying preferences, competitive products, advances in technology. In the meantime, the penalty for not responding fast enough to changing circumstances seems to grow ever more severe.

If you're doing battle in the arena of time-based competition, Microsoft Office can be a hidden weapon. Using the applications' built-in programming languages, you can construct an automated updating mechanism that feeds data to your PC from a "real environment"—a place where important events are happening quickly. The following business situations fit this definition:

- Financial markets (such as stock, bond, or international currency exchanges)

- A computer network with numerous servers and hundreds of workstations

- An industrial process such as automobile assembly or petroleum refining

- An order processing or customer service center with hundreds of representatives fielding telephone orders or inquiries

- A nationwide network of automated teller machines

This chapter addresses high-pressure environments where the stakes are high and, accordingly, where managers need to monitor events very closely. For simplicity, such an environment—whether it be the New York Stock Exchange, a nuclear power plant, or a long-distance telephone network—will be referred to as the "site." The site might be localized, or it could be geographically spread out. Events occurring at a site might be recorded by a person (as when a factory worker keys production data into a workstation on the shop floor) or by machine (as when a transaction in an automated teller machine is transmitted via a communications network).

One of the most sophisticated examples of this concept is NASA's manned space command center in Houston. Data is captured in space by sensors, then transmitted to display terminals on the ground. The kind of integrated decision-support environments exemplified by NASA's control room are driven by a pressing need to monitor fast-changing conditions.

Creating Your Own Operations and Command Center

The device that displays the information to the operator (who could be a money market trader, lumber broker, or computer network administrator) must have two key elements:

- A computer interface that helps the operator *visualize* what is happening at the site, rather than view rows and columns of numbers

- "Push-button" controls that facilitate instantaneous response by the operator to changing conditions

In the high-pressure situations described earlier, the operator doesn't have time to analyze multiple what-if scenarios. This chapter demonstrates a particular type of solution, using a manufacturing plant as an example. The purpose, however, is not to show you how to use Excel in manufacturing, but to show you how to apply Excel's unique automation and interface features to a classic rapid-response problem. Because of continuing developments in networks and databases, it is possible (if you have the expertise) to bring data from a variety of sources into a central database. With help from Access, Query, and ODBC, selected subsets of the data can be provided to Excel. Operators can watch the data as it streams into Excel and determine if and when action is required.

Monitoring Operations by Computer

In order to make rapid decisions, human beings need to have data fed to them in digestible chunks. Crucial to realizing this concept is a computer system that captures the raw data and then sorts, massages, and summarizes it. Then, only the relevant data is presented to the user. The computer system mediates between the sea of amorphous measurement data and the user, as illustrated in Figure 14-1.

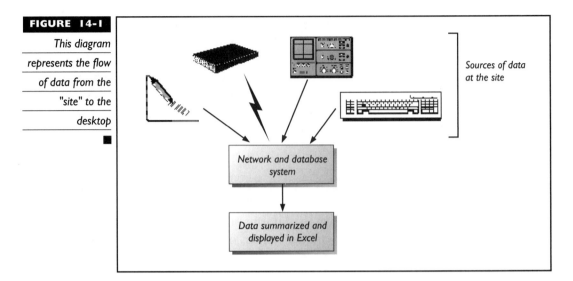

FIGURE 14-1
This diagram represents the flow of data from the "site" to the desktop

A well-designed system of this kind will support the idea of *management by exception*. The word "exception" means a situation that is out of the ordinary. The most pressing exceptions are negative ones, such as below-normal sales and over-budget expenses; however, even "good" exceptions should be investigated if they are very abnormal. A system that highlights exceptions allows managers to prioritize their time and focus their attention where it will have the most impact.

Understanding the Components of a Rapid-Response System

A rapid-response monitoring system of the type discussed in this chapter should include the following three components:

- One or more systems for gathering or entering data at the site
- A network or other communications link, including a database engine, between the point of initial data capture and the rapid-response workstation (hereinafter referred to as simply the "workstation")
- A visually intuitive interface

The three components are represented from top to bottom in Figure 14-1. The top level shows examples of data input and transmission devices that feed data from the site into a database. The database stage might itself consist of several intermediate steps. For instance, the first stop for "site" data might be an old mainframe. The mainframe might communicate with an SQL Server database, which in turn might update an Access database on a workstation PC.

From this point, the chapter will use the example of a factory that produces chocolate candy to show how to construct the last component—the interface—in Excel. Using a factory as an example provides a useful physical metaphor to visualize whatever form of activity is being monitored. You are likely to work somewhere other than manufacturing—perhaps in a financial trading room or on the support staff for a wide-area network. However, since abstract operations such as these are highly technical and often difficult for nonexperts to visualize, the chocolate factory can provide a useful archetype you can relate to intellectually. Just remember as you walk through the example that the factory is only a stand-in, a symbol, for the kind of site you monitor in your operation.

Acquiring Data at the Site

The first component of the overall system performs some kind of data acquisition. In sites that are transaction-oriented (such as communication networks, retail stores, and toll-free telephone service centers), a series of discrete events is recorded. Often the transactions are recorded by electronic equipment without any human action.

In other cases, such as power plants and oil refining, the current "state" of things (in terms of, say, pressure, temperature, and quantity) is continuously recorded. Sometimes remote sensing devices such as oscilloscopes, counters, and gauges capture the data; sometimes operators at the site enter measurements manually.

Hooking the data acquisition devices to a computer system can often be the most challenging part of the system. Microsoft Office doesn't include tools to solve that problem; accordingly, detailed instruction on this subject is well beyond the scope of this book. This chapter will assume that the software and hardware to transmit data from the site has been installed and is working reliably.

Processing the Production Data

The second component of the operations center typically consists of a computer network running one or more databases that receive the data recorded on the shop floor. If the operations center draws information from multiple networks, some method of communication among the various networks must be implemented.

Because Microsoft Access can connect to a variety of data sources, it can perform the database processing on the data that is supplied by the network link from the production area to the operations center. Implementing this part of the system will usually require a high level of database design expertise. Typically, a database application designer will create tables to "receive" the data and design queries that summarize that data.

Designing the User Interface

The final piece of the rapid response system is the *user interface*, which tells the system operators what's going on "out there." The interface should highlight the exceptional situations that demand attention. In the next section, you will learn about the features of Office—particularly Excel—that you can take advantage of to create a rapid response user interface.

note *Because this chapter teaches you only how to create the interface with Excel, you will not have a complete production monitoring system that will be working with actual data. You will, however, be able to work with the interface.*

Creating a Rapid Response Workstation with Office and Visual Basic for Applications

Microsoft Office contains several features that make it a good choice for a Rapid response development platform. The examples you studied in the first two sections of this book illustrated numerous ways to automate your work without the use of macro code—using OLE 2, ODBC, and other Office features. Macros, however, provide the ultimate in automation.

The example in this chapter will require the use of Visual Basic, Applications Edition (known as *VBA*), the object-oriented macro language included with version 5 of Excel. Eventually, all the Office applications will contain VBA. At the time of this writing, however, only Excel and Microsoft Project (which is not included in the Office suite) have VBA.

Although Access 2.0 and Word 6.0 don't have VBA yet, they each have programming languages that include a great deal of the power of VBA. Both derived from the BASIC programming language, Access Basic and WordBasic are also similar in many respects. Once you know how to program in one of them, learning the other is somewhat easier.

VBA is an extremely powerful macro language. The sheer number of objects, properties, and methods that can be managed with VBA might seem overwhelming initially. Mastering the language to its full breadth and depth does take time. Once you learn how, though, you will be able to control the Office applications more completely than you ever thought possible.

This purpose of this chapter is to demonstrate how to use Excel, Access, and VBA to solve a particular business problem.. The instructions assume that you have a good familiarity with Excel and a basic understanding of

VBA. The absence here of any generic introduction to VBA should not, however, discourage VBA novices from reading the chapter. Most VBA experts say that the best way to learn the language is by active experimentation. The examples of VBA code in this chapter provide excellent opportunities for such learning, so don't let your unfamiliarity with VBA discourage you from working through this example.

For more information on using VBA in Excel, please refer to *Excel for Windows: The Complete Reference*, from Osborne/McGraw-Hill.

The Scenario: Monitoring a Manufacturing Process

The star attraction of this chapter is a Visual Basic, Applications Edition (VBA) module that creates a production monitoring workstation for the fictitious Megachunk Chocolate Factory, which makes chocolate candy kisses. A complex manufacturing process like this generates a lot of data. To avoid overwhelming you with detail, this chapter focuses on only part of the overall example. Still, you need to see the big picture before zeroing in on the details.

Making Sweet Stuff: The Megachunk Chocolate Factory

The entire candy-making consists of several stages. The following diagram lays out the process:

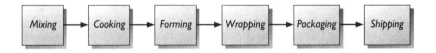

Some of the six stages include subprocesses that are also monitored by the workstation.

Recording Data During Processing

The types of data collected during manufacturing vary depending on the particular stage. Sometimes operators on the factory floor key data into terminals; at other times, electronic and electromechanical controls feed measurements to the computer system. Each of the production stages described in the following paragraph is a "site" where production occurs and original data is captured.

During mixing, for instance, gauges and thermometers record the "vital statistics" of each batch. In the forming and wrapping stages, where the cooked batch of chocolate is formed into individual candies, good and rejected pieces are counted. In packaging, where the individually wrapped candies are placed into various package sizes, operators enter batch numbers and Product ID numbers. In the shipping area, packages of the product are picked from available inventory, assigned to an order, and placed on a truck to be shipped. Typical data collected include the order ID, customer ID, and shipping method.

Now that you have an idea what happens on the factory floor (the site), let's see how it looks from the workstation, after Access and Excel have massaged the production data.

The Workstation in Action

The workstation personnel (referred to collectively as "the user" in this chapter) are responsible for monitoring all the production lines, along with some other necessary steps in filling a customer's order. The production process is highly automated. Halting production, even briefly, can be very expensive to the company. When a production line is down, the company makes no money, while the rent, loan interest, and personnel costs associated with that line continue unabated.

Management expects the operators at the workstations to closely monitor the whole process through the automated display, and to alert responsible personnel whenever performance varies from certain limits. Given timely notice of upcoming production snags, management can correct minor problems before they mushroom into unsafe or production-stopping disasters.

Because of the many processes tracked by the workstation, the first question is how to limit the quantity of data to an amount that can be readily understood. It's usually most effective to have a top-level screen—analogous to a main menu—that provides quick access to all production monitoring screens.

The system has to effectively flag exceptions. Color is a great device for drawing a user's attention to problem areas. The top-level screen for the Megachunk Chocolate Factory monitoring application, which is shown in Figure 14-2, uses color to highlight the status of each major area under its watchful eye. (Naturally, colors are represented in this book by varying shades of gray.)

Though you can't tell by simply looking at the screen, the monitoring application uses Microsoft Excel to provide the interface, or "front end." Microsoft Access collects production data from the server database (as described earlier in the chapter), accumulates it into a database, and reports summary figures to Excel as needed.

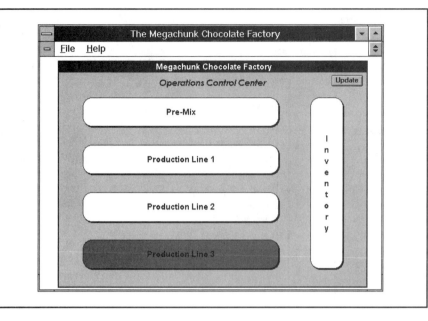

FIGURE 14-2
The top-level Summary screen of the production monitoring application

The top-level screen shown in Figure 14-2 uses color to indicate the status of the departments monitored by the workstation. Table 14-1 shows what each of the three colors means to the operator.

The colors displayed on the workstation screens are updated periodically based on data supplied by Access to Excel. Megachunk Chocolate has three production lines in its facility, in addition to the central setup (Pre-Mix) and order fulfillment (Inventory) operations. The colors of the text labels indicate the condition of each department.

Based on what is shown in Figure 14-2, it looks like there is a problem with Production Line 3 that needs immediate attention. The production monitoring application can provide more information about the problem. Clicking the Production Line 3 box will "drill down" to the next level of detail—that is, it will expand the view to show all production stages—as

Color*	Description
Green (medium gray)	Everything is fine; all readings are within normal ranges.
Yellow (white)	Readings are creeping outside normal ranges; the operator should monitor the situation closely if nothing else is more pressing.
Red (dark gray)	Immediate management attention is necessary.

*The color in parentheses is the color as it appears in the grayscale illustrations used in this book.

TABLE 14-1 Color Codes That Indicate Production Line Status

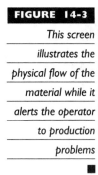

FIGURE 14-3

This screen illustrates the physical flow of the material while it alerts the operator to production problems

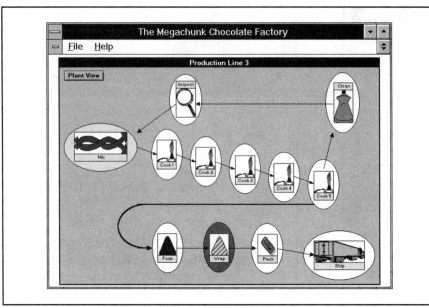

shown in Figure 14-3. Based on what you see there, you can take corrective action or investigate further, as appropriate.

The Production Line 3 screen (Figure 14-3) has several yellow-colored areas, including cooking stages 1 and 5 and the packaging stage. One area, the wrapping stage, is colored red, which indicates a need for immediate attention. Again, by clicking a button located within the colored ovals, the user can display a still more detailed view: a supplemental worksheet that shows detailed information for the selected production stage. By pressing the Wrap button shown in Figure 14-3, the user can see more detail and perhaps pinpoint the cause of the red indicator, as shown in Figure 14-4.

As you can see in Figure 14-4, batches 349 and 351 contained an unusually high proportion of rejects. Based on this information, managers can review the entire process for these batches in an attempt to determine what is causing the defects.

To envision how such a visual interface might help you monitor conditions in your business, think about the factory as a metaphor for your business operation. If you work for a large mortgage company, the mixing, forming, and other stages are analogous to the steps in approving a mortgage application. In the freight and delivery business, the main processing points would be the airport locations; under the airports would be the individual delivery routes. You can easily imagine how useful it would be to click on an icon for O'Hare airport to see a screen with icons representing the various delivery routes in the Chicago area. In such a scenario, if the O'Hare icon

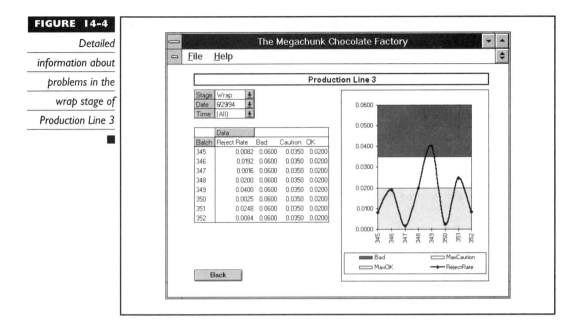

FIGURE 14-4

Detailed information about problems in the wrap stage of Production Line 3

■

turned yellow or red, a dispatcher would naturally want to see which drivers were running late on their deliveries.

Now that you are familiar with how a rapid-response workstation can represent what's happening at a site, let's take a close look at the necessary programming and at the worksheet setup to make the system work.

Looking at the Entire Macro

This section lists the entire example macro, which includes the VBA code behind the top-level screen and one of the detail screens. Use this listing as a reference; it contains numerous embedded comments, indicated by a leading single quote character. However, for detailed explanation of several key parts of the macro, refer to the following section, "Taking a Closer Look at the Macro," which repeats (in several smaller listings) parts of the macro. The following complete listing is cross-referenced to the other listings by numbers shown in the margins.

Some macro commands are not discussed in detail in this chapter; however, you can see how those parts work by reading the annotations embedded in the code. Some technical topics are explained in notes.

Remember that the purpose of the macro is to change Excel's appearance to make it look like a sleek custom application, in a way that provides rapid access to supporting data. Though the factory example might not appear to apply in your particular industry, it will show you how to create a rapid response interface and to connect graphical screen objects with Excel worksheets that receive and process live data from a site.

```
' Type Declarations, Public Variables and Constants.
```

note *Type declarations are custom variable types. The following code defines a custom variable that contains a component that is a string data type and a component that is a long integer data type.*

```
Type Warning
    ObjectName As String
    WarnColor As Long
End Type
```

note *Public variables are visible to all of the procedures in a module. This public variable defines an array of 11 variables of the Warning data type defined above.*

```
Public Warnings(11) As Warning
' The constants below are used to make the
' code that assigns colors more understandable.
' Constants are string representations of a value
' that does not change during code execution.
```

Listing 14-4

```
Global Const WARNGREEN As Long = 32768      'results of RGB(0,128,0)
Global Const WARNRED As Long = 255          'results of RGB(255,0,0)
Global Const WARNYELLOW As Long = 65535     'results of RGB(255,255,0)
```

Listing 14-2

```
Sub Auto_Open()
' Change the Excel application window title.
    Application.Caption = "The Megachunk Chocolate Factory"
    ' Set the default window caption to a zero length string (so
    ' that it doesn't display the filename).
    ThisWorkbook.Windows(1).Caption = ""

    ' Run the SecureEnvironment subroutine, which hides the standard
    ' Excel interface.
```

note *Auto_Open procedures execute code whenever the file is opened.*

Listing 14-2 (continued)

```
    SecureEnvironment

    ' Set up each worksheet in the workbook so that when the sheet
    ' becomes active, the custom menus will be displayed.
    For Each WS In ThisWorkbook.Worksheets
        WS.OnSheetActivate = "LimitedMenuActivate"
    Next

    ' Restore the default menus when the developer accesses
    ' the module code.  Users will not see the module
    ' as it will be hidden.
    ThisWorkbook.Modules("Module1").OnSheetActivate = _
            "RestoreDefaultMenus"
End Sub
```

' The following procedure hides the standard Excel interface.

Listing 14-1

```
Sub SecureEnvironment()
    With ActiveWindow
        .DisplayGridlines = False
        .DisplayHeadings = False
        .DisplayHorizontalScrollBar = False
        .DisplayVerticalScrollBar = False
        .DisplayWorkbookTabs = False
    End With
    With Application
        .DisplayFormulaBar = False
        .DisplayStatusBar = False
    End With
End Sub
```

```
' The following procedure restores the standard module
' menus for developer use.
Sub RestoreDefaultMenus()
MenuBars(xlModule).Activate
End Sub

Sub LimitedMenuActivate()
    ' Show the custom (limited') menu.
    MenuBars("LimitedMenu").Activate

    ' Show the default menus.  Useful during development.
    ' Comment out or remove this line in the production
    ' version.
    ' MenuBars(xlWorksheet).Activate
End Sub

Sub ShowRejectPivot()
    ' This routine displays a different pivot table based on
    ' the button that calls it.  The supplemental sheets for
    ' the Forming and Wrapping stages are actually two different
    ' configurations of the same pivot table.
    Select Case Application.Caller
        Case "btnWarnForm"
            DisplayRejectPivot ("Form")
```

```
            Case "btnWarnWrap"
                DisplayRejectPivot ("Wrap")
        End Select
    End Sub

    Sub DisplayRejectPivot(StageName As String)
        ' This routine changes the selected page field in the pivot
        ' table on the supplemental sheet.
        With ActiveWorkbook.Sheets("Reject Chart")
            .PivotTables("RejectPivot").PivotFields("Stage"). _
                CurrentPage = StageName
            .Activate
        End With
    End Sub

    Sub UpdateAllSheets()
```

note *This routine could be executed using an OnTime event. Due to the space limitations, however, the following code updates only one part of one department. In actual practice, all updates would be executed from this procedure.*

```
        ' This routine, which is called by the button on the "Operations
        ' Control Center" sheet, controls the updating of all values in
        ' the user interface.
    FillWarningArray
```

note *In a complete application, several routines would be run here to update each of the department-level detail sheets. In this sample code, only two such procedures are shown.*

```
        UpdateWarnWrapColor
        FillWarningColors ("Production Line 3")

        ' After all of the department-level sheets are updated, update
        ' the Control Center and make it the active sheet.
        UpdateControlCenterColors
        ActiveWorkbook.Sheets("Operations Control Center").Activate
    End Sub

    Sub FillWarningColors(SheetName As String)
        ' This routine initializes the Warning array variable, retrieves
        ' current data from the data source, and updates the color of the
        ' ovals on the Production Line Detail screens.

        ' Activate the required sheet.
        ActiveWorkbook.Sheets(SheetName).Activate

        ' For each element in the array variable.
```

```
            For x = LBound(Warnings) To UBound(Warnings)

                ' Select the active sheet's drawing objects (one by one).
                ActiveSheet.DrawingObjects(Warnings(x).ObjectName).Select

                ' Set the selected object's color based on a value in the
                ' Warning array.
                Selection.Interior.Color = Warnings(x).WarnColor
            Next
        End Sub
        Sub FillWarningArray()
            ' This routine fills the ObjectName field of the Warnings array.
            Warnings(0).ObjectName = "WarnMix"
            Warnings(1).ObjectName = "WarnCook1"
            Warnings(2).ObjectName = "WarnCook2"
            Warnings(3).ObjectName = "WarnCook3"
            Warnings(4).ObjectName = "WarnCook4"
            Warnings(5).ObjectName = "WarnCook5"
            Warnings(6).ObjectName = "WarnClean"
            Warnings(7).ObjectName = "WarnInspect"
            Warnings(8).ObjectName = "WarnForm"
            Warnings(9).ObjectName = "WarnWrap"
            Warnings(10).ObjectName = "WarnPack"
            Warnings(11).ObjectName = "WarnShip"
        End Sub
```

Listing 14-8

```
Sub UpdateWarnWrapColor()
    ' This routine is used to update the Wrapping stage.

    ' Calculate the warning color and set the oval to that color
    Worksheets("Production Line 3").DrawingObjects("WarnWrap"). _
            Interior.Color = CalcPLine3Color()

    ' Set the appropriate color value in the warning array.
    Warnings(9).WarnColor = Worksheets("Production Line 3"). _
            DrawingObjects("WarnWrap").Interior.Color
End Sub
```

Listing 14-9

```
Function CalcPLine3Color() As Long
    ' This function calculates and returns the most critical color
    ' in the Wrap Stage supplemental sheet.
    Dim ChtPL3 As Chart, x As Integer
    Dim MaxOK As Single, MaxCaution As Single
    Dim MostCriticalColor As Long

    ' Make sure the pivot table is up to date.
    UpdatePivot

    ' Set an object variable to reference the chart based
    ' on the pivot table in the supplemental sheet.
    Set ChtPL3 = Worksheets("Reject Chart"). _
            ChartObjects("RejectChart").Chart
```

Listing 14-10
```
    ' Calculate the OK and Caution thresholds.
    MaxOK = Application.Max(ChtPL3.SeriesCollection("MaxOK").Values)
    MaxCaution = Application.Max(ChtPL3. _
            SeriesCollection("MaxCaution").Values)

    ' Calculate the maximum reject rate in the chart and assign
    ' a color based on that value.
    Select Case Application.Max(ChtPL3.SeriesCollection("RejectRate") _
            .Values)
        Case Is > MaxCaution
            CalcPLine3Color = WARNRED
        Case Is > MaxOK
            CalcPLine3Color = WARNYELLOW
        Case Else
            CalcPLine3Color = WARNGREEN
    End Select
End Function
```

Listing 14-7
```
Sub UpdatePivot()
    ' This routine requeries and updates the pivot table.
    Worksheets("Reject Chart").PivotTables("RejectPivot").RefreshTable
End Sub
```

Listing 14-3
```
Sub UpdateControlCenterColors()
    ' This routine updates the colors of the textbox "buttons" on
    ' the "Operations Control Center" screen.

    ' Dimension an object variable of the Textbox type.
    Dim Dept As TextBox

    ' Loop through the Textboxes collection of the "Operations
    ' Control Center" sheet.
    For Each Dept In ActiveWorkbook. _
            Worksheets("Operations Control Center").TextBoxes

        ' Pass the textbox name to the GetDeptColor function,
        ' which will return the proper color.
        Dept.Interior.Color = GetDeptColor(Dept.Name)
    Next
End Sub
```

Listing 14-5
```
Private Function GetDeptColor(DeptName As String) As Long
    ' This function accepts a department name (which is
    ' the name of a department-level detail sheet) and
    ' returns the "most critical" color on the sheet.

    ' Dimension the necessary variables.  One variable is a
    ' long integer; the other is an Oval object.
    Dim MostCriticalColor As Long, WarningOval As Oval

    ' Set the default warning color to green.
    MostCriticalColor = WARNGREEN
```

Listing 14-5 (continued)

```
        ' For each oval on the designated sheet, look for
        ' an oval that is colored red or yellow.
        For Each WarningOval In Worksheets(DeptName).Ovals
            Select Case WarningOval.Interior.Color
                Case WARNRED
                    MostCriticalColor = WARNRED
                    Exit For
                Case WARNYELLOW
                    MostCriticalColor = WARNYELLOW
            End Select
        Next

        ' Return the MostCriticalColor variable value.
        GetDeptColor = MostCriticalColor
End Function
```

Listing 14-6

```
Sub GoToSheet()
    ' This routine is called from the "Operations Control
    ' Center" and activates the appropriate department-level
    ' worksheet when a departmental button is pressed.
    ActiveWorkbook.Worksheets(Application.Caller).Activate
End Sub
```

```
Sub Auto_Close()
    ' Display the standard Excel interface.
    With ActiveWindow
        .DisplayGridlines = True
        .DisplayHeadings = True
        .DisplayHorizontalScrollBar = True
        .DisplayVerticalScrollBar = True
        .DisplayWorkbookTabs = True
    End With
    With Application
        .DisplayFormulaBar = True
        .DisplayStatusBar = True
    End With
End Sub
```

Taking a Closer Look at the Macro

To use the Megachunk Chocolate Factory macro as a prototype for your own system, you need to break it down and look at some of its key parts. First you'll learn how to change Excel's appearance.

Disguising Excel

Though the screens that display the production information are Excel worksheets, they've been stripped of the normal Excel accoutrements, so they look more like part of a custom application. Removing the Excel menus and toolbar buttons from the screen simplifies the interface for users. That reduces the chance of error and creates a less intimidating look for users who are not familiar with Excel.

To completely disguise Excel from the user in this manner, you can perform the following actions:

- Remove the following telltale Excel objects from the display: gridlines, row and column headings, scroll bars, sheet tabs, the formula bar, and the status bar.
- Create custom menus and/or toolbars that apply to each screen.
- Create a customized caption for the application title bar.

Removing the Excel Interface with Commands

Any or all of the Excel display objects referred to in the preceding list can be removed with Excel commands. Simply display Excel's Options dialog box (shown below) and deselect the items you want removed from the screen display.

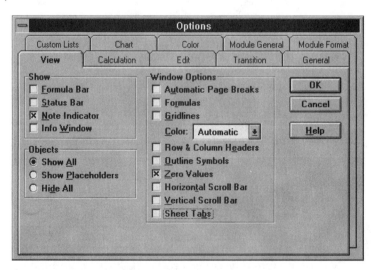

Determining Production Standards

The whole point of the production monitoring application is to continuously compare current production figures with a standard. The first step in setting the standard is to determine what unit of measure you will use. In manufacturing, you would use such statistics as number of units produced, dollar value produced, and yield percentage. If you are processing loans, you will track number of applications processed and perhaps some sort of quality indicators. If you are a network administrator, you might track server uptime percentage, amount of network traffic, and response time on support calls.

You also have to determine an acceptable, or standard, level of performance for each of the measures you use. When performance falls below the standard, the application will display appropriate warning indicators. This example computes one production statistic: units that do not meet the quality standard (rejects) as a percentage of units produced. In a real application, this measure of production would be only one of many variables tracked by the system.

This example will assume that a reject percentage of 2.0% is acceptable. A percentage of 2.0% to 3.5% is considered cautionary; that is, it calls for at least some cursory investigation, but is not serious enough to drop everything else. If the percentage is greater than 3.5%, management should be notified as soon as possible.

Removing the Excel Interface with Visual Basic Code

In creating a custom application, you will usually write VBA code to perform the Excel face-lift automatically. The VBA instructions in Listing 14-1 remove the Excel-specific objects from the display. (Remember, Listing 14-1 and the remaining listings in the chapter are simply segments of the entire module repeated in the text for convenient reference.)

note *If you were creating an Excel 4 macro, you would use macro functions to carry out operations. In VBA, you invoke* methods *to cause objects to "do something," and you set* properties *to change certain things about objects. Invoking methods and setting properties is done with* statements *(which constitute the actual VBA code). A group of statements that accomplishes a certain task is called a* procedure. *Individual procedures are demarcated by* Sub *and* End Sub *statements.*

How the VBA Routine Customizes the "ActiveWindow" Object

The code in Listing 14-1 provides an excellent opportunity to review some basic principles behind Visual Basic, Applications Edition and how it relates to the OLE 2.0 object model.

LISTING 14-1

This procedure hides the normal Excel interface

```
Sub Secure Environment()
    With ActiveWindow
        .DisplayGridlines = False
        .DisplayHeadings = False
        .DisplayHorizontalScrollBar = False
        .DisplayVerticalScrollBar = False
        .DisplayWorkbookTabs = False
    End With
    With Application
        .DisplayFormulaBar = False
        .DisplayStatusBar = False
    End With
End Sub
```

All the display elements (the gridlines, row headings, and so on) are properties of the Window object that can be manipulated by VBA. The statement

```
With ActiveWindow
```

tells Excel that you are working with the Active Window object. Objects, as you remember from Chapter 2, have *properties* and *methods*. The code in Listing 14-1 sets the display properties of the "unwanted" screen properties to "False," meaning you want them removed from the screen.

"ActiveWindow" is the object that has the Display properties you want to control. However, DisplayFormulaBar and DisplayStatusBar are *not* properties of the active window, but of the application object. Each group of property "settings," therefore, is bracketed by **With** and **End With** statements that identify the objects whose properties are being changed.

An Auto_Close procedure (at the very end of the complete macro listing) has the opposite effect: it redisplays the Excel screen objects by setting the display properties to True.

Customizing the Excel Interface

Using VBA, you can add instructions that apply the custom interface to selected worksheets rather than to all worksheets. This can be useful when you are developing the Excel worksheets; during that phase you will want to use the procedure shown in Listing 14-2. To eliminate the Excel interface within the active window only, use the VBA statement in Listing 14-2 in an Auto_Open subprocedure where the code in Listing 14-1 has been incorporated into a subprocedure named "LimitedMenuActivate." First, though, you have to create the custom caption and menus.

Creating Custom Captions and Menus

To create custom menus for the production monitoring application, follow these steps:

1. Select a module sheet.

2. From the Tools menu, choose Menu Editor. This displays the Menu Editor dialog box, shown below:

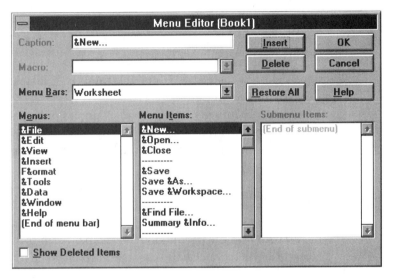

3. Press DEL repeatedly until you have removed all menu items from the Main Menu list.

4. Add new main menu and submenu items by selecting the Menus or Menu Items list (respectively) then choosing Insert, and typing a name in the Caption box.

5. When you are done revising the menu, choose OK.

Once you have created and named a custom menu, you can assign the menu to a particular worksheet using the VBA code in Listing 14-2.

To replace the "Microsoft Excel" caption on the title bar with a more descriptive caption, set the Caption property from within VBA. The second line of code in Listing 14-2 demonstrates this; it sets the caption for the Megachunk application.

The OnActivateSheet and OnDeactivateSheet properties replace Excel's menu with the custom menu when the specified worksheet is opened, then reestablish the standard Excel menu when another sheet is selected.

LISTING 14-2

This procedure creates a custom caption and a custom main menu

```
Sub Auto_Open()
    Application.Caption = "The Megachunk Chocolate Factory"
    ThisWorkbook.Windows(1).Caption = ""
    Secure Environment
    For Each WS in ThisWorkbook.Worksheets
        WS.OnSheetActivate = "LimitedMenuActivate"
    Next
    ThisWorkbook.Modules ("Module1").OnSheetActivate = _
                "RestoreDefaultMenus"
End Sub
```

Once you have performed these steps, the application will essentially be unrecognizable as Excel. Users will think of it instead as the "Megachunk Control Center" program.

By experimenting with the code examples just presented, you can create a blank-slate look for a custom Excel application. Now it's time to show you how to design some of the working screens for the application.

Designing the Main Screen

The top-level, or main, screen is the central observation post from which the user surveys the production landscape. From this screen the production monitoring personnel will scan the horizon for early warnings of trouble ahead.

The construction and operation of the Megachunk Chocolate Factory main screen are quite simple in principle. The screen, as you know from the introduction to the example, consists of an Excel worksheet, sans most of the characteristic visual elements of worksheets. What the user sees is a collection of text boxes and other objects created with Excel's drawing tools.

Each text box is labeled with a department name and sports one of three colors. The color of any individual box is determined by computations in another sheet in the workbook. Macros have been assigned to all the text boxes. Clicking a text box displays the detail screen (another sheet in the workbook) that corresponds to the department represented by the text box.

Applying Colors to Objects to Indicate Possible Trouble

Two VBA macros control the operation of the main screen. One macro updates the colors of the text box objects to reflect the most critical state of the detail sheet. For example, if the object representing one of the production stages on a detail sheet is coded red (the worst case), the macro changes the

LISTING 14-3

This part of the macro highlights trouble spots by displaying "warning" colors

```
Sub UpdateControlCenterColors()
    Dim Dept As TextBox
    For Each Dept In ActiveWorkbook.Worksheets _
        ("Operations Control Center").TextBoxes
        Dept.Interior.Color = GetDeptColor(Dept.Name)
    Next
End Sub
```

color of the related text box object on the main screen to red. If all stages on a particular detail sheet are either green or yellow, and at least one is yellow, the color of the corresponding oval on the main screen will be yellow—the "most critical" color displayed on the Production Line Detail screen. The other main screen macro displays the related detail sheet when a text box on the main screen is clicked.

note *GetDeptColor is a private function. It is shown in Listing 14-5.*

The macro that updates the colors of the text box objects is shown in Listing 14-3.

Declaring Constants and Variables

Const statements in the first three lines of code (shown in Listing 14-4) use constants to define color numbers. This technique makes it possible to refer to the colors by intuitive names (WARNGREEN, WARNYELLOW, and WARNRED) in other parts of the macro, making the code more readable.

These **Const** statements must come before any SUB procedures or the macro will not recognize the global constants.

The SUB procedure UpdateControlCenterColors uses a simple *dimension statement* to define an object and a loop that processes each text box on the worksheet. The **Dimension** statement (Dim) declares a variable that is a

LISTING 14-4

These statements define the colors for normal and abnormal situations

```
Global Const WARNGREEN As Long = 32768    'results of RGB(0,128,0)
Global Const WARNYELLOW As Long = 65535   'results of RGB(255,255,0)
Global Const WARNRED As Long = 255        'results of RGB(255,0,0)
```

specific object type in Excel. Declaring the variable **Dept** in this manner tells Excel that when your code uses that term, it is referring to a text box. This enhances the efficiency of the code as it executes. It also provides a small amount of quality control; if you inadvertently try to use a method on a **Dept** that is not appropriate for a text box, the VBA module will generate an error message.

Using "For Each" Statements to Process Object "Collections"

Also notable in this code excerpt is the **For Each** statement referencing each text box object in the Textboxes collection. A *collection* is a group of objects that are related sibling-style, such as all the worksheets in an Excel workbook. A collection is itself an object that can be manipulated.

For Each statements are an essential tool in automating operations in VBA. Use this statement when you want your macro to reference each item in a collection. In this case, the collection consists of all the "Dept" variables (previously declared to be text boxes) in the active workbook.

For each text box in the workbook, the Dept.Interior.Color statement sets the Interior.Color property. However, instead of setting the color to a constant, this statement calls a separate function, GetDeptColor, to calculate and return the color.

The function uses a clever trick to apply the color of the object on the detail sheet to the corresponding text box on the main screen. The argument to the GetDeptColor function (Dept.Name) is the Name property of the Textbox object. For this technique to work, you must assign identical names to each matched pair of text boxes and production line detail sheets. That is, each text box on the main screen must have the same name as the worksheet tab of its corresponding detail sheet. This trick not only allows us to easily access the underlying detail sheet, it also is used in the macro that makes the detail sheet active.

Determining the Correct Color for an Object

Next you need to create the code for the GetDeptColor function. Essentially, this function examines the color of each of the oval graphical objects on the detail sheet and determines the most "critical" color on the sheet. (Remember, we are assuming that Access "uploads" the production data to Excel at frequent intervals. Excel computes the oval colors from this data; you'll see how in a few minutes.)

WARNRED is the most critical color; that is, it signifies the highest priority for corrective action. WARNYELLOW is next most critical. WARNGREEN, the default value, indicates no action is required.

The code for the GetDeptColor function is shown in Listing 14-5.

A **For...Next** loop controls the examination of the object colors. The **For Each** statement causes the macro to determine the color of an oval and then set the value of the MostCriticalColor variable according what it finds. Then it moves to the "Next" oval and performs the procedure again.

Once the macro has computed the color of each oval object on the sheet, the macro then examines these colors. When the macro first encounters an oval object with the color WARNYELLOW, the MostCriticalColor variable is set to the value of that constant. The macro then continues to examine the remaining ovals in the collection. If any Oval object is found to be WARNRED, the most critical condition, the MostCriticalColor variable is set to WARNRED and processing of the Ovals collection stops. (This is accomplished with the "Exit For" statement.) There is no need to examine any more objects because the most critical condition has already been found.

The function then returns the appropriate color value—the most "critical" color found in the collection. That color value is applied by the macro (by the code sample shown in Listing 14-3) to the appropriate object on the top-level screen.

Displaying More Detail

The final VBA procedure controlling the operation of the main screen activates the appropriate detail screen when the Textbox "button" is clicked. The code in Listing 14-6 can be used with any of the buttons. The trick to getting it to work with any button is to use the Application.Caller method to determine the object name of the Textbox object "button." As mentioned earlier, each text box on the main screen is named the same as the worksheet tab of the underlying detail sheet.

LISTING 14-5

This function determines the appropriate color to display

```
Private Function GetDeptColor(DeptName As String) As Long
    Dim MostCriticalColor As Long, WarningOval as Oval
    MostCriticalColor = WARNGREEN
    For Each WarningOval In Worksheets(DeptName).Ovals
        Select Case WarningOval.Interior.Color
            Case WARNRED
                MostCriticalColor = WARNRED
                Exit For
            Case WARNYELLOW
                MostCriticalColor = WARNYELLOW
        End Select
    Next
    GetDeptColor = MostCriticalColor
End Function
```

LISTING 14-6

This procedure displays a particular sheet based on which button is clicked

```
Sub GoToSheet()
    ActiveWorkbook.Worksheets(Application.Caller).Activate
End Sub
```

Creating a Production Line Detail Screen

Each of the five departments on the main screen is associated with a Production Line Detail screen. The screen is a worksheet you create in Excel, but its purpose is not to calculate numerical results. Instead, it provides a "quick read" of how a particular production line is performing. The data in this worksheet consists primarily of graphic objects. You can attach VBA code to graphic objects in Excel, so that clicking the object carries out the associated code. You'll learn to do this at the end of this chapter; first, though, you will create the graphical objects for the wrapping stage of the production line. Then you will create VBA code that will display a supplementary worksheet when you click the associated object.

Creating the Detail Worksheet

Each graphical object you see on the Production Line Detail screen (that is shown in Figure 14-2) is actually a group of three objects. To create this type of object, you would follow these steps:

1. Create or obtain graphic objects that visually represent each of the production stages on the detail screen. (You could use any drawing program, or the Microsoft ClipArt gallery, to create these graphic objects. See Chapter 7 for more details on using graphics.)

2. Open the production monitoring workbook and display Excel's Drawing toolbar.

3. Display a blank worksheet.

4. Draw an oval on sheet. (The purpose of the oval is to display the appropriate warning color.)

5. Insert the appropriate graphic objects that stage on top of the oval. Using graphics facilitates quick identification of each of the production stages by the user.

6. Under the pictorial graphic, insert a text box and enter a label for the production stage.

7. Group the bitmap and text box together by clicking the arrow button in the Drawing toolbar and drawing a rectangle that surrounds the two objects, as shown below:

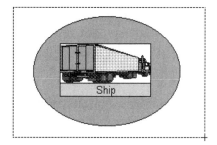

8. Repeat steps 4 through 7 above for each of the production stages in the department.

Creating the Production Line Detail worksheets does not require macros. However, as you saw earlier, you need macro code to control the color of the oval-graphic objects (called "oval objects" hereinafter) by setting the Ovals Interior.Color property to a defined color value. You also need a VBA routine to help the user navigate to the detail screen associated with any oval object that is colored red or yellow.

Updating the Color Indicators

Each of the oval objects representing production processes is associated with a second-level detail screen (referred to hereinafter as the "supplementary screen") containing production statistics. The VBA code for updating the color of the oval objects needs to address two major questions:

- At what point is the color updated; that is, what is the "triggering" event?
- How are the colors determined from the incoming data?

The trigger that causes the Excel data to be updated could be one of many events. Depending on how time-critical the data is, you could have the macro update the color indicators whenever new data is received, at predetermined intervals of time, or only when the user clicks a button or performs some other action. This example updates the color indicators every five minutes by means of the OnTime Method of Excel's Application object.

For Production Line 3, the supplementary worksheet includes a pivot table and a chart. The production statistics from the Access database flow into the pivot table. The data then flows through the supplementary sheet to the Production Line Detail screen. Finally, the macro will update the colors on the main screen.

The flows of data within the Excel workbook are driven by macros. First, let's take a look at the routine that updates the colors. To update all screens in the monitoring application, the macro must do all of the following:

1. Update the pivot table in the supplementary sheet, which will automatically update the linked chart.

2. Calculate the proper color for the oval object associated with the supplementary sheet.

3. Apply the calculated color to the oval object.

note *Since the updating of color indicators is something that is done for each of the production departments represented on the main screen, the preceding steps would normally be part of a comprehensive macro procedure that updates all the items on the main screen. For simplicity's sake, however, the VBA code examples will apply specifically to Production Line 3.*

Calculating the Color in a Pivot Table

The first step in updating the production monitoring main screen is to update a pivot table on the wrapping stage supplementary screen (Figure 14-3). To cause a pivot table in a supplementary sheet to query the Access database, enter the statement in Listing 14-7.

LISTING 14-7
This procedure updates the figures in Excel

```
Sub

Worksheets("sheet_name").PivotTables("pivot_table_name").RefreshTable

End Sub
```

LISTING 14-8

This procedure calls the function that calculates the appropriate color

```
Sub
    Worksheets("Production Line 3").DrawingObjects("WarnWrap"). _
       Interior.Color = CalcPLine3Color()
    Warnings(9).WarnColor = Worksheets("Production Line 3"). _
            DrawingObjects("WarnWrap").Interior.Color
End Sub
```

tip *Pivot tables can be created on the basis of other pivot tables. When you create a pivot table based on another pivot table, the two tables share the same data. This not only reduces file size, but also saves time. Running the RefreshTable Method once for any of the pivot tables refreshes all pivot tables sharing the data.*

After the pivot table has been updated, you want the macro to recompute the appropriate color for the related oval object. To apply the appropriate warning color to the oval object, insert the code in Listing 14-8 after the statement that refreshes the pivot table.

The code in Listing 14-8 calls a user-defined function, CalcPLine3Color(), to determine the color. The function compares the maximum value in the series values array for selected series on the reject chart.

The user-defined function contains several key elements. First, appropriate variables are declared and object variables are set, as shown in Listing 14-9.

Declaring the object variables essentially creates alternative names for the objects in the active sheet, making it easier to refer to them in the macro. (It also makes the code run faster.) The Chart Object "ChtPL3," for instance, is now set to reference the Reject chart.

Comparing the Result to the Standard

The chart in the supplementary sheet incorporates the production standards discussed earlier. The monitoring application compares the actual results to predetermined Normal and Minimum Acceptable levels to determine whether a warning color is warranted. Listing 14-10 shows the code

LISTING 14-9

Statements that declare objects and variables for a function

```
Function CalcPLine3Color() As Long
Dim ChtPL3 As Chart, MostCriticalColor As Long
Dim MaxOK As Single, MaxCaution As Single
    Dim MostCriticalColor As Long
Set ChtPL3 = Worksheets("RejectChart").ChartObjects _
        ("RejectChart"). Chart
```

LISTING 14-10

The part of the function that determines the correct color

```
        MaxOK = Application.Max(ChtPL3.SeriesCollection("MaxOK").Values)
        MaxCaution = Application.Max(ChtPL3.SeriesCollection _
            ("MaxCaution").Values)
        Select Case Application.Max(ChtPL3.SeriesCollection _
            ("RejectRate").Values)
        Case Is > MaxCaution
            CalcPLine3Color = WARNRED
        Case Is > MaxOK
            CalcPLine3Color = WARNYELLOW
        Case Else
            CalcPLine3Color = WARNGREEN
        End Select
    End Function
```

for the function. In this part of the macro, variables are set, using the Excel MAX function, to determine the maximum value of the values that plot the OK and Caution series on the chart. These values are then compared with the maximum value in the Reject Rate series. The procedure then computes the appropriate color.

This is a simple but powerful example of using the built-in functionality of Excel to update the Production Line 3 Detail screen. The only remaining VBA code we need for the detail screen is the code to navigate further down to the supplementary screen for the wrapping stage. To navigate to this sheet, you can use the same approach as used in the GoToSheet() subroutine in Listing 14-6.

Attaching VBA Code to Graphic Objects

To each of the graphics representing a production step, you have to attach the related VBA code. Then, when the user clicks the object (that is, within the outline of the oval), the associated code will run.

Follow these steps to transform a graphic object into a macro button:

1. Select (click) the graphic object. (Note that if a macro has previously been assigned to the object, you must hold down the CTRL key while you click.)

2. From the Tools menu, choose Assign Macro. This brings up the following dialog box:

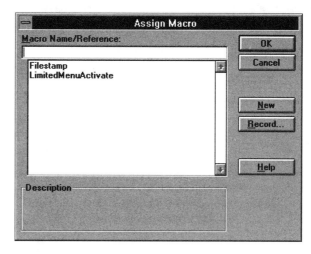

3. From the Macro Name/Reference box, select the macro name, and then choose OK.

If you want to record a new macro instead of using an existing one, choose the Record button in the Assign Macro dialog box, then record the macro.

Creating the Supplementary Screen

Though the example macro applies to only one Production Line Detail screen and the related supplementary screen, you can copy and modify it to create screens for the other departments and production steps in the factory.

Conclusion

This chapter harnessed Excel's Visual Basic programming language to convert database information into a display that anyone can use. Not included, of course, was code for using Access to manage the flow of production data into the system. In the final chapter of the book, you will see how smoothly Access can integrate with Excel and Word.

First, though, the next chapter will cover some complex and troublesome topics not previously addressed in the book.

CHAPTER 15

Advanced Topics and Troubleshooting

THE OLE 2 coverage in Section I gave you an overall understanding of the subject and prepared you for the business-oriented examples presented later. Now, it's time to examine other aspects of OLE, such as nesting and packaging objects, that were not touched on earlier. These topics are covered in the first part of this chapter.

You have also probably discovered that things occasionally go awry in the world of linking and embedding. The second part of this chapter is a compilation of ways to avoid trouble and techniques to recover from errors, bugs, and other gremlins that can creep into your work with Office.

Nesting Objects

Until now, you've worked mostly with examples wherein one object is linked or embedded into a client application. You are not limited, however, to linking or embedding an object into an application. You can link or embed an object within another object, and then link or embed the latter object somewhere else. OLE clients can *nest* objects within objects.

This means you can create compound documents like the one shown in Figure 15-1. OLE 2 does not impose any theoretical limit to the number of nesting levels a document can contain. However, if you are running version 3.1 of Windows or any version of Windows for Workgroups, a lack of system resources will stop you before you create more than a few levels.

Another reason for not arbitrarily daisy-chaining object and documents together is the difficulty of keeping track of source documents. OLE 2 does not provide any way to trace from source documents to destination documents, making it difficult to determine whether you can safely remove a file from your hard disk. Accordingly, it's best to avoid overindulgence in object nesting.

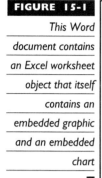

FIGURE 15-1

This Word document contains an Excel worksheet object that itself contains an embedded graphic and an embedded chart

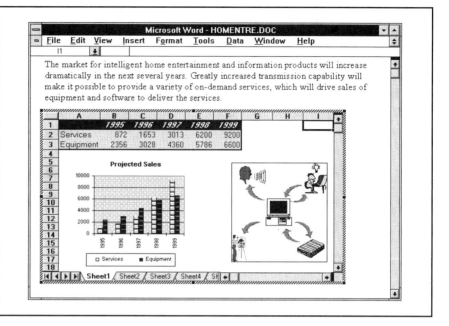

Packaging Objects

OLE 2 allows you to embed *packages*. Packages are very eclectic entities, not easy to describe comprehensively. In one sense, a package is a way of disguising non-OLE objects so that OLE can be fooled into sharing them with other applications. In another sense, packages are a bit like window dressing—they are decorative containers.

Why Would You Package Objects?

In many ways, packaging a single object is similar to linking or embedding an object as an icon, which you learned about in Chapter 4. Packages, however, have several unique features that are useful in certain situations. The following paragraphs summarize the benefits of using packages.

REDUCING DEMANDS ON THE NETWORK   Including packaged linked objects in Mail messages is much kinder to your network resources than attaching files to messages. A linked object contained in a package contains only a reference to a file.

PACKAGING DOS COMMANDS   You can package DOS commands and batch files. The recipient can execute a file by activating the packaged object.

PACKAGING NON-OLE ITEMS You can package such items as text files and data files created by non-Windows applications such as 1-2-3 for DOS, without first having to convert them in Word, Excel, or Access.

CREATING CUSTOM ICONS OR CUSTOM LABELS With the Object Packager application, which you'll learn about in a moment, you can select different icons—even design your own—for packages. You can also apply longer, more descriptive labels to packages than when you link or embed an object as an icon.

PACKAGING FILES WITHOUT STARTING THE SERVER APPLICATION You can package a file by simply dragging or copying the file from the Windows File Manager.

Understanding the Object Packager

Packages are created by a program called the Object Packager, included in Windows 3.1 and higher. Sometimes the Object Packager works entirely in the background, so you don't necessarily see it on screen when you package an object. Often, though, the Object Packager appears as a result of your choosing an Insert Object command. You'll see an example in a little while.

Packaging Documents

The simplest way to package an object is to package an entire file using the Windows File Manager. This helps when you are in a hurry; you don't have to take the time to start up the server application and open the file.

Inserting a Packaged Document into a Mail Message

Packaging is especially convenient when you want to attach a file to a Mail message. Follow these steps:

1. In the Windows File Manager, select the file you want to link or embed in the Mail message.

2. Choose File, then Copy.

3. In the Copy dialog box, select the Copy to Clipboard option, and then choose OK. (Don't enter anything in the To box.)

4. Activate Mail and open the message to which you want to attach the document.

5. Choose Edit, then Paste Special. This displays the following dialog box:

[Paste Special dialog box]

6. Select Packaged Link, and then choose OK.

This embeds a package containing a link to the source file.

The preceding example contained not one but *two* new techniques. First, it demonstrated how to embed or link files from the File Manager. Second, it showed you how to attach a link (rather than a file or partial file) to a Mail message. Selecting the Packaged Link does not embed or attach the file to the message. Instead of attaching a large file to a message, consider packaging a link instead. This will save file space and, usually, reduce network traffic. Remember, though, the source file must reside on a shared directory to which all recipients have access.

When you paste from the Object Packager, the Attached File option attaches the file, just as if you had used the Attach button in the Send Note window. Selecting Packaged Object embeds a packaged file, which is essentially the same as an attached file, except that you can change the icon or label of the package.

Packaging Files in Word, Excel, PowerPoint, and Access

Word, Excel, PowerPoint, and Access won't let you paste files from the Clipboard as you can in Mail. Consequently, packaging files into documents other than Mail messages is a bit different.

To paste a file from File Manager to Word, Excel, PowerPoint, or Access, follow these steps:

1. In the Windows File Manager, select the file you want to link or embed.

2. Choose File, then Copy.

3. In the Copy dialog box, select the Copy to Clipboard option, and then choose OK. (Don't enter anything in the To box.)

4. Activate the client application and open the file in which you want to package the file.

5. Choose Insert, then Object.

6. In the Object dialog box, select Package and choose OK. This displays the Object Packager (shown next).

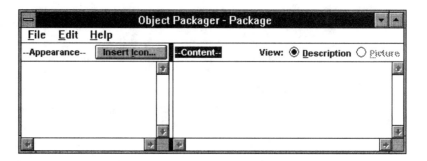

7. Choose Edit, then Paste.

8. Choose File, then Exit.

9. Choose Yes to confirm that you want to update the destination document.

Object Packager inserts the packaged document as an icon.

Packaging Part of a Document

Let's say that instead of packaging an entire file, you want to package a range in an Excel worksheet. Follow these steps to package the range:

1. In Excel, copy the range you want to package.

2. Activate Word and open the destination document.

3. Choose Insert, then Object.

4. In the Object dialog box, select Package and choose OK.

5. In the Object Packager dialog box, change the icon or label as desired.

6. Choose Edit, then Copy Package.

7. Choose File, then Exit.

8. Choose Yes to confirm you want to update the Word document.

Inserting a Packaged Object

You don't have to copy objects in order to package them. You can insert a package by choosing Insert, then Object (or Edit, then Insert Object), and then selecting Package in the Insert Object dialog box. You'll see this sequence of steps in the next example.

Packaging a DOS Program File in a Mail Message

To package a DOS command or program file (ending with an EXE or a COM extension) in a Mail message, follow these steps:

1. In Mail, choose Edit, then Insert Object. This displays the Insert Object dialog box.

2. In the Object Type list, select Package. This starts the Object Packager.

3. In the Object Packager dialog box, choose Edit, then Command Line.

4. In the Command box, type the path, and filename of the file you want to package and choose OK.

5. Choose the Insert Icon button in the Appearance window. This displays the following dialog box:

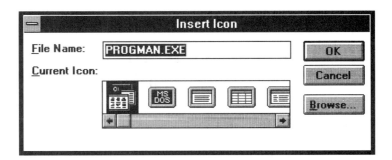

6. Choose OK. (Alternatively, you can select a different icon for the object. You'll learn how to do this in a moment.)

7. Choose Edit, then Label.

8. In the Label box, type a label for the icon, and choose OK.

9. Choose File, then Exit. Confirm that you want to update the Mail message.

Selecting Your Own Icons

Having the flexibility to assign alternative icons and custom labels to packaged icons allows you to say more about the contents than with an ordinary iconized object. The following steps illustrate how you would select a different icon when packaging an Excel document:

1. Copy or insert an Excel object into the content window of the Object Packager.

2. Choose the Insert Icon button.

3. Select the icon you want, and choose OK.

Figure 15-2 shows how you might use alternative icons along with labels to clarify what's contained in a document with several packaged objects.

tip *You can create an icon of your own design by creating it in Paintbrush (or another drawing program) and copying it to the Appearance window of the Object Packager.*

Editing an Existing Package

To modify a package (for instance, to change the icon or label), follow these steps:

1. Choose Edit, then Package Object.

2. From the submenu that appears, choose Edit Package. This starts the Object Packager.

3. In the Object Packager, change the icon or label as desired.

Restoring a Corrupted REG.DAT File

In the first part of Chapter 2, you learned that OLE 2.0 keeps track of objects that might potentially be created by installed applications. It does this by maintaining a list of such applications, and the types of objects they can create, in a special registration file named REG.DAT. OLE-compliant applications (regardless of which version of OLE they support) automatically register their objects upon installation.

FIGURE 15-2

Custom icons and labels advise the reader what to expect after opening the packaged objects

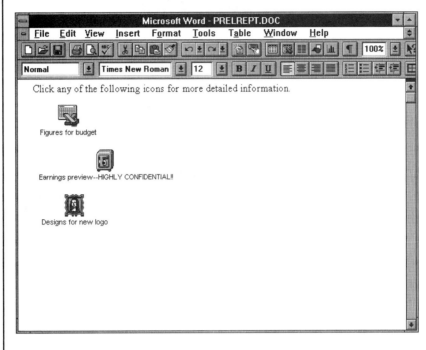

REG.DAT is also the repository of the Windows *file associations*. File associations are like cross-references between application programs and the corresponding three-letter DOS filename extensions of their data files. To illustrate this: because the Windows setup program creates an association between Paintbrush and the PCX extension, double-clicking a PCX file in the File Manager will open the file in Paintbrush.

You usually don't have to pay any attention to REG.DAT, because it works behind the scenes. It is possible, however, for the REG.DAT file (like any file) to become corrupted if there is an abnormal exit from Windows or a cutoff of electrical power to your PC. A corrupted REG.DAT file will disable some or all of OLE's data-sharing capability. One possible consequence is that the Paste or Paste Link options in the Paste Special dialog box might become unavailable. You might also receive one of the following error messages when you try to link or embed:

There is no application associated with this file. Choose Associate from the file menu to create an association.

There is a problem with REG.DAT. Delete REG.DAT and restart Windows.

When you see either of these messages, suspect a corrupted REG.DAT. To remedy the problem, you must rebuild the damaged file.

Rebuilding REG.DAT for the Applications

To rebuild REG.DAT for applications, you must disable your existing REG.DAT and allow Windows to rebuild it from scratch. Follow these steps to clear the way for Windows to rebuild REG.DAT:

1. Open the WIN.INI file in Word or another text-editing application such as Windows Write or Notepad.

2. Make sure that all the paths entered in the [embedding] section in WIN.INI are entered correctly. Make corrections as needed.

3. Remove all program icons from the Startup group. This ensures that no OLE-capable applications will start automatically when you start Windows next. (Alternatively, you could rename the file STARTUP.GRP on the Windows directory. Later, you can name the file STARTUP.GRP again to "recover" your original startup group.

4. Exit Windows.

5. In MS-DOS, rename REG.DAT. (This is a precaution. If something goes wrong, or if a corrupted REG.DAT turns out not to have been the problem, you can name the file REG.DAT again and use it.)

Now start Windows again. Follow these steps to rebuild the registration database information on your installed OLE-capable applications:

1. Start the File Manager.

2. Choose File, then Search.

3. In the Search For box, type *.reg. The results will be listed in a dialog box similar to this one:

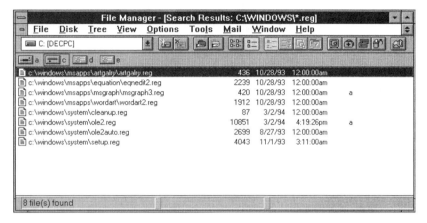

4. Select one of the listed files.

5. Choose File, then Associate.

6. From the Associate With list, select REGEDIT.EXE, and then choose OK.

7. In the File Manager, double-click the OLE2.REG, SETUP.REG, and WORDART2.REG files. (After each file, click OK to acknowledge the confirmation message.)

8. Double-click all other registration files in the File Manager window. This procedure re-registers all your OLE server applications.

note *REG.DAT is not rebuilt when you reinstall Windows, so you don't have to worry about wiping it out when you upgrade to the next version of Windows.*

Restoring REG.DAT to the Default Setup

Microsoft's Knowledge Base contains an article (Q80393) on restoring REG.DAT to the default Windows setup parameters using the REGEDIT program. The procedure outlined in the article, however, affects only the OLE embedding applications included with Windows. Consequently, use the procedure outlined in the preceding example, which rebuilds REG.DAT from scratch.

Troubleshooting Common OLE Problems

The Microsoft Office suite makes your life simpler by integrating the applications into a unified product. However, there is no such thing as 100% OLE 2 functionality in any application program today. Occasionally, you will encounter some unconventional implementations of OLE 2 in particular application programs, sometimes yielding unexpected results.

Chapters 3 and 4 pointed out some quirks in the implementation of OLE links between Excel and Word. Fortunately, they don't usually show themselves except under fairly unusual circumstances. This section discusses some of the more common trouble spots.

Losing the Formatting of Linked Excel Objects

When you copy data from version 5 of Excel and link or embed it into a Word document as formatted text, formatting attributes such as fonts, text alignment, and borders are copied along with the returned values in the cells. However, if you have linked the Excel data, only the data—not the formatting—will update when the source data changes.

That is because the LINK field created when you paste-link an Excel range into Word contains the * MERGEFORMAT switch by default. That is often desirable; it allows you to completely control formatting in Word, as pointed out in Chapter 12.

At times, this feature might cause you some consternation, however. For instance, you might be working with the worksheet in Excel and decide to right-align the text in certain cells. When you update the link in Excel, you might be surprised that the change in alignment does not carry through to the Word document.

If you decide you want to control the formatting of linked Excel objects from Excel rather than Word, press ALT+F9 to display field codes, and then delete the * MERGEFORMAT switch LINK from the field code. Then, when the LINK field is updated, changes in both data and formatting will flow through to the linked object.

Linking the Same Item More Than Once

When you link the same Excel object to the same Word document more than once, all the instances of the linked object might not appear to update correctly in some circumstances. This happens when part of the Word document, including a second (or later) instance of a linked Excel object, is visible at the time you make a change in the source Excel document that affects the linked cell(s). In these circumstances, the second instance of the linked object in the Word document might not immediately update to reflect the change in the source. This can happen even when the link is set to automatic updating. The problem does not occur consistently, but it can be disconcerting when it does.

Fortunately, the problem is only one of appearance. When you activate the Word document, all instances of the linked object will update correctly on the screen.

Making Corrections When Excel Feeds "Incorrect" Data to Word

There are few things more disturbing than having a colleague or superior come to you with a frantic look and claiming that you provided wrong figures. However, as was pointed out in Chapter 4, it is possible for a cell in an Excel source file to change and for a Word document linked to that cell to reflect old information and still give every indication that the information is current. This can happen even if the Word document contains an automatic-update link to the Excel document. The following circumstances can cause this unhappy result:

- While the source and destination files are closed, the source file, but not the destination file, is moved to a different subdirectory, renamed, or removed from the hard disk.

- The source file is subsequently reopened and changed.

Even though you try to keep your OLE links intact by scrupulously avoiding moving source files, it's easy to lose track of which documents are sources. Source files are not marked by any special indicators in the File Manager window. Furthermore, you can't always prevent other users from unknowingly moving or deleting your source files.

Unfortunately, Word does not advise you when you have opened a document containing an "orphaned" link. The link, in fact, will behave normally even when you update it by selecting the link and pressing F9. Only by displaying the Links dialog box can you determine for sure if a link is still intact. (You'll learn how in a moment.)

Consider adopting some basic quality assurance procedures to protect yourself against the dangers of unknown broken links. For instance, you might store vitally important source documents in a special directory. Saving them on your local hard disk, if possible, is the safest move.

Another effective security measure is to examine all LINK fields in all important documents containing links before submitting the documents to management. To find and test links, follow these steps while the Word document is open:

1. Press ALT+F9 to display field codes.
2. Choose Edit, then Find.
3. In the Find What box, type **LINK** (all caps).
4. Select the Match Case option, and choose OK.
5. For each LINK field you find, press F9, and choose Edit, then Links. If the Open Source button is dimmed, the link is broken and must be re-established.

Speeding Up File Saves

One drawback to OLE 2 is that OLE 2-capable applications, including those in the Microsoft Office suite, save files very slowly to a floppy disk. This is because of OLE 2's new, more complex, file storage technology. The new format, called DocFile, saves objects in "data streams" that are separate from the data created by the client application.

If you frequently save files to floppy disks, you might want to speed up the process. You can use Microsoft's SMARTDrive disk-caching utility to save files to floppy disks up to five times faster. Use one of the techniques described next (depending on what version of MS-DOS is installed on your computer) to create a disk cache on your floppy drive:

- If you use version 6.0 or higher of MS-DOS, add the following command to your AUTOEXEC.BAT file:

```
C:\DOS\SMARTDRV.EXE a+ nnnn
```

where *nnnn* is the cache size (between 256 and 2048 bytes).

- If you use version 5.0 or lower of MS-DOS, add the following command to your AUTOEXEC.BAT file:

```
DEVICE=C:\DOS\SMARTDRV.EXE a+ nnnn
```

where *nnnn* is the cache size.

In the next chapter you'll learn how to use OLE automation to create solutions that integrate multiple applications. You have now learned everything this book has to teach you about OLE proper.

CHAPTER 16

Creating Solutions with Visual Basic for Applications and OLE Automation

By now, no one has to sell you on the collective power of the Office applications. The one element of Office we have not covered, however, is its facility for automating operations that involve multiple applications. OLE Automation is the OLE 2.0 feature that allows users to use one application's macro language to program objects in another application.

There are few limits to what you can do with OLE Automation and an individual application's macro language. That is, if you can do something in the application's native macro language, you can usually do it from another application with OLE Automation. (One major exception is Access, which cannot be controlled by other applications.) You can also automate operations within certain applets, such as Microsoft Graph 5.0. In effect, you can control one application by using the macro language of another application, creating a program that uses the best features of two (or more) applications.

Integrating features in this way greatly enhances the power of the individual components of the Office suite. Using OLE Automation, you could automate the creation of daily reports in Word containing data tables or charts created in Excel. You could create a custom application that summarizes data in Excel on the basis of choices a user makes from an Access form. There are numerous other examples of how OLE Automation can automate your work.

OLE Automation is complex, however; before you can use it to full advantage, you must learn some basic principles. In this chapter, you will learn:

- What an "object model" is and why it is vital to mastering OLE Automation

- How OLE Automation's terminology and syntax differs from Visual Basic for Applications

- Some practical examples of using OLE Automation

Getting Started with OLE Automation

OLE Automation per se is relatively easy to use. The technical challenge lies primarily in mastering the macro language in the *underlying* application. OLE Automation is not a separate and distinct macro language. Rather, it's an umbrella term for a number of programming techniques. These techniques are implemented, in a consistent manner, within the native macro language of the OLE Automation *controller* application.

Understanding Controllers and Objects

Every OLE Automation session involves a *controller* and an *object*. The controller is the application that uses OLE Automation techniques to take control of another application. The controller creates an object in its own macro language that references, as an object, a second application. The application being "controlled" in this manner is known as the OLE Automation *object*. The OLE Automation controller sends commands that the object application executes as if those commands originated in the latter's own macro language.

The following table indicates which applications in Microsoft Office 4.2 can be OLE Automation controllers and objects. Since the Visual Basic language (version 3.0 or higher) and Microsoft Project now support OLE Automation, they are also included in the table. PowerPoint and Mail, since they do not have their own macro languages, cannot be controllers or objects.

OLE Automation Controllers	OLE Automation Objects
Excel 5.0	Excel 5.0
Access 2.0	Word 6.0
Visual Basic version 3.0 or higher	Project 4.0
Project 4.0	

OLE Automation is a major milestone in Microsoft's goal of creating a universal macro language for all its application programs. As you learned in Chapter 7, this language, called Visual Basic, Applications Edition (or VBA), was first introduced in Excel 5.0. A short time later, VBA was added to Microsoft Project.

Even though Excel 5.0 is the only program in Office 4.3 that features VBA and fully supports OLE Automation, you can still use OLE Automation within Microsoft Office. Access and Word have partially implemented the OLE Automation concept even though they don't have VBA. OLE Automation controllers (Excel, Access, Project, and Visual Basic 3.0 and higher) can control Word 6.0 as an OLE Automation object. Access Basic, the programming language built into Access 2.0, can manipulate Excel, Word, and Project objects.

Understanding Object Models

There are three distinct ways to implement OLE Automation:

- Using one standalone application to control another standalone application—Access controlling Excel, for instance.

- Using one application to control another application, with the latter application embedded in the controller application—for instance, an Excel worksheet or chart object embedded into an Access form.

- Programmatically manipulating *OLE custom controls*, which are self-contained program objects that work in conjunction with standalone applications. Currently, OLE custom controls (commonly referred to as OCXs) can be used only with Access 2.0.

Later in this chapter you will see examples of each of these variants.

One thing all three styles of OLE Automation have in common is the use of the macro language belonging to the controller to manipulate another application using the object application's *object model*. An object model is the collection of objects available in an application *and* the relationships between those objects. To become proficient in using OLE Automation, it is very important that you understand the object model of the OLE Automation object application.

If you want to become a doctor, you must attend medical school. As part of your early training, you will take a basic course that teaches you human anatomy—knowledge that is absolutely necessary if you are to learn how to treat illness and injuries. In the same way, if you want to automate operations that involve more than one application, you must learn how the "parts" of an application fit and function together.

A Simple Example

The OLE Automation example in Listing 16-1 will demonstrate how the object model permeates all parts of a Visual Basic procedure. The following code, when entered into a module in Access Basic, VBA, or Visual Basic version 3.0 or higher, will start Excel, place the words "Hello World" in cell B2, save the file, and quit Excel.

LISTING 16-1

A simple macro that starts Excel, enters data, and then quits

```
Sub HelloWorldFile ()
    Dim XL As Object
    Set XL = CreateObject("excel.application")
    XL.visible = True
    XL.workbooks.add
    XL.range("B2").formularlc1 = "Hello World"
    XL.activeworkbook.saveas "c:\hellowor.xls", 33, , , True
    XL.[Quit]
    Set XL = Nothing
End Sub
```

The first line,

```
Dim XL As Object,
```

uses VBA's Dimension statement to declare a variable to be of a particular type. In the previous chapter, you learned that defining a dimension for a variable safeguards against errors and improves processing speed. In many cases, a Dimension statement is optional; it is, however, mandatory in this case. OLE Automation objects must be declared as the type "Object."

Creating an Excel Object

The second line of the macro,

```
Set XL = CreateObject("excel.application"),
```

is used to create a variable that refers to the object program. (This chapter will use the term "setting an object" to refer to this procedure.) Setting an object in this manner is similar to naming a range in Excel. Using the (usually shorter) variable name makes your code more understandable.

The CreateObject function creates an Excel Application object. This means that subsequently (within the procedure) the variable "XL" will mean the Excel application in its role as an OLE application object. In this scenario, the application in whose macro language this statement appears—and that can be Access, Visual Basic, or Project—is the controller; Excel is the object.

The CreateObject function must be used in conjunction with the Set statement. (The Set statement explicitly tells the program that, instead of assigning the variable a value, you are instead filling the variable with a reference to another object.) Using the CreateObject function without the Set statement will generate an error.

To understand what the macro does, you need to understand what comprises the Excel application object. Figure 16-1 is a graphical representation of the Excel Object Model. As illustrated in the figure, the Application object is the *top-level* object in Excel. That is, the application sits atop the object hierarchy, subsuming all the other Excel objects.

An object at a given level "owns" (in a matter of speaking) the lower-level objects connected to it. Excel *exposes* three objects to OLE Automation; that is, it makes these objects available to programmatic control by external application programs. Every object exposed by an application has a specific *programmatic ID*—a name that is used in the code to refer to the object. (More precisely, a programmatic ID is a string identifier associated with a particular exposed object that is registered in the OLE registration database.) By including a Set statement with a CreateObject function as in the preceding example, in a macro, you make it possible to create an instance of any of the objects listed in Table 16-1.

Manipulating the Excel Object

Now that you know how to create an Excel object, you need to know a few of the ground rules for navigating around the object model using OLE Automation. All the statements in Listing 16-1 following the Set statement

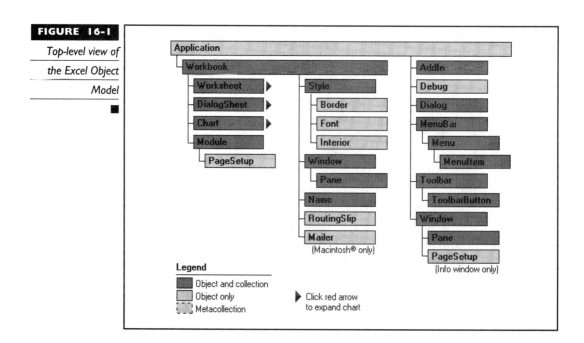

FIGURE 16-1

Top-level view of the Excel Object Model

OLE Automation Object	Programmatic ID
Excel Application	excel.application
Excel Worksheet	excel.sheet
Excel Chart	excel.chart
Word Basic	word.basic
MSProject Application	msproject.application
MSProject Project	msproject.project

TABLE 16-1 *OLE Automation Objects and Their Programmatic IDs* ■

begin with "XL," indicating that they manipulate the Excel object. The part of the statements following the "XL" are Excel VBA commands.

The next statement,

```
XL.visible = True,
```

sets the **visible** property of the application object to True (that is, it displays Excel). By default, an Excel application object you create is not visible. (You don't always want an OLE Automation object to be visible; for instance, you might want to use Excel's recalculation engine for financial calculations, but not want Excel to appear on the screen.) The **visible** property is a property of the top-level application object.

How OLE Automation Statements Interact with the Object Model

The statement

```
XL.workbooks.add
```

reaches down past the application into the Object Model. It executes the **add** method on the workbooks collection, which is a method of the application object. The "XL.workbooks" portion of the command references the workbooks object, which is a collection. The **add** method then affects the workbooks object.

The statement

```
XL.range("B2").formular1c1 = "Hello World"
```

sets the **formular1c1** property of a Range object on a worksheet. Since no particular worksheet is specified, the Range method applies, by default, to the active worksheet in Excel. (More precisely, it applies to the **activesheet** property of the application object. The **activesheet** property is a reference to an Excel worksheet object.) The Range itself is an object whose property, `formular1c1`, stores the formula for the Range.

It's instructive to trace this statement through the object model in both Figure 16-1 and Figure 16-2. You will see that the preceding statement extends *four* levels deep into the Object Model. That is the Range Object is three levels down from the top-level Application object.

Especially when creating OLE Automation macros, you must know "where you are" in the Object Model of the application object. To use the medical analogy again, a doctor needs to know all the side effects of a medicine before prescribing it. If, for instance, a particular allergy medicine has the side effect of increasing blood pressure slightly, no doctor would prescribe that particular drug to someone who has a blood pressure problem.

Another way to illustrate this principle is to draw an analogy between the application object and the root directory of a hard disk. If you move a directory with the Windows File Manager, you also move all the directories and files underneath that directory. In the same way, you need to know the structure of the Object Model in order to anticipate the effects of the statements, methods, and properties in your macro code.

The statement

```
XL.activeworkbook.saveas "c:\hellowor.xls", 33, , , True
```

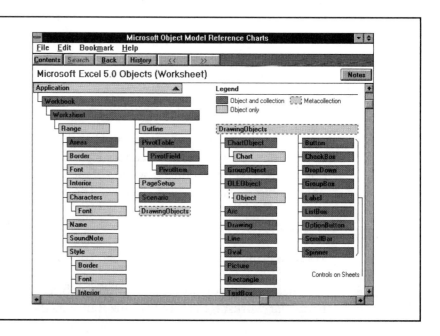

FIGURE 16-2
The Excel Worksheet Object Model

saves the workbook that you are currently operating to a specified filename. **Activeworkbook** is a property of the Excel application object; it returns a reference to the workbook that is currently activated. The **saveas** method, which applies to any workbook object, will save the workbook to the specified filename (in this case, HELLOWOR.XLS) in Excel 4.0 worksheet format. The "True" argument causes the worksheet to be saved with a "read-only recommended" notation.

This statement illustrates how the syntax of VBA OLE Automation commands can differ from that of equivalent native VBA commands. A numeric code (33) used in conjunction with the argument "c:\helloworld.xls" causes the file to be saved as an Excel 4.0 worksheet. In an Excel VBA module, by contrast, the equivalent statement would use the intrinsic constant "xlExcel4." In OLE Automation, any intrinsic constants in the object application must either be defined constants in the controller application or be referenced by value. That means that VBA-named arguments such as "xlExcel4" are not currently supported in OLE Automation. When you use the CreateObject function (or the GetObject function) to initialize the OLE Automation object variable, you must use a comma-separated list of arguments, as illustrated by the preceding statement.

To determine the order in which the arguments must be listed, display the help file for the method you are using in the statement. The sequence for the **saveas** method is shown under the Syntax heading in Figure 16-3.

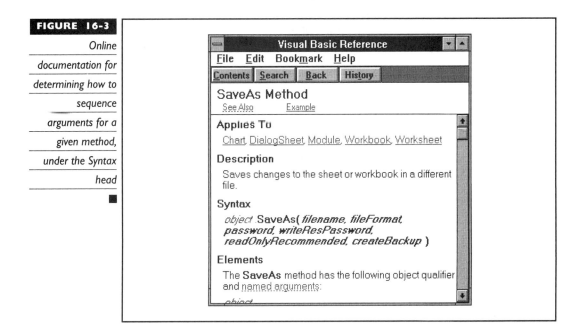

FIGURE 16-3

Online documentation for determining how to sequence arguments for a given method, under the Syntax head

The line

```
XL.[Quit]
```

quits the Excel application and removes it from memory. The Quit method was delimited by square brackets so that it would apply to the Excel application object. If not for the brackets, Access would interpret the statement to be its own Quit method.

Finally,

```
Set XL = Nothing
```

recovers the memory reserved for the XL object variable.

The preceding example macro doesn't do anything earthshaking. However, it does highlight the mental state of "object awareness" you will need to attain if you hope to perform more momentous tasks with OLE Automation. You might already have thought of a dozen ways to apply what you have learned so far, but hold tight a while longer. First you need to know more about how to refer to OLE Automation objects.

Manipulating Objects in OLE Automation

The three styles of OLE Automation you can use with your applications are very similar. In fact, the primary difference is in the way you create the object to reference. This section will teach you how to create an object variable and to reference existing objects in each of the variants of OLE Automation.

Creating and "Getting" Objects

As illustrated in the preceding example, you use a CreateObject function to create an object variable. You can then use that variable name as a sort of nickname for an object that is native to an object application. Generally, you use a related function— GetObject—to create a reference to an existing object. However, it would be an oversimplification to say that CreateObject is for creating new instances of objects, and that GetObject is used for referring to existing objects. A more precise way to put it is shown in the following table:

Function	When Used
CreateObject	When the object application *is* registered with the controller macro language
GetObject	When the object application is *not* registered with the controller macro language

In practice, that means that when you want to create a new instance of Excel, perform an Excel operation, and then close the application, you would use CreateObject. To open a new object (such as a worksheet) within an already running instance of Excel, use the GetObject function.

note *You can always use a direct reference rather than a variable to set an OLE Automation object. You'll see how later in the section "Using Object Libraries in VBA."*

The effects of either the CreateObject or the GetObject functions can vary depending on the condition of the object application and, in some cases, whether you include an optional argument in the function. You must master the syntax of these two functions to achieve the intended result.

Table 16-2 describes the results attained with the CreateObject function when used to create references to the Excel's Application and Sheet objects and a worksheet object under different circumstances.

Table 16-3 shows the results of using the GetObject function to refer to an Excel object under various conditions. The GetObject function takes an optional first argument; entering a set of double quotes (" ") as the value of that argument specifies that a new instance of the object should be created. (Inserting a filename as text between the quotes opens the named file rather than creating a new document.)

Object Created	Status of Object Application	Result
excel.application	(Does not matter)	The XL variable references a newly started instance of Excel. Excel is not visible.
excel.sheet	Running	The XL variable references a newly created worksheet in the running instance of Excel. Object inherits the visible status of the running instance.
excel.sheet	Not running	The XL variable references a newly created worksheet in a newly started instance of Excel. Excel is not visible.

TABLE 16-2 *Results Produced by CreateObject Function in Different Contexts* ■

Object Referred To	Status of Object Application	First Argument (" ") Entered	Result
excel.application	(Does not matter)	Yes	The XL variable references a newly started instance of Excel. Excel is not visible.
excel.application	Running	No	The XL variable references the running instance of Excel. Object inherits the visible status of the running instance.
excel.application	Not running	No	The function returns an error because an Excel application object does not already exist.
excel.sheet	Running	Yes	Creates a new sheet object in the running instance of Excel. Sheet Object is visible.
excel.sheet	Running	No	The function returns an error because, in this case, a filename is mandatory.
excel.sheet	Not running	Yes	The XL variable references a newly started instance of Excel. Excel is not visible.
excel.sheet	Not running	No	The function returns an error because an Excel sheet object does not already exist.

TABLE 16-3 *Results Produced by GetObject Function in Different Contexts* ■

The remarks in the Result column of Tables 16-2 and 16-3 assume you are using a variable named "XL" to refer to an Excel application object.

note *Remember, you can only use the GetObject function in a Set statement.*

Using Object Libraries in VBA

Each of the Microsoft applications that incorporate VBA (currently Excel and Project) include an *object library*. An object library is a file that contains detailed information on the objects, methods, properties, arguments, and constants of the application. An OLE Automation controller can refer to the object application's object library to simplify writing macro code.

If an application has an object library, you can use direct references to initiate OLE Automation sessions. Referring to an object directly makes it unnecessary to create object variables for the application being controlled; no Dimension statements or Set statements are needed. To illustrate how

LISTING 16-2

A procedure that starts Excel

```
Sub ExcelReference()
    Excel.Workbooks.Add
    Excel.Application.Visible = True
End Sub
```

this works, Listing 16-2 shows how you would instruct version 4.0 of Microsoft Project, as the OLE Automation controller, to start Excel and make it visible.

note *Using the same syntax, you can access Project by using the keyword "MSProject" in a VBA macro created in Excel.*

Though you might have little reason to use Project to control Excel, the technique of referring to an object library will become important when VBA is eventually added to all the Office applications. Once this happens, referring to objects in other applications will be standardized and very straightforward. To reference the objects in the Excel application from any VBA-enabled controller application, you need only use the keyword "Excel."

The only requirement is that the controller application have a reference set to the object library of the desired object application. When using Excel as a controller, for instance, you would set a reference by following these steps:

1. Activate a VBA module sheet.

2. Select Tools, References. This displays the following dialog box:

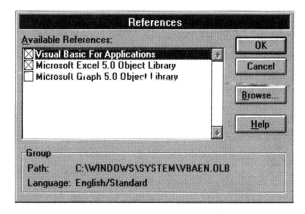

3. Select the object library for the desired application.

The reference is stored with the file containing the VBA module.

note *You can use named arguments (predefined names for objects such as Excel.Range ("C3")) when using direct referencing to create an object from a VBA-enabled object application. Because the named arguments refer directly to the object library, you do not need to enclose common object, property, and method names in square brackets, as in the XL.[Quit] statement in Listing 16-1.*

Controlling Embedded Applications

So far this chapter has dealt primarily with the most common form of OLE Automation: using one application to control an object application that runs independently. However, there are two other ways to implement OLE Automation: controlling embedded applications and embedded OLE Custom Controls. You implement these two types a bit differently.

Understanding Object Containers

When one application is embedded in another, the object application is actually embedded in a *container*. The first thing you must do in order to control an embedded object with OLE Automation is to determine the name of the object container in the controlling application.

When Access is the controller, embedded object applications are contained in an Access object called an *object frame*. Object containers have an **object** property, and you can set an object variable to reference that property.

Understanding Object Frames

You never see an object frame; it's just a container. It is, however, an object that has properties.

An object frame can be *bound* or *unbound*. A bound object frame is tied to a field and record in a table. The pictures of the Northwind Traders employees you looked at in Chapter 6, for instance, were in bound object frames. An unbound object frame is part of the form itself; it is not stored in a table. To add a logo to a form, you would use an unbound object frame.

Embedding an Excel Object in Access

Let's suppose you want to put an Excel worksheet named "Budget95" in an unbound object frame control on an Access Form named "OperPlan." To create an OLE Automation session with the embedded Excel file, you can include the following lines of Access Basic code:

```
Dim objXLSheet as Object
Set objXLSheet = Forms!OperPlan!Budget95.object
```

Alternatively, if you only needed to reference the object for one operation, such as to set the value of a cell, it would usually be more efficient to bypass the step of setting an object. Instead, you would directly reference the object, as in the following code:

```
Forms!MyForm!MyExcelSheet.object.cells(1, 1).value = "some
value"
```

Now that you have learned a variety of techniques (and some niggling details) for creating OLE Automation code, it's time to look at some practical examples of using OLE Automation.

Solving Business Problems Using OLE Automation

This section of the chapter will help you break out of the somewhat theoretical mindset that attends the rigorous study of OLE Automation's syntax and mechanics. To understand these examples, start the controller application and enter the code shown in the listings. Then execute the code in step mode so you can see what's happening.

Three of the examples involve Access; these presuppose some knowledge of Access Basic. The examples are provided to help those who are familiar with Access programming to integrate the database program with other Office applications. Unfortunately, the scope of this book does not include instruction on programming in Access. For more information on this topic, consult the *Building Applications* manual in the Access program documentation.

Automating the Creation of a Word Document from Excel

Remember the proposal automation example in Chapter 12? Entering the VBA code shown in Listing 16-3 can improve it by automatically opening the Word proposal template from Excel. Before you run this macro successfully, you must first create a Word template called PROPOSAL.DOT.

This procedure starts by opening a Word document using the PROPOSAL.DOT template. It then updates all fields in the document. (It thus replaces the AutoOpen macro you created in Chapter 12.) After the user responds to a series of prompts, the macro prompts the user to save the document by bringing up Word's Save dialog box.

LISTING 16-3

Procedure to create a new document from a template and update all fields ∎

```
Sub CreateProposal()
    Dim objWordBasic As Object
    Set objWordBasic = CreateObject("Word.Basic")
    With objWordBasic
        .filenew Template:="Proposal"
        .EditSelectAll
        .UpdateFields
        .LineUp 1
        .FileSave
    End With
End Sub
```

This basic macro can be extended with additional labor-saving features. For instance, you could add code that would prompt for the addresses of Excel ranges that would be linked to the Word document, providing key computations.

Controlling Excel with Access

You can perform amazing feats using Access to control an Excel object. One of Excel's important uses, after all, is to analyze data stored in databases. As you learned from Chapter 5, you can query a single data source from Excel with the Query add-in. Often, however, all the data you want to analyze is not conveniently stored in a single data source. You might want to combine the data stored in a large corporate database with some data you have in an ASCII file or in Access.

The Access Basic macro in Listing 16-4 creates a query that places the results in an embedded Excel worksheet. In this manner, Access brings Excel's computational powers to bear on data from such databases as Oracle, BTrieve, or Informix—something that the Query add-in cannot do. This method can be used to access more than one data source if needed—though this is not demonstrated in the example.

As you read the Access Basic code in the remaining listings in this chapter, note that any text preceded by single quotes is not code, but explanatory comments.

Incidentally, you'll notice in the listing that the code uses a counter (y) that starts from zero rather than one. (The counter is used to keep track of which fields have been processed.) The counter starts from zero because fields, like most collections, are numbered from zero to *n*-1, where *n* is the number of fields in the collection.

LISTING 16-4

Procedure to query a database and place the results in an Excel worksheet

■

```
Sub CrossTabQueryToExcel ()
    Dim db As Database, rstmp As Recordset
    Dim xl As Object, SQLCode As String
    'Set the sheet object variable.
    Set xl = CreateObject("excel.sheet")

    xl.application.visible = True    'Make Excel visible.

    Set db = dbengine(0)(0)   'Set the database object variable.

    'Create a recordset based on the stored query.
    Set rstmp = db.OpenRecordset("ProductSalesByCountry")

    'Move through the entire recordset.
    rstmp.MoveLast
    rstmp.MoveFirst

    'Put the field names at the top of columns.
    For y = 0 To rstmp.fields.count - 1
        xl.cells(1, y + 1).value = rstmp.fields(y).name
    Next y

    'Place the data in the excel worksheet for each row.
    For x = 2 To rstmp.recordcount
        'Place the data for each column in each row.
        For y = 0 To rstmp.fields.count - 1
            xl.cells(x, y + 1).value = rstmp.fields(y)
        Next y
        'Move to the next record in the recordset.
        rstmp.MoveNext
    Next x

    'Calculate the range address just filled by using the
    'record and field count.
    FillRange = xl.cells(1, 1).address & ":" &
xl.cells(rstmp.recordcount, rstmp.fields.count).address

    'Autofit the range.
    xl.range(FillRange).EntireColumn.AutoFit

    'Delete a file, if it exists, using the Access Kill Statement.

    If Len(Dir("c:\temp.xls")) > 0 Then
```

LISTING 16-4

Procedure to query a database and place the results in an Excel worksheet (continued)

```
        Kill "c:\temp.xls"
    End If

    'Save the file and overwrite any changes.
    xl.application.activeworkbook.saveas "c:\temp.xls"

    'Quit Excel
    xl.application.[quit]

    'Release the object pointer.
    Set xl = Nothing
End Sub
```

Executing the procedure in Listing 16-4 against the Northwind Traders sample data in Access 2.0 creates an Excel sheet similar to that shown in Figure 16-4.

Note that the procedure in Listing 16-4 runs a stored crosstab query. The query design is shown in the following QBE grid:

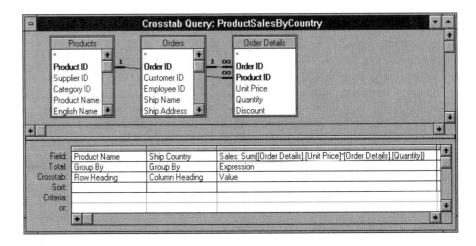

(See chapter 10 for an explanation of crosstab queries.)

tip *You can embed actual SQL code in a procedure. An easy way to do this is to create a query in Access, and then display the query in SQL view. You can then copy the SQL code into your module.*

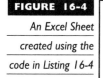

FIGURE 16-4

An Excel Sheet created using the code in Listing 16-4

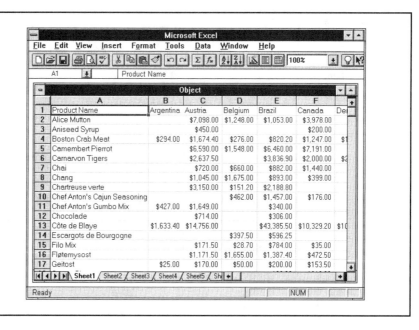

Embedding an Excel Object in an Access Form

Another useful way to turn loose Excel's number-crunching power on Access data is to embed an Excel sheet into an Access form. Suppose you work with a great many mortgage files, and have to answer frequent inquiries about payoff amounts and past transactions. You might have data such as the loan number, mortgagor name, loan date, original loan amount, interest rate, and term of loan stored in a database. Rarely, however, will you find the capability to generate an amortization schedule stored in a database. The mortgage files do contain all the necessary information, but in the absence of OLE Automation, the only way to get the job done is to plug the mortgage data into an Excel worksheet.

By using OLE Automation to control an Excel worksheet embedded in an Access form, you can have your cake and eat it, too. That is, you can display records *and* automatically view an amortization schedule, as illustrated in Figure 16-5.

The Access form consists primarily of a combo box, named "cbxSelectedMortgage," and an embedded Excel worksheet, named "objMortSheet." Listing 16-5 contains an example of a *form module*—Access code that is attached to a form. This code is executed upon the AfterUpdate event of the "cbxSelectedMortgage" combo box. That means that after the user enters

FIGURE 16-5

An Excel Sheet object embedded into an Access form

■

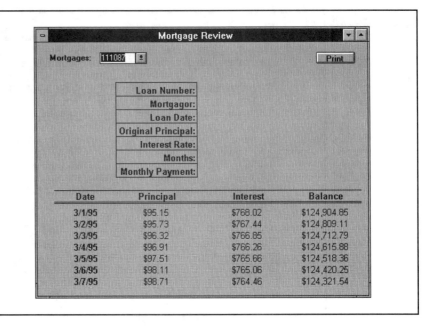

or changes the value displayed in the combo box, Access executes the code. The code does the following:

- Selects mortgage data from the database based on the entered or revised value.

- Sets the values of Excel ranges (cells in the worksheet) to the values returned by the query.

Excel then recalculates the worksheet. The results are shown in the bottom half of the form.

Controlling an OLE Custom Control

Executing OLE Automation to an OLE Custom Control is very much like executing OLE Automation to the embedded Excel sheet as illustrated in Listing 16-5. The major difference between an embedded object and an OLE Custom Control is that the OLE Custom Control returns events where an embedded object doesn't. ("Returning an event" means taking action in response to some event like a keypress or mouse movement. For instance, when you click on an OCX it notifies Access that the Click event has occurred. That causes Access to execute the procedure in the OnClick property of the control.)

LISTING 16-5

Procedure to query a mortgage loan database and supply values to an embedded Excel worksheet object

■

```
Sub cbxSelectedMortgage_AfterUpdate
    Dim db As Database, rstmp As Recordset, embxl As Object
    Dim SQLCode As String

    Set db = dbengine(0)(0)

    'Set the SQL string based on the value in the combo box.
    SQLCode = "SELECT DISTINCTROW Mortgages.[Loan Number], "
    SQLCode = SQLCode & "Mortgagors.MortgagorName ,
        Mortgages.[Loan Date], "
    SQLCode = SQLCode & "Mortgages.[Original Principal] ,
        Mortgages."
    SQLCode = SQLCode & "[Interest Rate], Mortgages.Months "
    SQLCode = SQLCode & "FROM Mortgagors INNER JOIN Mortgages ON "
    SQLCode = SQLCode & "Mortgagors.MortgagorID =
        Mortgages.MortgagorID "
    SQLCode = SQLCode & "Where Mortgages.[Loan Number] = "
    ' Note that the variable "Me" refers to the Access Basic
    ' module to which this procedure belongs.
    SQLCode = SQLCode & Me!cbxSelectedMortgage

    'Create a recordset based on SQL string created above.
    Set rstmp = db.OpenRecordset(SQLCode)

    'Set the OLE Automation object by referring to the object
    'property of an unbound OLE Object frame.
    Set embxl = Me!objMortSheet.object

    'Set the value of cells in Excel to values returned by the
    'SQL statement. Note that the amortization schedule in Excel
    'references these cells.
    embxl.range("loannumber").value = rstmp.[Loan Number]
    embxl.range("mortgagor").value = rstmp.[MortgagorName]
    embxl.range("loandate").value = rstmp.[Loan Date]
    embxl.range("origprincipal").value = rstmp.[Original Principal]
    embxl.range("interestrate").value = rstmp.[Interest Rate]
    embxl.range("months").value = rstmp.Months
End Sub
```

The code example in Listing 16-6 executes OLE Automation to an OLE Custom Control. The OCX used in the example is the Data Outline Control included with the Access Developers Toolkit. (To execute the procedure, you must have this particular OCX installed on your computer. However, if you don't have the Access Developers Toolkit, don't despair. Most OCXs will use the methodology illustrated by Listing 16-6.) A wide variety of available OCX's should be commercially available by early 1995.

The purpose of the Data Outline Control is to provide a mechanism for developers to allow users to "drill down" to obtain more detail relating to displayed summary information. An example of the Data Outline Control is shown in Figure 16-6.

LISTING 16-6

Access Basic macro to add a button to an OLE custom control

```
Sub btnCollapse_Click ()
    Dim objDoc As Object, Result As Integer

    'Set up the Data outline control object
    Set objDoc = Me!objDataOutline.Object

    'Hide the action!
    Me.painting = False

    'Invoke the MoveFirst method and move to the first
    'row in the first level.
    Result = objDoc.[MoveFirst](1)

    'Loop through each row in the control and collapse each level.
    While Result
        If objDoc.isexpanded Then
            objDoc.collapse
        End If
        Result = objDoc.[movedown]
    Wend

    'Move back to the top when done.
    Result = objDoc.[MoveFirst](1)

    'Show the results!
    Me.painting = True

End Sub
```

In the following example with the Data Outline OCX, collapsing a level of detail will trigger the Collapse event of the OCX. Any code associated with that event would then execute. For instance, you might want the procedure to close a form related to a given level in response to the Collapse event. To accomplish this, attach the code in Listing 16-6 to the "Collapse All Levels" button shown in Figure 16-6. When the button is pressed, all data *not* in the first level will be hidden, or collapsed.

You can expect to see third-party vendors bring hundreds of OCXs to market in the next year or two. These will extend the Office applications well beyond their standard functionality. Many of these add-ons will allow you to replace specific application features with features that better fit your needs. The example in Listing 16-6 shows how you will be able to manipulate OCXs programmatically to make them work the way you want them to.

Chapter 16: Creating Solutions with Visual Basic for Applications and OLE Automation

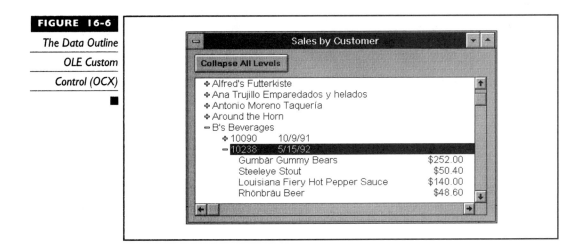

FIGURE 16-6

The Data Outline OLE Custom Control (OCX)

Conclusion

This chapter has presented a variety of ways to use multiple applications to solve business problems. These brief examples, however, are but tidbits compared to what can be done with OLE Automation. You have seen how OLE Automation easily integrates multiple applications to make them look like a single one. You have also seen that success in using OLE Automation depends on your knowledge of the underlying applications. As VBA is introduced into more Microsoft products, knowledge of OLE Automation will become an increasingly valuable skill.

The next and final chapter will present a capstone example that pulls Access, Excel, and Word together to automate the client accounting and communication functions of a money management firm.

CHAPTER 17

The Ultimate Office

THE initial chapters in this book have painted a picture of a smooth-running data "factory" on the desktop—one that required little attention to mechanical details such as entering data or converting file formats. In this, the final chapter, you'll examine an Access Basic application that creates, in simplified fashion, the kind of automated, push-button environment that Office makes possible.

This chapter does cover some new techniques, such as how to control Word from Access, but the main lesson is how to put the pieces together to create a comprehensive solution to a complex business problem.

What You Need to Know

As the Introduction pointed out, this chapter is not what you would call a quick read. To make use of the techniques demonstrated, you need to be a near-expert with Microsoft Access. The material assumes familiarity with Access' development language; the chapter consists largely of Access Basic code.

To implement an automated solution like the one in this chapter, you also need to know how to design forms. Much of the sample code in the example belongs in special Access Basic modules attached to forms. You must be experienced in Access form design to implement such "code-behind-forms" modules. Attaching code to forms can increase efficiency because such code is not loaded into memory until the form itself is loaded. This conserves memory, which is vital when you run large applications.

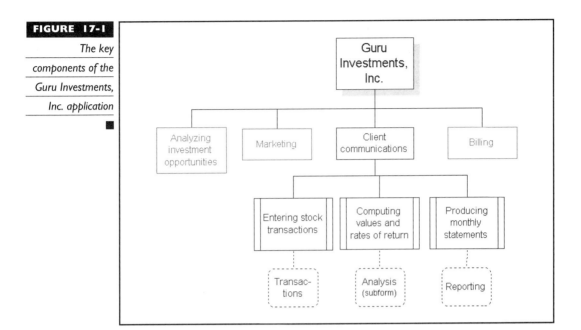

FIGURE 17-1

The key components of the Guru Investments, Inc. application

The Scenario: The Money Manager

The purpose of the Access application demonstrated in this chapter is to manage some of the client-oriented activities of Guru Investments, Inc. Figure 17-1 illustrates the overall structure of the Guru Investments application presented in the chapter. The second row of the diagram illustrates the four major business activities carried out by the fictitious company in the example. This chapter will focus on the client communications function (outlined in solid black in the figure).

The presentation of the example begins by discussing the global options that are used in all modules in the Guru Investments application. Each of the three client tasks in the example is performed by a different Access module. The modules, shown in the third row of Figure 17-1 are each explained in subsequent sections in this chapter. Each module has a form or subform (shown in the last row of the diagram).

Guru Investments, Inc. is a one-person money management company. The company offers money management services, investing clients' money in stocks and bonds for maximum return.

To render its service, Guru Investments performs a variety of tasks. The proprietor must do a great deal of research on investments. Purchases and sales of securities on the clients' accounts must be recorded accurately. The company has to send regular reports to keep clients informed of its activities.

Finally, Guru Investments must carry out the long list of mundane but vital marketing and administrative tasks that attend the operation of any successful business.

As you saw from Figure 17-1, this chapter will focus on the client-oriented activities of the business. That includes the recording of securities transactions in clients' accounts, computation of portfolio values, rate of return computations, and the production of monthly statements. The example is an Access Basic application that uses OLE Automation to control Excel and Word for computation and reporting functions, respectively.

Figure 17-2 shows the Access form where Guru Investments' proprietor enters stock transactions. You'll see the Access Basic code attached to this form in the section called "Entering Transactions" later in this chapter.

The Customer Investments form also provides a platform for inquiry and analysis. Figure 17-3 shows the Customer Investments form with a subform displayed. In the subform, an embedded Excel object values the stocks by referring to a table of closing prices for a given date. Cell formulas in the Excel Worksheet multiply the client's current number of shares by the price as of the selected valuation date, computing the value of the client's holding in each security. It also computes summary totals.

The remainder of this chapter consists almost exclusively of Access Basic code with annotations. Most of the annotations, following good programming practice, are included in the code itself. Other annotations—containing explanations of techniques and background information on OLE Automation—are in Notes scattered throughout the code.

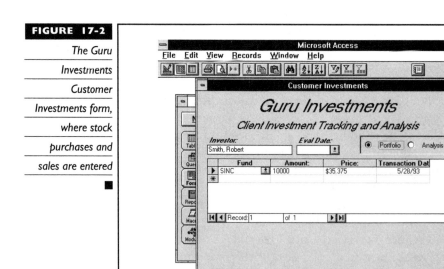

FIGURE 17-2

The Guru Investments Customer Investments form, where stock purchases and sales are entered

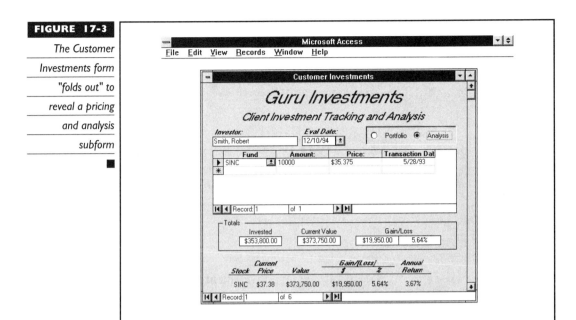

FIGURE 17-3

The Customer Investments form "folds out" to reveal a pricing and analysis subform

Please note that the example presented in this chapter is not a complete, production-quality application. The example was limited in its scope to make it easier to focus on the key principle: how to combine Office applications to create a business solution. Among the features that you would expect to see in a production-quality application that you will *not* see in the example are

- A form for editing customer master files
- Extensive error-trapping
- Security features such as prompts for the user to save files
- Support for ad hoc reporting

Setting Global Options for the Application

The Access Basic code starts with some preliminaries. By default, new modules in Access all contain an initial Option Compare Database statement. Leave this statement in the module; it establishes a default sort order.

This example also declares the Excel object so it can be "seen" and used by all the code in this module. This saves the effort of declaring it in every procedure in which you want to use it.

```
Option Compare Database    'Use database order for string comparisons
Option Explicit
' Declare the Excel object at the module level.
Dim Excel As Object
```

note *Option Explicit is used to force explicit declaration of all variables. This helps prevent mistyping variable names that can cause hard-to-locate bugs. It also forces you, as developer, to determine the variable type in advance in order to minimize data-type errors.*

Entering Transactions

The first component of the Guru Investments application is a code-behind-form module associated with the Customer Investments form. In the Customer Investments form, the user records purchases and sales of stocks on behalf of clients. The Customer Investments form, which is used to generate the investment analysis data, is a subform of the Customer Investments form. For more information on forms and subforms, please refer to the *Microsoft Access Handbook*, from Osborne/McGraw-Hill, or the Microsoft documentation for Access.

```
Option Compare Database    'Use database order for string comparisons
Option Explicit

Sub Amount_AfterUpdate ()
    ' This code executes after the Amount field is updated.
    ' It calls the GetPrice subroutine.
    GetPrice

End Sub
```

note *GetPrice is a subroutine in this module. Several of the Event Procedures in this module call the same subroutine (which gets the price for a stock for a selected date).*

```
Sub BuyorSellDate_AfterUpdate ()
    ' This code executes after the BuyorSellDate field is updated.
    ' It calls the GetPrice subroutine.
    GetPrice
End Sub
```

```
Sub GetPrice ()
    ' This subroutine gets the price for a selected stock on a
    ' selected date.
    ' The End statement unconditionally stops code execution. In the
    ' case below, if any of the named text boxes are blank, it wouldn't
    ' be possible to get a price so the code execution is stopped.
    ' Can't get the price if the FundID, Transaction or Amount text
    ' boxes have no values, so don't execute the code.
    If IsNull(Me!FundID) Or IsNull(Me!TransactionDate) Or
Isnull(Me!Amount) Then
        End
    End If

    ' Dimension the necessary objects and variables.
    Dim db As Database, qdtmp As QueryDef, rstmp As Recordset

    ' Set the database variable to the default workspace and database.
    Set db = dbengine(0)(0)
    ' Create a new query. Because the query has no name (i.e. the
    ' name is defined as a zero length string, it will not be saved.
    ' In other words, this opens a temporary query.
    Set qdtmp = db.CreateQueryDef("")

    ' Dimension a variable to contain the SQL string.
    Dim SQLCode As String

    ' Create the SQL string using string concatenation. Note how the
    ' second and all following lines set the variable "SQLCode" equal
    ' to the variable "SQLCode" and ("&" is the "and" operator for
    ' concatenating text) another part of the string. If you use this
    ' technique, remember to include spaces between words (note the
    ' spaces at the end of each line in the variable creation.
    SQLCode = "SELECT StockData.Close "
    SQLCode = SQLCode & "FROM StockData "
    SQLCode = SQLCode & "WHERE ((StockData.Date=#" & Me!Transaction-
Date & "#) "
    SQLCode = SQLCode & "AND (StockData.StockID=" & Me!FundID & ")) "

    ' Set the sql property of the querydef object to the string
    ' created above.
    qdtmp.sql = SQLCode

    ' Set the recordset object to the recordset returned by executing
    ' the query.
    Set rstmp = qdtmp.OpenRecordset()

    ' Set the BuyorSellPrice text box to the close field in the
    ' recordset. Note the square brackets are necessary to tell Access
    ' that "close" refers to the recordset field named "close", which is
    ' a reserved word in Access
    Me!BuyorSellPrice = rstmp![close]
```

```
        ' Refresh the records in the forms recordset.
        Me.Refresh
End Sub

Sub TransactionDate_AfterUpdate ()
        ' This code executes after the TransactionDate field is updated.
        ' It calls the GetPrice subroutine.
        GetPrice
End Sub
```

Analyzing Investment Data at the Touch of a Button

The next module you will examine is one of many *event procedures* in the application. Event procedures are executed upon the occurrence of a triggering event. (In the following procedure, the event is the selection of a button.) You must use a certain convention for event procedure names. First comes the name of the control (Analysis in the following example), then an underscore character, then the name of the event (GotFocus in the following example).

Also note the use of the variable name "Me," which is shorthand for the module in a procedure that is associated with a form. The following procedure is associated with (or *behind*) the Customer Investments form.

```
        ' This code executes whenever the Analysis button in the
        ' optDisplay option group gets the focus (i.e. when a user selects
        ' the button). The procedure checks to make sure that an
        ' evaluation date has been picked. If not, alert the user and
        ' then go to the Evaluation Date drop down.
Sub btnAnalysis_GotFocus ()
    If IsNull(Me!EvalDate) Then
        MsgBox ("You must first enter an evaluation date.")
        DoCmd GoToControl "EvalDate"
    End If
End Sub

Sub EvalDate_AfterUpdate ()
        ' This code executes after the value is changed in the "EvalDate"
        ' combo box (and after the code in "Sub EvalDate_AfterUpdate").
        ' After updating the Evaluation Date combo box, set the option
        ' group to display the Portfolio view and make the embedded Excel
        ' sheet invisible.
```

note *When a button–any button–in an option box is selected, it returns a value to the option group. The value represents the currently selected button. The next line of code sets the option group "selected" button to be the button with its Option Value property set to "1." In the Customer Investments form, that is the Portfolio button.*

```
    Me!optDisplay = 1
    Me!objxl.visible = False
End Sub

Sub EvalDate_BeforeUpdate (cancel As Integer)
    ' This code executes before the value in the "EvalDate" combo box
    ' is updated (but after the user chooses a new value). After
    ' updating the Evaluation Date combo box, make sure the date
    ' selected is later than the latest client investment date.

    ' Dimension the necessary objects and variables.
    Dim rstmp As Recordset, DateOK As Integer

    ' Set the recordset object to be a copy of the Client Transactions
    ' subform recordset using the recordsetclone property.  This
    ' property returns a recordset that is a duplicate of the
    ' recordset underlying a form (or subform).
```

note *The Form property of a subform object refers to the active form associated with a subform.*

```
Set rstmp = Me!sfmTransactions.form.recordsetclone

    ' Move to the first record in the dataset.
    rstmp.MoveFirst

    ' Initialize the DateOK variable. The DateOK variable is used as
    ' a "flag" to indicate whether only valid dates exist for the
    ' requested evaluation period.
    DateOK = True
    ' Loop through the recordset and look for transaction dates that
    ' are later than the selected Evaluation Date.
```

note *The most reliable way to perform a recurring procedure on a recordset is to loop through the recordset until an "end-of-file" condition is reached. Some users employ an alternative method: count the number of records, then create a For/Next procedure, but that is not recommended. It can be slow, because the entire query must be executed to get an accurate record count. Moreover, the results might not be reliable in table or dynaset type recordsets because other users might be updating records in your recordset during your loop.*

```
            While Not rstmp.eof
                ' Use the DateValue function to convert the "text" dates to
                ' serial date values for comparison purposes.
                If DateValue(rstmp.TransactionDate) > DateValue(Me!EvalDate)
        Then
                    ' If a transaction date later than the evaluation date is
                    ' found, change the value of the DateOK variable.
                    DateOK = False

                    ' Since an invalid date has been located, it is
                    ' unnecessary to examine any more records.  Move to the
                    ' last record to break the loop.
                    rstmp.MoveLast

                End If

                ' Move to the next record and then loop to test it.  If the end
                ' of the dataset is reached, the While loop will terminate.
                rstmp.MoveNext
            Wend

            ' Test the DateOK variable to see if it is false.  If it is false
            ' (meaning a record was found in the test above), alert the user,
            ' cancel the event and end code execution.
            If Not DateOK Then
                MsgBox ("The evaluation date must be after the most recent in-
        vestment date.")
                DoCmd CancelEvent
```

note *The CancelEvent action essentially cancels the event from completing. Because this is a macro action (instead of an Access Basic method), you must use the DoCmd keyword. (The DoCmd statement executes Access menu commands.)*

```
        End
            End If

            ' Display the Portfolio view of the form by setting the option
            ' group (optDisplay) equal to the value 1.  Note the default
            ' property for an option group control is the value property;
            ' hence it is not necessary to specify the property name as in
            ' "Me!optDisplay.value = 1".
        Me!optDisplay = 1

        End Sub

        Sub Form_Current ()
            ' This code executes whenever a new record is selected in the
            ' main form. First it displays the Portfolio view by setting the
            ' option group (optDisplay) equal to the variable 1. Then it
```

```
          ' hides the embedded Excel sheet and all the controls in the
          ' Totals group.
          Me!optDisplay = 1
          Me!objxl.visible = False
          Me!TotLabel1.visible = False
          Me!TotLabel2.visible = False
          Me!TotLabel3.visible = False
          Me!TotLabel4.visible = False
          Me!TotInvested.visible = False
          Me!TotCurrent.visible = False
          Me!TotGainDollars.visible = False
          Me!TotGainPercent.visible = False
          Me!optTotals.visible = False
End Sub

' The following procedure executes whenever the Customer Investments
' form is loaded into memory.
Sub Form_Load ()
Me!objxl.visible = False
          ' Set the Excel object, which is defined at the module level, to
          ' the object property of the objxl control.  If Excel is not
          ' running, this line of code will cause it to launch.
```

note *Setting an object variable to the object property works somewhat like using GetObject(,"excel.sheet") in that if Excel is running, it will reference the existing object in the running instance of Excel. If Excel is not running, however, it does launch Excel before making the reference.*

```
          Set Excel = Me!objxl.object

          ' Clear the contents of the indicated range in the embedded Excel
          ' sheet.  Note the clearcontents method was used instead of Excel's
          ' clear method. The latter would clear formats as well as values.
          Excel.range("A4:F100").clearcontents
End Sub
Sub optDisplay_BeforeUpdate (cancel As Integer)
          ' This code executes after a user selects a button in the optDisplay
          ' option group but before the value of the option box is changed.

          ' If the "Analysis" button is selected (returning a value of 2),
          ' make sure an analysis can be prepared.  If it can be successfully
          ' prepared, prepare and display it.
          If optDisplay = 2 Then

               ' If the "EvalDate" combo box doesn't have a value selected,
               ' tell the user to select one before running an analysis,
               ' cancel the event and terminate code execution.
               If IsNull(EvalDate) Then
                    MsgBox ("You must enter an evaluation date before
```

```
            performing an analysis.")
                DoCmd CancelEvent
                End
            End If

            ' The "EvalDate" combo box doesn't contain a value that can be
            ' converted to a date, tell the user the value is bad, cancel the
            ' event before running the analysis, and terminate code
            ' execution. Note that variant type 7 is the date data type.
            If Not (VarType(DateValue(EvalDate)) = 7) Then
                MsgBox ("Invalid Evaluation Date.")
                DoCmd CancelEvent
                End
            End If
            ' Keep running code in case an error occurs.
            On Error Resume Next

            ' Make sure the Excel object is still valid by getting the
            ' application property. If the object is active, the application
            ' property will return the string "Microsoft Excel". If the
            ' the object is inactive, it will return a trappable error
            ' (Error 91 - Object variable not Set)
            Dim AppName As String
            AppName = Excel.application
            ' If the Excel object variable is not properly set, reset it.
            If Err = 91 Then
                Set Excel = objxl.object
            End If

            ' Dimension the necessary objects and variables.
            Dim db As Database, qdtmp As QueryDef, rstmp As Recordset
            ' Set the database variable to the default workspace and
            ' database.
            Set db = dbengine(0)(0)
```

note: *dbengine(0)(0) is shorthand for dbengine.workspaces(0).databases(0). In the Access 2.0 object model, the DBEngine object is the Microsoft Jet database engine and is the top-level application object. Under this object, you can have a collection of workspaces, which are roughly equivalent to "user sessions." Each workspace can have a collection of databases; in other words, one user can be simultaneously using multiple databases. Workspaces collection item "0" and Databases collection item "0" are the default items in these collections (that is, the workspace and database the user has logged into through the user interface).*

```
' Set the query object equal to the "TransactionValues"
' query. This query joins the client's transaction data
' records with the stock  valuation records for the requested
' evaluation date. Open the saved parameter query named
' "TransactionValues" and provide values for its parameters.
Set qdtmp = db.OpenQueryDef("TransactionValues")
        qdtmp.PARAMETERS("EvaluationDate") = Me!EvalDate
        qdtmp.PARAMETERS("CustID") = Me!CustomerID
```

The preceding three lines of code provide a good example of setting the value of the query's parameters "on the fly," based on data in the form. Normally, when Access Basic executes a query, the user is prompted for the query parameter values. The Qdtmp statements, however, read the values for Evaluation Date and CustomerID from fields in the form, saving the user time.

This technique also allows more flexibility for using parameter queries within code. With the preceding three Access Basic statements, you can execute the following SQL code:

```
PARAMETERS EvaluationDate DateTime, CustID Long;
SELECT DISTINCTROW Transactions.*, Securities.*,
StockData.Close, StockData.Date
FROM (Securities INNER JOIN StockData ON
Securities.SecurityID = StockData.StockID) INNER JOIN
Transactions ON Securities.SecurityID = Transactions.FundID
WHERE ((StockData.Date=[EvaluationDate])
AND (Transactions.CustomerID=[CustID]))
ORDER BY Transactions.TransactionDate
```

```
' Set the recordset object to be the recordset of the query.
Set rstmp = qdtmp.OpenRecordset()
```

note   *The conventional procedure is to put the Dim statements at the top of the procedure or function. To make the example code easier to follow, however, the Dim statements for most variables in this example have been placed near where the variables are used.*

```
' Initialize a counter that indicates the row in Excel that
' current data will be copied to, to the beginning row
' number. In this case, the first row of data in the recordset
' will be placed into row 4 in the embedded Excel sheet.
Dim Counter As Integer
Counter = 4

' Clear the contents of a range of cells in the embedded
' Excel sheet.
Excel.range("A4:F100").clearcontents

' The following several statements (preceding the Wend
' statement) execute a "do while" loop until each record in the
' recordset has been processed. By setting the cells in the
' embedded Excel sheet equal to values in the current form and
' recordset, the macro essentially copies those values into the
' worksheet. The Counter value of the Excel.cells statement
' indicates the row number into which the data will be pasted.
' Note that in all but the fifth Excel.cells statement, the
' data comes from the recordset (the query results).
While Not rstmp.eof
        Excel.cells(Counter, 1).value = rstmp.TransactionDate
        Excel.cells(Counter, 2).value = rstmp.SecuritySymbol
        Excel.cells(Counter, 3).value = rstmp.Amount
        Excel.cells(Counter, 4).value = rstmp.BuyorSellPrice
        Excel.cells(Counter, 5).value = Me!EvalDate
        Excel.cells(Counter, 6).value = rstmp.[close]
```

note *The square brackets in the preceding statement are necessary to indicate that "close" is a field name in the recordset. This is so Access won't confuse the field name "Close" (which contains the closing price of a given stock) with the Close method.*

```
        ' Move to the next record in the recordset.
        rstmp.MoveNext

        ' Increment the Counter variable.
        Counter = Counter + 1
Wend

' Calculate all open Excel worksheets.
Excel.application.calculate

' Set the value of text boxes in the Access form equal
' to values in the Excel sheet. Row 3 in the Excel sheet
' contains SUM formulas that return column totals. (The cells
' being summed are located below row 3.)
Me!TotInvested = Excel.range("D3").value
Me!TotCurrent = Excel.range("G3").value
```

```
            Me!TotGainDollars = Excel.range("H3").value
            Me!TotGainPercent = Excel.range("I3").value
            ' Display the embedded Excel sheet and the controls in the
            ' Totals option group.
            Me!objxl.visible = True
            Me!TotLabel1.visible = True
            Me!TotLabel2.visible = True
            Me!TotLabel3.visible = True
            Me!TotLabel4.visible = True
            Me!TotInvested.visible = True
            Me!TotCurrent.visible = True
            Me!TotGainDollars.visible = True
            Me!TotGainPercent.visible = True
            Me!optTotals.visible = True
    ' In case OptDisplay <> 2 then do the following.
    Else
            ' If the Portfolio button is selected, hide the embedded Excel
            ' sheet and the controls in the Totals option group.
            Me!objxl.visible = False
            Me!TotLabel1.visible = False
            Me!TotLabel2.visible = False
            Me!TotLabel3.visible = False
            Me!TotLabel4.visible = False
            Me!TotInvested.visible = False
            Me!TotCurrent.visible = False
            Me!TotGainDollars.visible = False
            Me!TotGainPercent.visible = False
            Me!optTotals.visible = False
    End If

End Sub
```

Printing Reports for Clients

The clients of Guru Investments, Inc. are always interested in whether the firm is making money for them. The last module in the Guru Investments application produces a monthly account statement, like the one shown in Figure 17-4, for each client in the database. Guru Investments sends these reports out monthly to clients.

Creating these reports combines OLE Automation with linking and makes use of three applications. First Access queries the client files. Excel then performs the mathematical computations. The module then creates a WordBasic object (remember, WordBasic is the only OLE 2 object exposed by Word) that opens a Word template. The template contains LINK fields that refer to data in the Excel object, so the Excel data appears in the template automatically once the fields are updated. Word then prints the statements.

FIGURE 17-4

A monthly statement of account produced by the reporting module

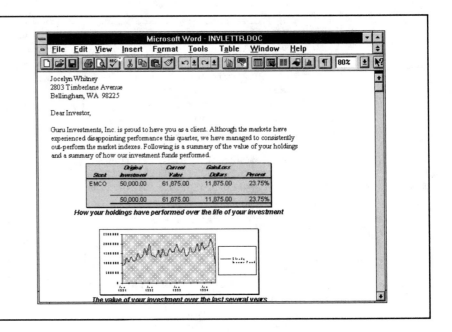

```
Option Compare Database    'Use database order for string comparisons
Option Explicit
Sub PrintInvestorReports ()

    ' This subroutine prepares the periodic investor
    ' reports by using OLE Automation to manipulate
    ' an Excel worksheet, named report1.xls, and a Word
    ' document, named invreprt.doc. The Word document
    ' contains both boilerplate text and linked data from
    ' the Excel worksheet.

    ' Define objects and open object applications.
    Dim Word As Object, Excel As Object
    Set Word = CreateObject("word.basic")
    Set Excel = GetObject("C:\EXCEL\ACCOUNTS\REPORT1.XLS", _
"excel.sheet")

    Word.FileOpen "C:\WINWORD\CLIENTS\INVREPRT.DOC"
    ' Dimension the necessary objects and variables and
    ' initialize. Note the recordset rsCustInv will be re-created
    ' for each customer.
    Dim db As Database, qdCustInvest As QueryDef
    Dim rsCustList As Recordset, rsCustInvest As Recordset

    Set db = dbengine(0)(0)
    ' Create a recordset based on a simple, complete SQL statement
```

```
        ' embedded in the code itself.
        Set rsCustList = db.OpenRecordset("select * from Customers")
        Set qdCustInvest = db.OpenQueryDef("TransactionValues")

        ' Get the date to use for the evaluation. It must be a date-type
        ' variant in order to be used as a parameter in the Transaction
        ' Values query.
        Dim EvaluationDate As Variant, ValidDate As Integer

        ' Initialize the ValidDate variable to false.
        ValidDate = False

        ' Keep running code in case an error occurs. In the following
        ' loop, the expression "DateValue(EvaluationDate)" will create an
        ' error if the EvaluationDate variable (as input by the user)
        ' does not contain a string value that "looks" like a date.

        On Error Resume Next
        ' Request an evaluation date from a user. Loop until a valid date
        ' is input by the user. The ValidDate variable, which has been
        ' initialized to false above, will be set to true when the user
        ' types in a valid date.
        While Not ValidDate
             EvaluationDate = InputBox$("Please enter the evaluation
date:")

            ' If the user pressed the Cancel button, advise that the
            ' evaluation was cancelled and end code execution.
        If Len(EvaluationDate) = 0 Then
            MsgBox ("Evaluation Cancelled.")
            End
        End If

             ' Convert the value typed in to a date.
             EvaluationDate = DateValue(EvaluationDate)

             ' VarType 7 is a date, thus if the VarType of the
             ' EvaluationDate variable is 7, it is a date. In that case,
             ' set the ValidDate variable to True to break out of the
             ' While loop.
             If VarType(EvaluationDate) = 7 Then
                 ValidDate = True
             End If
        Wend

        ' Set the "EvaluationDate" parameter of the query equal to the
        ' date value of the EvaluationDate variable.
        qdCustInvest.Parameters("EvaluationDate") = DateValue(Evaluation-
Date)
        ' The following "do-while" loop creates a report for each
        ' customer, replicating the relevant Access data in the Excel
        ' worksheet.
```

```
        While Not rsCustList.eof
            ' Put the customer data over into the Excel worksheet.
            Excel.cells(77, 2).formular1c1 = rsCustList!FirstName
            Excel.cells(78, 2).formular1c1 = rsCustList!LastName
            Excel.cells(79, 2).formular1c1 = rsCustList!Address
            Excel.cells(80, 2).formular1c1 = rsCustList!City
            Excel.cells(81, 2).formular1c1 = rsCustList!State
            Excel.cells(82, 2).formular1c1 = rsCustList!PostalCode

            ' Set the CustomerID parameter and create a recordset.
            qdCustInvest.Parameters("CustID") = rsCustList!CustomerID
            Set rsCustInvest = qdCustInvest.OpenRecordset()

            ' The Excel file (REPORT1.XLS) that was opened at the outset of
            ' this module contains some charts. These charts, along with
            ' some cell values, are sources for linked Excel objects in
            ' the Word file (INVREPRT.DOC).

' Put each row of customer investment data into the Excel worksheet,
' starting with cell A63 (R63C1).
            Dim RowCount As Integer
            RowCount = 63

            While Not rsCustInvest.eof
                Excel.cells(RowCount, 1).formular1c1 = rsCustIn-
vest![Amount]
                Excel.cells(RowCount, 2).formular1c1 = rsCustInvest!Buy-
orSellPrice
                Excel.cells(RowCount, 3).formular1c1 =
rsCustInvest![close]
                Excel.cells(RowCount, 4).formular1c1 = rsCustInvest!Secu-
ritySymbol
                rsCustInvest.MoveNext
                RowCount = RowCount + 1
            Wend
```

Once the reporting module processes a client, the Excel worksheet for that client will resemble Figure 17-5. (Of course, the user will not actually view the worksheet, which operates behind the scenes.)

```
' Now that the data is complete, update the links and
' print the report in Word.
        Word.EditSelectAll
        Word.UpdateFields
        Word.FilePrintDefault
        ' Process the next customer.
        rsCustList.MoveNext
    Wend
        ' Explicitly quit Excel. The Excel.parent property for an Excel
        ' sheet returns a workbook. Setting the saved property for the
```

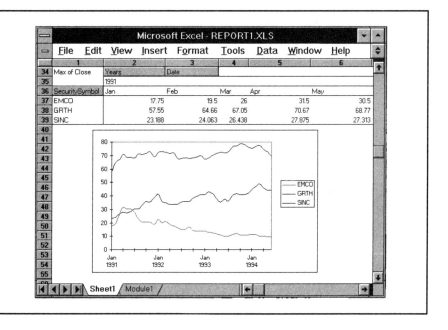

FIGURE 17-5

The embedded Excel worksheet showing data placed in cells by the Access Basic module

```
     ' workbook to true prevents Excel from asking if you want to save
     ' the workbook. Note you don't need to do this with Word 6.0.
Excel.parent.saved = True
    Excel.application.[Quit]
' Deallocated the object variable memory.
    Set Excel = Nothing
    Set Word = Nothing

End Sub
```

note: *Setting an object equal to Nothing frees up the memory resources associated with the referenced object. In other words, it's a necessary cleanup step.*

Creating Your Own Solutions

If you have worked all the way through the example in this chapter, you're well on your way to learning how to create comprehensive applications with OLE Automation, using Access as the controller.

If you have finished every chapter in the book, congratulations are in order. It hasn't been easy, but you have learned some advanced application features along with powerful automation techniques. The foundation was laid by familiarizing you with the way OLE manages the many and varied objects contained in the Office application programs.

Try to create solutions to your own specific business problems, using the examples in this book as creative springboards. This will keep you working with the Office macro languages, strengthening your awareness of the application object models. The "componentized" view of software will grow ever more dominant in the coming years. Soon even parts of the operating system will be available to the Office macro languages. Application-specific expertise will decline ever so slightly as a mark of status. Instead, a more holistic familiarity with the tools contained in applications will be highly prized. You have seen the future, and it is object-oriented.

INDEX

A

Access Basic, 381-389
  Dim statements, 403
  DoCmd statements, 400
  event procedures, 396-398
  object equal to Nothing, 409
  Option Compare Database statement, 395
  Option Explicit statement, 395
  Qdtmp statements, 403
  setting an object variable, 401
  square brackets, 404
Access Basic application (ultimate office), 392-410
Access program. *See* Microsoft Access
Add Criteria dialog box, 111
Add Fax Modems dialog box, 261
Add Tables dialog box, 105
Add-Ins dialog box, 103-104
Address book. *See* Personal address book
Address Book dialog box, 245-246
Address Book window, 247
Address dialog box (Microsoft Mail), 245
Analyze It button, 148-149
Applets, 161
Application vs. job orientation, 13-14
ASK fields (Word), 272-278
  avoiding blank lines when using, 274-275
  creating, 272-273
  syntax of, 272
  updating, 273-274
Assign Macro dialog box, 191-192, 348-349
Attach dialog box, 248
Auto Report button, 228
AutoCaption dialog box, 195

AutoContent Wizard (PowerPoint), 313-315
AutoFormats (Excel), 82
Automatic vs. manual links, 82-85
AutoOpen macro, 287-288
AutoQuery, using, 113
AutoQuery key, 113

B

Basic. *See* Access Basic; VBA code
Bitmapped graphics (bitmaps), 43
Bookmarks (Word), 66
  and ASK fields, 272, 274
  identifying all in a document, 94
  and REF fields, 275-276
  searching for, 66
Border dialog box (WordArt), 184
Borders, adding in Word, 185-186
Bound object frame, 380

Breaking a link, 33-34, 82, 85, 88
Build button, 143

C

Cairo operating system, 50
Calculations in Word, 229-233
Caption dialog box, 195
Captions, adding to embedded objects, 194-196
CAS modem, 260
Cell formulas, pasting text into, 91-92
Change Source dialog box, 85-86
Charts (Microsoft Graph), 59, 197-199
Charts/chart objects (Excel)
  embedding, 56-57
  embedding in a Word document, 58-61
  linking to a Word document, 61-62
  Microsoft sample data in, 58
  orphan markers and labels, 59
Check Errors button, 210
Checking and Reporting Errors dialog box, 210
Chocolate factory example, 325-349
  physical flow of material, 328
  process diagram, 325
  recording data, 325-326
  top-level Summary screen, 327
  workstation, 326-329
Client applications, 22
  drawing graphic objects in, 157-161
  putting objects into, 161-167
Clip art, 167-171, 344-345
Clipboard Viewer, 42
Code-behind-forms modules, 392
Command center for rapid response example, 321-325
Communications Application Specification (CAS), 260
Company logo
  adding to document header, 288-289
  creating with WordArt, 181-188
Comparison criterion (queries), 111
Comparison operators, 112, 119-120
Compound documents, 26
  example of creating, 26-29
  opening, 33
  printing, 95-96
  routing, 76
  saving, 32-36
Consulting proposal (*See also* Presentations; Sales proposal)
  cover page, 271
  enhancing accuracy, 278
  entering client information, 272-278
  generating, 269-290
  inserting an Access database, 281-285
  paste-linking Excel computations, 279-280
  personalizing, 277-278
  saving as a template, 287-289
Container applications. *See* Client applications
Container (object), 380
Controllers (in OLE Automation), 369-370
Conversing with colleagues, 11
Convert command, 78
Converting objects, 77-78
Copied data, viewing on the Clipboard, 42
Copy to Address Book button, 246

Copy Picture command (Excel), 89-90
Copying data from Microsoft Query, 126
Copying objects, 88
CorelDRAW image, inserting in a table, 172-173
Create Button button, 191
Create Labels dialog box, 215
CreateObject function (OLE Automation), 376-378
Criteria Equals button, 116-117
Criteria pane (query window), 112, 114-115
Criteria (query)
  adding, 113-116
  specifying, 110-113
Crosstab queries, 222-229, 384
Cue Cards window (Office Manager), 15
Custom Controls (OLE OCX), 386-389

D

Data items. *See* Objects
Data objects. *See* Objects
Data Outline Control, 387-388
Data pane (query window), 106
Data sharing. *See* Shared data
Data sources, 104
  editing, 127
  querying multiple, 146
  specifying for queries, 104-105, 131
Data Sources dialog box (Access), 140
Database applications, 133-134
Database dialog box (Word), 283
DATABASE fields, 286
Database management systems (DBMSs), 101
Database objects (Access), 132
Database tables (relational), join lines in, 118
Database window (Access), 132
Databases, 100-103, 117, 131, 138-140
Datasheet view of Access queries, 147, 226
Datasheet view of Access tables, 133, 135
DBEngine object (Access 2.0), 402
DCX fax-format files, 265-266
DDE (Dynamic Data Exchange) links, 21, 25-26, 66

Deleting objects, 68
Destination document, 26, 83
Dimension statements (VBA), 341
Dingbats, using, 173-175
Disk cache, creating on floppy drive, 364
Documents. *See* Compound documents; Files; Word documents
Dragging data between applications, 8
Drawing programs, third-party, 163-165
Drawing tools in Word, 157-158, 160
Drawn objects
  in the graphics layer, 158-159
  layering, 159-161
Drop Cap dialog box, 187
Drop caps, using, 187-188
Dynasets (Access), 143, 148

E

Edit Links command, 83
Edit Paste command, 44-45
Editing in place, 32
Electronic mail messages, 242 (*See also* Microsoft Mail)
  attaching files and objects to, 247-251

checking for, 6-7
composing, 244-245
deleting, 255, 260
with documents and
routing slips,
252-254
with packaged
document, 354-355
reading, 255-260
replying to, 255-256
responding to routed
documents, 254
searching for, 259-260
sending, 243-251
sending to a group,
246-247
storing in folders,
256-258
Electronic mail system.
See Microsoft Mail
EMBED fields, 79-80, 90
Embedded Excel objects,
editing and resizing,
60-63, 74
Embedded Excel
worksheet, saving in
Excel, 89
Embedded graphics,
framing, 171-172
Embedded vs. linked
Excel range, 48-49
Embedded objects, 23
(*See also* Objects)
adding captions to,
194-196
editing, 31-32

and File Close, 52
in Mail messages,
249-250
managing 72-78
storage requirements
of, 75-76
type conversion of, 78
using, 31
Embedding, 25 (*See also*
Embedded objects;
OLE Automation)
advantages of, 25
an Excel chart into
Word, 56-61
Excel objects in
Access, 380-381,
385-389
an Excel range into
Word, 45-48
limitations of, 74-75
an object as an icon, 44
picture objects, 43
vs. plain-pasting, 43
power of, 72-74
Word picture objects
in Excel, 92-93
Embedding applications,
161-162, 380-381. *See
also* WordArt
Envelope Address dialog
box, 237
Envelopes, printing,
237-239
Event procedures (Access
Basic), 396-398

Excel (*See also* Excel
objects; Excel ranges)
controlling with
Access, 382-385
creating picture charts,
170-171
creating a Word
document from,
381-382
creating a worksheet,
188-190
graphics and text
layers, 158-159
managing Word
objects in, 95
object types, 40-44
rapid response
interface example,
319-349
returning query results
to, 8-9
role of, 12
sending files from, 251
sharing data with
Word, 39-68
suppressing printing of
objects, 96
using data in Word,
87-90
using Word data in,
91-96
Word documents in, 92
Excel charts/chart objects
(*See also* Excel objects)
with clip art, 171

embedding in Word, 56-61
linking to Word documents, 61-62
vs. Microsoft Graph charts, 59
orphan markers and labels, 59
sample data provided, 58
Excel modules, 75
Excel object model, top-level view, 372
Excel objects (See also Excel charts/chart objects)
creating, 371-372
editing embedded, 62-63
editing linked, 63-64
embedding in Access, 380-381
embedding in an Access form, 385-389
fitting large, 76-77
manipulating, 372-373
Excel ranges (See also Excel)
data type options for, 44
embedding in Word, 45-48
inserting in an active Word document, 50-56

inserting in a Word document, 6-7, 54-56
inserting the wrong range, 56
linked vs. embedded, 48-49
linked with Word documents, 24, 79-82
linking, 48-50
pasted in a Word document, 26-29
redirecting a link to, 85
sharing, 27
Excel server, using Word as, 64-67
Excel text box, Word text in, 92-93
Excel for Windows: The Complete Reference, 325
Excel workbooks, attaching to a PowerPoint presentation, 10
Excel worksheet object model, 374
Excel worksheets, paste-linking into Word documents, 279-280
Executing a query, 146
Expiration dates for source files, 34

Exposing an object, 21-22, 372
Expression Builder, 143-144
Expression fields, 229

F

Fax modems
configuring, 260-261
specifying the active modem, 262
Fax Modems dialog box, 260-261
Fax Viewer window, 265
Faxing documents, 263-264
Faxing messages, 242-243, 260-266
Field lists in query windows, 106, 108-109, 142
File associations, 359
File Close command, 52
File dialog box (Word), 54-55
File Open command, 74-75
File Save command, 126
File Send command, 8
Files
faxing, 263-264
opening linked, 87
sending with Microsoft Mail, 247-254

speeding up saving of, 364
Filling out forms, 9
Floppy drive disk cache, creating, 364
Flowcharts, Visio, 164
Folders, Mail message, 256-258
Foreign objects, 63
Form fields (Access), 136-137
Form filling, 9-10
Form letters, creating, 201-216. *See also* Mail Merge scenario
Form module (Access), 385
Form Object dialog box (Excel), 95
Form view (Access tables), 133, 135
Format Data Series dialog box, 170
Formatted text, embedding, 43
Forms (Access), working with, 135-137
Forms list (Access), 135
Frames, using, 193-194
Framing embedded graphics in Word, 171-172
Functions, using in Access queries, 144-146

G

Gallery clipart, 167-168, 344-345
Genigraphics software, 311-312
Get External Data command, 103
Get External Data dialog box, 124-125
GetObject function (OLE Automation), 376-378
Go To dialog box, 66
Graphics/graphics objects (*See also* Pictures/picture objects)
    attaching VBA code to, 348-349
    creating, 158
    drawing in the client application, 157-161
    framing in Word, 171-172
    putting in text boxes, 172-173
    using placeholders for, 96
    using in tables, 165, 172-174
    working with, 155-175
Graphics layer (Word and Excel), 158-159
Graphics printing in Word, turning off, 96
Graphics techniques in Word, 171-175

H

Handouts (presentation), 299
Header (document), adding a logo to, 288-289
Header and Footer toolbar, 288
Hidden text, formatting paragraphs as, 274
Hiding computations in Word, 231
Historical data, researching and assembling, 7-8

I

Icons
    assigning to packaged objects, 358-359
    embedding objects as, 44
IF fields (Word), 276
Inbox window (Microsoft Mail), 244, 255
Increase Decimals tool, 189
In-place activation, 32
Insert Chart button, 198
Insert Column dialog box, 108
Insert Data dialog box, 284
Insert File command (Word), 54-56

Insert Icon dialog box, 357
Insert Microsoft Excel Worksheet button, 50
Insert Object command, 8, 51-53, 56, 67, 87
Insert Picture dialog box, 166
Install Drivers dialog box (Access), 140
Installation routine, choosing, 17
Installing Microsoft Office, 16-17
Installing the Microsoft Query add-in, 103-104
Installing ODBC drivers, 139-141
International letters, addressing, 232-233
Intrinsic functions (Access), 144
Invalid Merge Field dialog box, 210-211

J

Job vs. application orientation, 13-14
Join lines
    in Access query windows, 142-143
    in relational database tables, 118
Joining tables manually, 119

K

Key fields (in relational databases), 117

L

Label Options dialog box, 214-215
Labels (mailing), creating, 213-216
Large Excel objects, fitting on a page, 76-77
Letters, creating. See Mail Merge scenario
LINK fields, 405
    creating, 80
    editing directly, 86-87
    switches, 81
    syntax, 80-81
    troubleshooting, 362
Linked vs. embedded Excel ranges, 48-49
Linked objects, 23-24 (See also Linking data; Links)
    control of, 81-82
    editing, 31-32
    editing Excel, 63-64
    Excel range with Word document, 24
    fields in relational tables, 118
    locked, 82
    managing, 79-87
    source file access, 88
    using, 30-31

Linking data (See also Linked objects; Links; OLE Automation)
    an Access database to a Word document, 281-285
    basic steps for, 30
    Excel chart objects to Word documents, 61-62
    Excel ranges to Word documents, 48-50
    Excel worksheet objects to Word documents, 192-193, 279-280
Links (See also Linked objects; Linking data)
    breaking, 33-34, 85, 88
    changing automatic to manual, 82-85
    locking, 84-85
    modifying, 35-36, 82-87
    opening a file containing, 87
    redirecting, 35-36, 85-86
    safe, 34-35
    to the same item more than once, 362-363
    storage requirements for, 75-76
    suppressing updating of, 84
    updating, 84

Links dialog box, 35-36, 83
Locked linked objects, 82, 84-85
Logos
　adding to document header, 288-289
　creating with WordArt, 181-188
Long text, sharing, 92-94
Lost links, 34. *See also* Links

M

Macro language of Excel, 190
Macros, Visual Basic. *See* OLE Automation; Visual Basic macros
Mail. *See* Microsoft Mail
Mail Merge Helper button, 214
Mail Merge Helper dialog box, 204-205, 225-226
Mail Merge reports, generating, 219-239
Mail Merge scenario, 202-216
　adding merge fields, 208-209
　checking for errors, 209-212
　creating mailing labels, 213-216
　creating the main document, 203-205

merging to a document, 212-213
merging name and address data, 207-213
　printing the letters, 212
　specifying the data source, 205-207
　viewing merged data, 209-210
Mail Merge toolbar, 207-208
Mail Merge Wizard, 227
Mail messages. *See* Electronic mail messages
Mail Sign In dialog box, 243
Mailing labels, creating, 213-216
MailMerge command, 203
Main document (form letter), creating, 203-205
Management by exception, 322
Manual links, 82-85
Master document (template), saving, 287-289
Mathematical operators, 119
Memos in Word, 8, 57-58. *See also* Word documents

Menu Editor dialog box, 339
Merge fields, 207-209, 227
Merge It button, 149, 229
Merge to New Document button, 212, 236, 239
Merge to Printer button, 212, 239
Merging data, using Access for, 227-229
Message Finder dialog box, 259
Message Finder window, 259-260
Messages, faxing, 260-266
Messages, sending. *See* Electronic mail messages
Microsoft Access, 8, 129-152. *See also* Access Basic; Tables (Access)
　attaching external database tables, 138-141
　connecting to with Mail Merge Wizard, 227
　controlling Excel with, 382-385
　creating a database, 131
　creating queries in, 141-147, 222-229, 282, 384, 405

customizing the toolbar, 150
database as report data source, 222-229
DBEngine object and workspaces, 402
dynasets of queries, 143, 148
embedding an Excel object in, 380-381
embedding an Excel object in a form, 385-389
exporting data, 147-149
form module, 385
forms, 135-137
inserting a database in a Word document, 281-285
intrinsic functions, 144
MDB extension files, 131
merging data from, 227-229
opening files, 131-132
query in datasheet view, 226
query window, 142-143, 145-146
recordsets, 147-148
required fields, 133
role of, 11
Select Query window, 141-142
using clip art in, 168-169
using Report Wizard, 227-229
viewing and editing data, 132-138
Microsoft Access Handbook, 131
Microsoft At Work PC Fax, 260-266
Microsoft Clipart Gallery, 167-168, 344-345
Microsoft Excel. *See* Excel
Microsoft Graph, 197-199
Microsoft Graph charts vs. Excel charts, 59
Microsoft Mail, 9, 242-266 (*See also* Electronic mail messages)
  attaching files and objects to a message, 247-251
  composing messages, 244-245
  creating a personal address book, 245-246
  creating a personal group, 247-248
  deleting messages, 255
  Inbox window, 244, 255
  post office, 242
  reading messages, 255-260
  replying to messages, 255-256
  responding to routed documents, 254
  routing documents, 252-254
  searching for messages, 259-260
  sending messages, 243-251
  sending a note to a group, 246-247
  storing messages in folders, 256-258
Microsoft Office Manager, 14-16
Microsoft Powerpoint. *See* PowerPoint
Microsoft Query add-in, 8, 99-127
  copying data from, 126
  as a data import tool, 103
  data sources in, 131
  editing data in, 127
  and the ODBC standard, 102-103
  returning data from, 124-125
Microsoft Word. *See* Word; Word documents; Word fields
Modem specifications, 260
Modules (Excel), 75
Money manager scenario, 392-410

analyzing data, 398-405
Customer Investments form, 393-398
entering transactions, 395-398
printing reports, 405-410
setting global options, 395
Mutual fund report scenario, 180-199

N

Named text blocks. *See* Bookmarks
Native objects, 42
Nesting objects, 352-353
New Folder dialog box, 257
New Query button, 141
New Slide dialog box, 297
New User dialog box (Address Book), 264
Notes (presentation), 299
Null values vs. zero values, 114

O

Object containers, 380
Object dialog box, 51, 53, 67, 162-163
Object frames, 380
Object libraries, 378-380
Object models, 370, 373-376
Object Packager, 354-358
Object pollution, 76
Object properties and methods, 338
Objects, 21-23 (*See also* Embedded objects; Excel objects; Linked objects; OLE Automation)
  adding captions to, 194-196
  classification scheme, 23
  converting, 77-78
  copying, 88
  creating with embedding applications, 161-162
  deleting, 68
  editing in place, 62-64
  embedding as icons, 44
  examples of, 22
  exposing, 21-22, 372
  hierarchy of, 23
  inserting, 162-163
  integrating with Word text, 193-199
  manipulating in OLE Automation, 376-381
  nesting, 352-353
  in OLE Automation, 369-370
  packaging, 353-358
  programmatic IDs for, 372-373
  putting into client applications, 161-167
  top-level, 372
OCXs (OLE Custom Controls), 386-389
ODBC drivers, 138-141
ODBC (Open Database Connectivity) standard, 102-103, 138
Office Manager, 14-16
OLE Automation, 14, 368-389
  with Access as controller, 392-410
  controllers and objects, 369-370
  controlling embedded applications, 380-381
  creating and getting objects, 376-378
  creating a Word document from Excel, 381-382
  manipulating objects in, 376-381
  object models, 370, 373-376
  programmatic IDs for objects, 372-373
  VBA commands, 375
OLE Custom Control (OCX), 386-389

OLE (Object Linking and Embedding) standard, 13-14, 22-23
OLE problems, troubleshooting, 362-364
OLE servers, 161
OLE 2 (version 2.0), 13-14, 22-23
One-to-many database table relationship, 142
Open Data Source dialog box, 206
Open Database Connectivity (ODBC) standard, 102-103, 138-141
Open Worksheet dialog box, 55
Opening Access files, 131-132
Opening Access forms, 135
Opening an Access table, 132
Opening a compound document, 33
Opening a file containing links, 87
Opening queries, 126-127
Operating system requirements, 16
Operations center for rapid response example, 321-325

Options dialog box (Word), 87-88
Or criteria, 120-122
Orphan labels and markers on Excel charts, 59
Outlines, presentation, 299-304

P

Packaged objects, assigning icons to, 358-359
Packages, 353
Packaging documents, 354-358
Packaging objects, 353-358
Page Setup dialog box (Excel), 76
Paintbrush program (Windows), 162
Paragraph Borders and Shading dialog box, 196
Password-protecting files, 49
Paste Special dialog box, 27-28, 40-41, 249
Paste-linking data, 30
  from a chart to its own sheet, 90
  Excel range in a Word document, 26-29
  Excel worksheet in a Word document, 192-193, 279-280

  an object in a Mail message, 249
  text into a worksheet cell, 64-66
  text into a worksheet cell formula, 91-92
Pasting data vs. sharing data, 40
PC Fax program, 260-266
Percent tool, 189
Personal address book
  creating, 245-246
  entering fax addresses, 264-265
Personal group (Microsoft Mail), 247-248
Pick a Look Wizard, 298-299
Picture Borders dialog box, 186
Picture placeholders, 61, 96
Pictures/picture objects (*See also* Graphics/graphics objects)
  creating in Excel, 170-171
  converting embedded objects to, 78
  embedding, 43, 47-48
  embedding Excel charts as, 60
  embedding Word objects in Excel, 92-93

inserting, 165-167
Pivot tables, 346-347
Placeholders, picture, 61, 96
Plain-pasting data, 43-45. *See also* Paste-linking data
PowerPoint, 10 (*See also* Presentations)
  applying Transition effects, 309
  assigning a presentation template, 295-297
  attaching Exel workbooks to, 10
  changing the slide sequence, 304-305
  choosing a slide layout, 297
  handouts in, 299, 311
  importing data from Word, 10
  importing an outline from Word, 302
  linking to worksheets and tables, 307-308
  modifying the Slide Master, 306
  notes in, 299
  numbering slides, 312
  outlines in, 299-304
  printing handouts, 311
  printing slides, 311-312
  role of, 11
  saving your files, 298
  slides scroll bar, 305-306
  using AutoContent Wizard, 313-315
  using Builds, 309-310
  using for a proposal presentation, 293-315
  using visual effects, 308-310
PowerPoint Viewer icon, 312
PowerPoint window, maximizing, 305
Presentation Template dialog box, 296
Presentations (*See also* PowerPoint)
  adding visual effects, 308-311
  assigning a template, 295-297
  automated, 311
  changing the slide sequence, 304-305
  choosing a slide layout, 297
  dating the slides, 306
  displaying parts of a slide, 309-310
  handouts, 299, 311
  linking slides to sheets and tables, 307-308
  making, 311-312
  notes, 299
  in Outline view, 299
  outlines, 299-304
  printing slides, 311-312
  rehearsing, 310-311
  reusing or modifying, 313-315
  running from a PC, 312
  slide numbering, 312
  slides scroll bar, 305-306
  types of template, 296
  using AutoContent Wizard, 313-315
  using PowerPoint, 293-315
  using slide transitions, 309
Press release Mail Merge scenario, 202-216
Printing
  compound documents, 95-96
  envelopes, 237-239
  Mail Merge letters, 212
  reports, 405-410
  suppressing, 96
Private mail message folders, 257
Professional Edition programs, 5
Programmatic IDs (for objects), 372-373
Proposals. *See* Consulting proposal; Sales proposal
Protecting source data, 49-50

Publication-quality reports, creating, 179-199
Publish It button, 148
Purge dates for source files, 34

Q

QBE grid (in queries), 117, 142-143, 224
Queries, 102 (*See also* Query result sets)
  in Access, 141-147, 151-152, 222-229, 282, 384, 405
  adding criteria, 113-116
  adding fields to, 106, 108-109
  adding tables to, 106
  creating, 103-121
  crosstab, 222-229, 384
  inserting fields in, 107-108
  Mail Merge, 234-236
  with multiple data sources, 146
  of multiple tables, 117-119
  need for, 100-103
  opening, 126-127
  Or criteria, 121-122
  phrasing, 105
  rearranging columns in, 122
  removing criteria, 116
  saving, 126-127
  setting up simple, 105-110
  specifying criteria, 110-113
  specifying a data source, 104
  super-quick, 116-117
  using DATABASE fields in, 286
Query design window, 144-145
Query by example, 117
Query Options dialog box, 234-235, 285
Query parameters, getting from a form, 403
Query program. *See* Microsoft Query add-in
Query on a query (Access), 146
Query result sets, 107 (*See also* Queries)
  filtering, 110-113
  managing columns in, 109
  inserting in Word, 284
  returning to Excel, 8-9
  returning to Excel and Word, 121-127
  sorting, 123-124
  sorting by field, 145-146
  updating, 126
Query window, 106-109, 112, 114-115, 122
Query window (Access), 142-143, 145-146
Query Wizards, 144

R

Rapid response interface example, 319-349 (*See also* VBA code)
  acquiring data at the site, 323
  components of, 322-324
  creating a workstation, 324
  creating your command center, 321-325
  designing the main screen, 340-343
  designing the user interface, 324
  disguising Excel, 335-340
  monitoring manufacturing, 325-349
  monitoring operations by computer, 321-322
  processing production data, 323-324
  top-level Summary screen, 327
  user interface, 324, 335-340

using color for status, 326-328
workstations, 326-329
Record Macro dialog box, 287
Record New Macro dialog box, 190
Record selector, 134
Records (database), 101
Recordsets (Access), 147-148. *See also* Tables (Access)
Redirecting links, 85-86
REF fields (Word), 274-276
References dialog box (Excel Tools), 379
REG.DAT file, restoring corrupted, 358-361
Registration Info Editor window, 41
Registration procedure, 41
Relational databases, 102, 117-118
Report Wizard (Access), 227-229
Report Wizards dialog box (Access), 228
Reports
 creating, 179-199
 creating in Access, 151-152
 creating the main document, 221
 with embedded Excel object, 26-29
 generating, 219-239
 printing, 405-410
 selecting records for, 234-236
 sending, 8
 specifying a data source, 222-229
 using crosstab queries, 222-229
 using Word computations, 229-233
 with worksheet embedded, 193
Required fields (Access), 133
Return Data to Excel button, 124
Reverse type, using, 196-197
Rich Text Format (RTF) codes, 43
Routing compound documents, 76
Routing Slip dialog box, 253
Routing slips for Mail messages, 8-9, 252-254

S

Sales activity report scenario, 219-239
Sales proposal (*See also* Consulting proposal)
 allowing international addresses, 232-233
 base period average, 230-231
 base period order level, 229-230
 creating the main document, 221
 current sales level, 231-232
 hiding computations, 231
 selecting customers, 234-236
 specifying a data source, 222-229
 viewing computations, 232
Save As dialog box, 126-127
Saving a compound document, 32-36
Saving files, 364
Saving files containing OLE objects, 77
Saving queries, 126-127
Select Data Source dialog box, 104
Select File dialog box (Access), 138
Select Query window (Access), 141-142
Send Note dialog box, 244
Sending files, 8
Server application, 22
Shading dialog box (WordArt), 184

Shadow dialog box (WordArt), 184
Shared data, 12-13, 23-26, 39-68 (*See also* Embedding; Linking data)
  Excel objects, 40-44
  an Excel range, 27
  long text, 92-94
  and OLE, 19-36
  vs. pasted data, 40
  tables, 94
  specifying, 40-45
  working with, 30-36
Show/Hide paragraph button, 274
SKIPIF fields (Word), 235-236
Slide Master (PowerPoint), 306
Slide Show button, 310
Slide shows. *See* Presentations
Slide Sorter view, 305
Slide Sorter View button, 304
Sort Ascending button, 123
Sort Descending button, 123
Sort dialog box, 123-124
Sorting query results, 123-124, 145-146
Source data, 26
Source documents, 26

access to for linked documents, 88
expiration dates for, 34
protecting, 49-50
Space-saving techniques, 76
Special Effects dialog box (WordArt), 185
SQL code examples, 141, 286, 384, 403
Standard Edition programs, 5
Stop Recording button, 191
Storage requirements, embedded vs. linked, 75-76
Structured Query Language (SQL), 141, 286, 384, 403
Summary Info dialog box, 34-35
Symbol dialog box, 174
System requirements, minimum, 16

T

Tables (Access)
  adding and deleting records, 134
  changing a value in a record, 134
  Datasheet vs. Form view, 133, 135
  editing data in, 133-135

using graphics in, 165
viewing, 132
Tables (database), 101
  adding to queries, 106
  attaching to Access, 138-140
  joining, 118-119
  linking relational, 102, 118
  querying multiple, 117-119
  sharing between Word and Excel, 94
  using graphics in, 172-174
Templates
  assigning, 295-297
  saving a proposal as, 287-289
  types of, 296
Text blocks, named. See Bookmarks
Text Box tool, 172
Text boxes
  graphics in, 172-173
  Word text in, 92-93
Text layer (Word and Excel), 158-159
Third-party drawing programs, 163-165
Thumbnail, 166
Top-level object, 372
Transition button (PowerPoint), 309
Translating data, 12-13

Troubleshooting common OLE problems, 362-364

U

Unbound object frame, 380
Unformatted text, embedding, 43
Unlinking a Word field, 85
Update methods, 83
Updating links, 84
Updating query results, 126
User interface (rapid response system), 324

V

Validation rules for form fields, 137
VBA (Visual Basic for Applications) code
  ActiveWindow objects, 337-338
  for applying colors to objects, 340-341
  attaching to graphic objects, 348-349
  auto_Open procedures, 330
  for calculating color in a pivot table, 346-347
  for comparing result to the standard, 347
  for custom variables, 330
  declaring constants and variables, 341-342
  declaring variables, 371
  for determining object color, 342-343
  Dimension statements, 371
  and OLE Automation commands, 375
  OnTime events, 332
  procedures, 337
  for processing object collections, 342
  public variables, 330
  for rapid response system, 329-349
  statements, 337
  type declarations, 330
  for updating color indicators, 345-346
  using For Each statements with, 342
  using object libraries in, 378-380
View Merged Data button, 209
Viewing copied data, 42
Visio (Shapeware Corporation) drawing program, 164
Visual Basic for Applications (VBA), 190, 369-389. *See also* VBA code
Visual Basic macros
  assigning to buttons, 191-192
  for the rapid response system, 329-349
  recording, 190-191

W

Windows Paintbrush program, 162
Windows setup registration procedure, 41
Windows for Workgroups, 242-243, 260
Wingding characters, using, 174-175
Word (*See also* Word documents; Word fields)
  adding borders in, 185
  calculations in, 229-233
  drawing tools, 157-158, 160
  graphics techniques in, 171-175
  graphics and text layers of, 158-159
  role of, 11-12
  as a server for Excel, 64-67

suppressing printing of objects, 96
turning off graphics printing, 96
Word data/objects, using in Excel, 39-68, 91-96
Word documents (*See also* Mail Merge scenario; Word)
with clip art, 168
creating from Excel, 381-382
pasting Excel ranges into, 6-7, 26-29
embedding Excel charts in, 56-61
exporting to PowerPoint, 10, 302-304
inserting Access databases, 281-285
integrating OLE objects into, 192-199

linked to Excel ranges or charts, 24, 61-62, 79-82, 92
linking Excel worksheet objects to, 192-193, 279-280
reports, 180-199
using Excel data in, 87-90
Word fields, 79 (*See also* ASK fields; LINK fields)
DATABASE, 286
EMBED, 79-80, 90
IF, 276
merge, 207-209, 227
\p switch in, 86-87
REF, 274-276
SKIPIF, 235-236
switches in, 81, 86-87
unlinking, 85
viewing codes, 79-80

WordArt
creating a company logo with, 181-188
formatting with, 182-185
toolbar buttons, 183
WordArt objects, inserting, 182
WordBasic macros, 287
WordBasic objects, 405
Workday activities, typical, 4-5
Worksheet objects, embedding and linking, 46-49, 50-56, 192-193
Worksheets (Excel), creating, 188-190
Workspaces (Access 2.0), 402

Z

Zero values vs. null values, 114

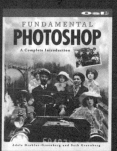

**Fundamental Photoshop:
A Complete Introduction**
by Adele Droblas-Greenberg
& Seth Greenberg
$27.95   ISBN: 0-07-881994-6

**dBASE for Windows
Made Easy**
by Jim Sheldon
$26.95   ISBN: 0-07-881792-7

**The Best Guide To
Business Shareware**
by Judy Heim, John Haib
and Mike Callahan
Includes Two 3.5-Inch Disks
$34.95   ISBN: 0-07-882076-6

The Visual C++ Handbook
by Chris H. Pappas and
William H. Murray, III
$34.95   ISBN: 0-07-882056-1

GET WHAT YOU WANT...

Expert Advice & Support 24 Hours A Day

Do you need help with your software?

Why pay up to $25.00 for a single tech support call!

Now, in conjunction with **Corporate Software Inc.**, one of the world's largest providers of tech support (they field more than 200,000 calls a month), Osborne delivers the most authoritative new series of answer books — **The Certified Tech Support** series.

- These books will bail you out of practically any pitfall.
- Find answers to the most frequently asked end-user questions, from the simple to the arcane.
- **Lotus Notes Answers: Certified Tech Support** is the next best thing to having an expert beside your computer.
- Watch for other books in the series.

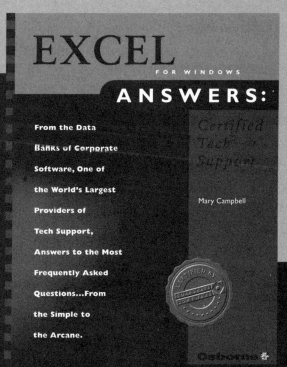

**Excel for Windows
Answers: Certified
Tech Support**
by Mary Campbell
$16.95
ISBN: 0-07-882054-5

Order Today!

BC640SL

MAKE THE RIGHT Connection

IT'S WHAT YOU KNOW THAT COUNTS. WITH INNOVATIVE BOOKS FROM LAN TIMES AND OSBORNE/MCGRAW-HILL, YOU'LL BE THE ONE IN DEMAND.

LAN TIMES GUIDE TO SQL
BY JAMES R. GROFF AND PAUL N. WEINBERG
$29.95 U.S.A.
ISBN: 0-07-882026-X

LAN TIMES ENCYCLOPEDIA OF NETWORKING
BY TOM SHELDON
AN AUTHORITATIVE REFERENCE ON ALL NETWORKING FACETS AND TRENDS.
$39.95 U.S.A.
ISBN: 0-07-881965-2
AVAILABLE NOW

LAN TIMES E-MAIL RESOURCE GUIDE
BY RICK DRUMMOND AND NANCY COX
$29.95 U.S.A.
ISBN: 0-07-882052-9

LAN TIMES GUIDE TO INTEROPERABILITY
BY TOM SHELDON
$29.95 U.S.A.
ISBN: 0-07-882043-X

BC640SL

Revolutionary Information on the Information REVOLUTION

Alluring opportunities abound for the global investor. But avoiding investment land mines can be tricky business. The first release in the Business Week Library of Computing lets you master all the winning strategies. Everything is here—from analyzing and selecting the best companies, to tax planning, using investment software tools, and more. Disks include MetaStock, Windows On WallStreet, and Telescan, the leading investment analysis software.

The Business Week Guide to Global Investments Using Electronic Tools
by Robert Schwabach
Includes Three 3.5-Inch Disks
$39.95 U.S.A.   ISBN: 0-07-882055-3

The Business Week Guide to Multimedia Presentations Create Dynamic Presentations That Inspire
by Robert Lindstrom
Includes One CD-ROM
$39.95 U.S.A.
ISBN: 0-07-882057-X

The Internet Yellow Pages
by Harley Hahn and Rick Stout
$27.95 U.S.A.
ISBN: 0-07-882023-5

BYTE's Mac Programmer's Cookbook
by Rob Terrell
Includes
One 3.5-Inch Disk
$29.95 U.S.A.
ISBN: 0-07-882062-6

Multimedia: Making It Work, Second Edition
by Tay Vaughan
Includes
One CD-ROM
$34.95 U.S.A.
ISBN: 0-07-882035-9

**The Internet
Yellow Pages**
by Harley Hahn and Rick Stout
$27.95 U.S.A.
ISBN: 0-07-882098-7

**The Internet
Complete Reference**
by Harley Hahn and Rick Stout
$29.95 U.S.A.
ISBN: 0-07-881980-6

**CorelDRAW! 5
Made Easy**
by Martin S. Matthews and
Carole Boggs Matthews
$29.95 U.S.A.
ISBN: 0-07-882066-9

**Teach Yourself C++,
Second Edition**
by Herbert Schildt
$24.95 U.S.A.
ISBN: 0-07-882025-1

When It Comes to CD-ROM...
We Wrote the Book

Everything You Always Wanted to Know About CD-ROMs and More!

This Exclusive Book/CD-ROM Package Includes
- Sound and Clip Art
- Samples of CD-ROM Applications
- Multimedia Authoring Tools

Part buyer's guide, part standards guide, and part troubleshooter, the **BYTE Guide to CD-ROM** discusses all aspects of this proliferating technology so you can take full advantage.

**BYTE
Guide to
CD-ROM**
by
Michael Nadeau,
BYTE Senior Editor

Includes CD-ROM
$39.95 U.S.A.
ISBN: 0-07-881982-2

Osborne
Get Answers—Get Osborne
For Accuracy, Quality and Value

BC640SL

Secret Recipes
FOR THE SERIOUS CODE CHEF

No longer underground...the best-kept secrets and profound programming tips have been liberated! You'll find them all in the new BYTE Programmer's Cookbook series — the hottest hacks, facts, and tricks for veterans and rookies alike. These books are accompanied by a CD-ROM or disk packed with code from the books plus utilities and plenty of other software tools you'll relish.

BYTE's Mac Programmer's Cookbook
by Rob Terrell
Includes One 3.5-Inch Disk
$29.95 U.S.A., ISBN: 0-07-882062-0

BYTE's Windows Programmer's Cookbook
by L. John Ribar
Includes One CD-ROM
$34.95 U.S.A.
ISBN: 0-07-882037-5

BYTE's DOS Programmer's Cookbook
by Craig Menefee, Lenny Bailes, and Nick Anis
Includes One CD-ROM
$34.95 U.S.A.
ISBN: 0-07-882048-0

BYTE's OS/2 Programmer's Cookbook
by Kathy Ivens and Bruce Hallberg
Includes One CD-ROM
$34.95 U.S.A.
ISBN: 0-07-882039-1

BYTE Guide to CD-ROM
by Michael Nadeau
Includes One CD-ROM
$39.95 U.S.A.
ISBN: 0-07-881982-2

BC640SL

Yo Unix!

INNOVATIVE BOOKS

FROM OPEN COMPUTING AND OSBORNE/McGRAW-HILL

Open Computing's Guide to the Best Free Unix Utilities
by Jim Keough and Remon Lapid
Includes One CD-ROM
$34.95 U.S.A.
ISBN: 0-07-882046-4
Available now

Open Computing's Best UNIX Tips Ever
by Kenneth H. Rosen, Richard P. Rosinski, and Douglas A. Host
$29.95 U.S.A.
ISBN: 0-07-881924-5
Available now

Open Computing's Unix Unbound
by Harley Hahn
$27.95 U.S.A.
ISBN: 0-07-882050-2

Open Computing's Standard Unix API Functions
by Garrett Long
$39.95 U.S.A.
ISBN: 0-07-882051-0

BC640SL

Think Fast
PASSING LANE AHEAD

Lotus Notes Answers: Certified Tech Support
by Polly Russell Kornblith
$16.95 U.S.A.
ISBN: 0-07-882055-3

What's the quickest route to tech support? Osborne's new Certified Tech Support series. Developed in conjunction with Corporate Software Inc., one of the largest providers of tech support fielding more than 200,000 calls a month, Osborne delivers the most authoritative question and answer books available anywhere. Speed up your computing and stay in the lead with answers to the most frequently asked end-user questions—from the simple to the arcane. And watch for more books in the series.

The Internet Yellow Pages
by Harley Hahn and Rick Stout
$27.95 U.S.A.
ISBN: 0-07-882023-5

Sound Blaster: The Official Book, Second Edition
by Peter M. Ridge, David Golden, Ivan Luk, Scott Sindorf, and Richard Heimlich
Includes One 3.5-Inch Disk
$34.95 U.S.A.
ISBN: 0-07-882000-6

Osborne Windows Programming Series
by Herbert Schildt, Chris H. Pappas, and William H. Murray, III
Vol. 1 - Programming Fundamentals
$39.95 U.S.A.
ISBN: 0-07-881990-3
Vol. 2 - General Purpose API Functions
$49.95 U.S.A.
ISBN: 0-07-881991-1
Vol. 3 - Special Purpose API Functions
$49.95 U.S.A.
ISBN: 0-07-881992-X

The Microsoft Access Handbook
by Mary Campbell
$27.95 U.S.A.
ISBN: 0-07-882014-6

ORDER BOOKS DIRECTLY FROM OSBORNE/MC GRAW-HILL.

For a complete catalog of Osborne's books, call 510-549-6600 or write to us at 2600 Tenth Street, Berkeley, CA 94710

Call Toll-Free: *1-800-822-8158*
24 hours a day, 7 days a week
in U.S. and Canada

Mail this order form to:
McGraw-Hill, Inc.
Blue Ridge Summit, PA 17294-0840

Fax this order form to:
717-794-5291

EMAIL
7007.1531@COMPUSERVE.COM
COMPUSERVE GO MH

Ship to:

Name _____

Company _____

Address _____

City / State / Zip _____

Daytime Telephone: _____
(We'll contact you if there's a question about your order.)

ISBN #	BOOK TITLE	Quantity	Price	Total
0-07-88				
0-07-88				
0-07-88				
0-07-88				
0-07-88				
0-07088				
0-07-88				
0-07-88				
0-07-88				
0-07-88				
0-07-88				
0-07-88				
0-07-88				

Shipping & Handling Charge from Chart Below	
Subtotal	
Please Add Applicable State & Local Sales Tax	
TOTAL	

Shipping & Handling Charges

Order Amount	U.S.	Outside U.S.
Less than $15	$3.45	$5.25
$15.00 - $24.99	$3.95	$5.95
$25.00 - $49.99	$4.95	$6.95
$50.00 - and up	$5.95	$7.95

Occasionally we allow other selected companies to use our mailing list. If you would prefer that we not include you in these extra mailings, please check here: ☐

METHOD OF PAYMENT

☐ Check or money order enclosed (payable to Osborne/McGraw-Hill)

☐ AMERICAN EXPRESS   ☐ DISCOVER   ☐ MasterCard   ☐ VISA

Account No. ☐☐☐☐☐☐☐☐☐☐☐☐☐☐

Expiration Date _____

Signature _____

In a hurry? Call 1-800-822-8158 anytime, day or night, or visit your local bookstore.

Thank you for your order   Code BC640SL